LOUIS VUITTON

CHA

CHA

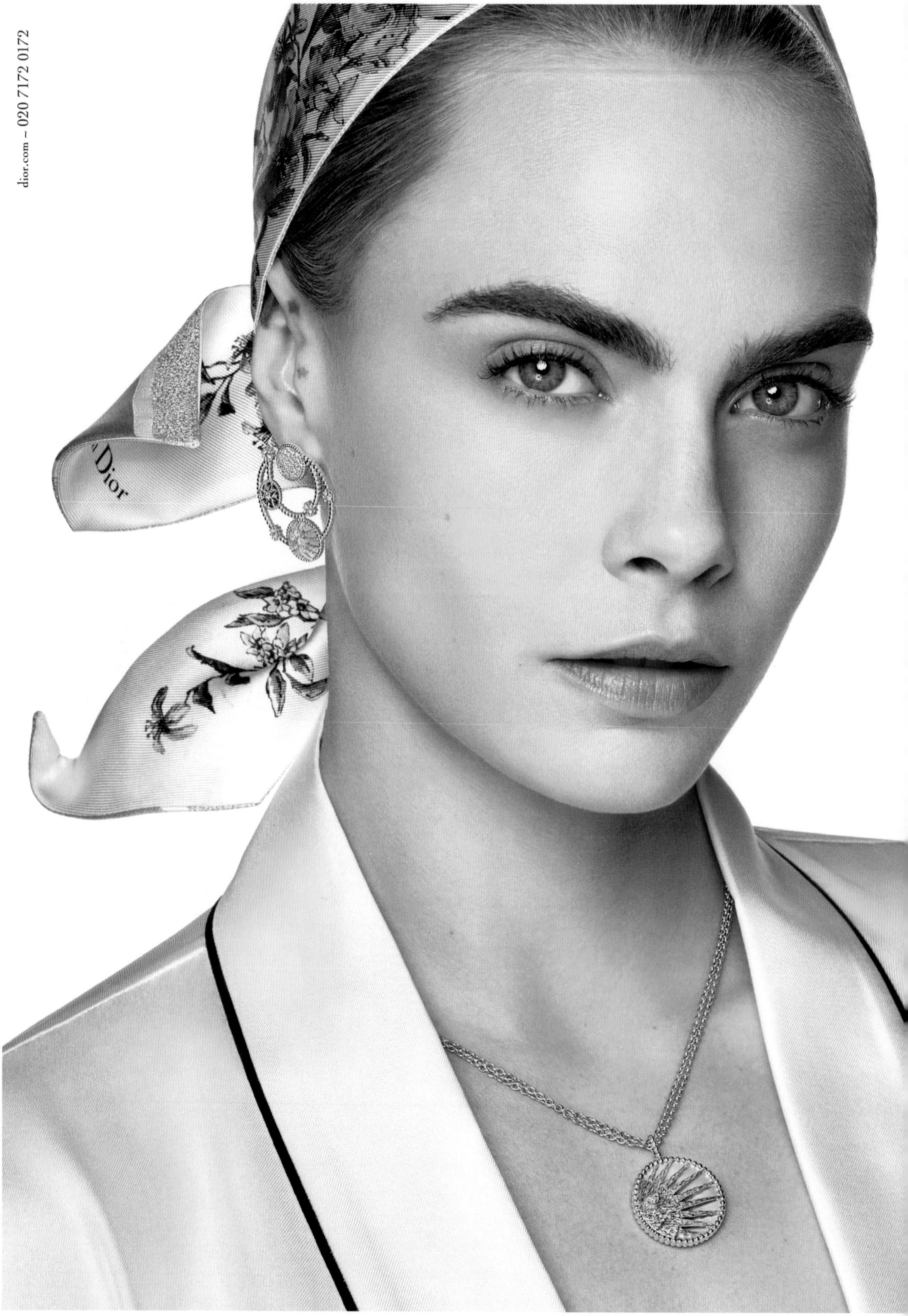
Dior

DIOR

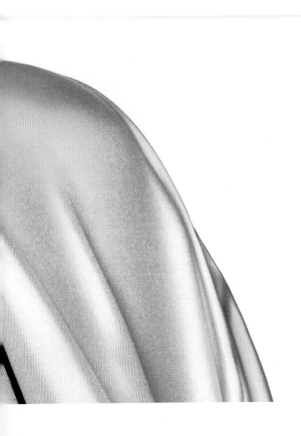

ROSE DES VENTS, ROSE CÉLESTE
AND *MIMIROSE* COLLECTIONS
Yellow gold, diamonds, mother-of-pearl and onyx.

CHANEL

FINE JEWELLERY

COCO CRUSH

SOME ENCOUNTERS YOU WEAR FOREVER.

RINGS AND EARRINGS IN BEIGE GOLD, WHITE GOLD AND DIAMONDS.

SAINT LAURENT

WINTER 22
COLLECTION
YSL.COM

GIORGIO ARMANI

FENDI

PRADA

FINE JEWELRY

ETERNAL GOLD

PRADA.COM

DOLCE & GABBANA

DOLCEGABBANA.COM

Liens Collection

YOUR STORIES OF LIENS

CHAUMET
PARIS

174 New Bond Street, London

NOVEMBER

KINGDOM COME, *page 180*

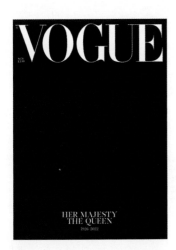

COVER

This month, Vogue is published with a cover dedicated to the life and service of Her Majesty Queen Elizabeth II

> 32

City HardWear Collection

TIFFANY & CO.

BURBERRY

LONDON ENGLAND

92% said tired eyes looked more rested.*
Fights the effects of blue light on skin's appearance.
FOR ALL AGES, ALL SKIN TONES AND ALL SKIN TYPES.

ESTĒE LAUDER

esteelauder.co.uk

SUPERCHARGE YOUR SKIN
WITH THE POWER RENEWAL DUO

NEW INNOVATION FOR EYES

ESTĒE LAUDER

Advanced Night Repair Eye
Supercharged Gel-Creme

Synchronized Multi-Recovery

ESTĒE LAUDER

Advanced Night Repair

Synchronized Multi-Recovery Complex
Complexe multi-réparation synchronisée

7 SERUMS IN 1

CONTENTS

FASHION & FEATURES

LEAGUES AHEAD, *page 182.*
Achenrin Madit wears tank top and shorts,
POLO RALPH LAUREN. *Skirt,* MAX
MARA. *Shoes,* CHRISTIAN
LOUBOUTIN. *Sunglasses,*
BALENCIAGA. *Earrings,* GUCCI *and*
PAULA MENDOZA

TREASURE
ISLAND,
page 202

VOGUE ASKS

FREE GIFTS*

SIX ISSUES FOR ONLY £9*
+ FREE HOME DELIVERY + FREE DIGITAL EDITIONS
+ FREE GIFTS FROM HERLUM, RRP £22

Take a sensory journey and experience the richness of Brazilian ingredients with Herlum. Made in England, this natural duo is enriched with Amazonian murumuru butter, known for its lauric and oleic acid properties, which leaves skin feeling soft and perfumed. The unique scent stems from upcycled flowers, uniting woody and spicy notes. Available at Cultbeauty.co.uk

WWW.VOGUE.CO.UK/SUBSCRIBE/4VO22165
ORDER NOW! CALL 01858 438 819   CODE: 4VO22165
WEEKDAYS 7.30AM-7.00PM, SATURDAY 8.00AM-4.00PM

YOUR DETAILS
With your email address we can manage your subscription and update you on services. Also, as a subscriber, you will automatically be eligible for exclusive offers, invitations and discounts from the publisher, Condé Nast Britain. If you do NOT want to receive these please tick this box ☐. If you WANT to receive special offers and promotions from our partners please tick this box ☐.
Email:

Mrs/Ms/Miss/Mr	Name:	Surname:
Address:		
		Postcode:
Telephone:		Mobile:

RECIPIENT/DELIVERY ADDRESS (IF DIFFERENT FROM ABOVE)
Mrs/Ms/Miss/Mr	Name:	Surname:
Address:		
		Postcode:
Telephone:		Mobile:

BEST DEAL: SIX ISSUES ONLY £9 + FREE GIFT – CANCEL ANYTIME*
(After the initial period, the subscription renews for six months at only £16, saving over 30%)

☐ **BY DIRECT DEBIT** DIRECT Debit
To the Manager (Bank name):   Originator's identification no: 850381
Bank address: Postcode:
Name of account holder:
Account number: Branch sort code:
Signature: Date:

INSTRUCTION TO YOUR BANK OR BUILDING SOCIETY: Please pay The Condé Nast Publications Ltd Direct Debits from the account details in this instruction subject to the safeguards assured by The Direct Debit Guarantee. I understand that this instruction may remain with The Condé Nast Publications Ltd and, if so, details will be passed electronically to my Bank/Building Society. Banks and Building Societies may not accept Direct Debit instructions from some types of account.

☐ **BY CREDIT CARD**   Please charge my VISA / AMEX / MASTERCARD
Card number: Start date: Expiry:
Signature: Date:

ONE YEAR ONLY £36   ☐ BY CHEQUE payable to The Condé Nast Publications Ltd.
☐ **BY CREDIT CARD**   Please charge my VISA / AMEX / MASTERCARD
Card number: Start date: Expiry:
Signature: Date:

*Offer is subject to terms and availability, limited to new subscribers at UK addresses until 29/11/2022. Savings are calculated against print & digital cover prices. Free welcome gifts are sent to payers. Customers can cancel a subscription at any time and receive a full refund on any issues yet to be mailed. Please tick this box if you DO NOT wish to receive direct mail from The Condé Nast Publications Ltd ☐ or other reputable companies ☐ For privacy notice and permission details, please visit condenast.co.uk/privacy.

Recycle

MAIL TO: FREEPOST CONDÉ NAST BRITAIN. NO STAMP NEEDED.

Perlée collection
Perlée signature bracelet,
rose gold.

Van Cleef & Arpels

Haute Joaillerie, place Vendôme since 1906

BIOCERAMIC
MOON**S**WATCH
COLLECTION

MISSION TO THE SUN

Ω
OMEGA
×
swatch✚

Only available in selected Swatch Stores

BIOCERAMIC
MOON**S**WATCH
COLLECTION

MISSION ON EARTH

Ω
OMEGA
×
swatch⊞

Only available in selected Swatch Stores

BVLGARI
ROMA

Tom Craig's images of HM QUEEN ELIZABETH II*'s funeral are accompanied by personal tributes, on page 170*

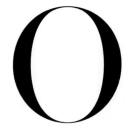

O n the morning of Her Majesty the Queen's funeral, on one of those September days in London when shafts of golden sunlight glint through the clouds and fall on the city's browning greens, I made my way to Hyde Park with friends to join the crowds and take it in.

It felt, as everyone noted, like living history. People were hushed but alive with the promise of the experience, as they gathered round large screens or inched as close as they could to the barricades by the funeral procession. Whatever your view of monarchy – having been born in a former colony and lived the immigrant experience first-hand, my own opinion is nuanced – it was extraordinary to see. There was so much beauty and pageantry. It felt like a farewell to a Britain of the past. Some people were ready for that, and yet that was the thing about the Queen: for most, there was always something to like. Personally, I responded to her steadiness, her dependable, joy-filled fashion choices, her kind but no-nonsense manners, her tireless devotion to others. She was, like all those who endure, curious and conscientious to the end.

In the weeks since her death was announced, the country has felt different. Granted it is neither a great surprise nor even a misfortune to die at a grand old age after an extraordinarily full life. Her passing did not > 40

A lighthearted day

HERMÈS
PARIS

EDITOR'S LETTER

On page 164, Robin Muir curates Vogue's defining royal imagery, including THE QUEEN *in 1972 and as a princess in 1934*

contain the electric shock of Diana, Princess of Wales's tragic death in 1997, but there has been a shift in its wake. A constant thread through our collective lives, throughout her 70-year reign she served not only her mission but as an almost touchable link to the fabric of history itself. Now she has gone and with her so many of our own memories – of our childhoods, of our parents and their childhoods – seem to have drifted a little further into the mist. As has been noted, with the Queen's passing it is as though the long tail of the 20th century has finally wagged its last.

British Vogue itself was already 10 years old when the Queen was born in 1926. Despite her record-breaking reign, she was, by the time of her Coronation in 1953, the fourth monarch in this magazine's life. In rare tribute, royal purple envelopes this month's special commemorative cover for the first time since 1952. On page 170, the worlds of fashion, culture and politics share their fondest memories of Her Majesty, while on page 164 we look at the special bonds that run through the generations of women who precede and succeed her, as captured in the magazine through the decades. On page 180, former press secretary Colleen Harris writes exclusively on the approaching reign of His Majesty King Charles III, a man she long worked with.

For Her Majesty Queen Elizabeth II, it is a farewell from Vogue. More than that, it is a thank you.

HAPPY SPORT CHRONO
Handcrafted in Ethical Gold

Chopard

THE ARTISAN OF EMOTIONS – SINCE 1860

Enjoy responsibly. Over 18s only.
be**drinkaware**.co.uk

MICHAEL KORS

COLLECTION

MICHAELKORS.COM

IN MEMORIAM

British Vogue has registered the passing of three monarchs in its 106-year history, commemorating the loss of George V, George VI and now Elizabeth II with a royal purple cover free from any adornment. In Her Majesty the Queen's case, the November 2022 issue reflects not only the continuity of her line, but also the much-mourned absence of Britain's longest-reigning sovereign. "The keynote of her character is a perfectly transparent sincerity: sincerity of purpose [and] sincerity of devotion to her duty," Vogue wrote upon her accession in 1952. Seventy years later, those words still rang true.

FEBRUARY 5 · 1936 (8)   PRICE ONE SHILLING

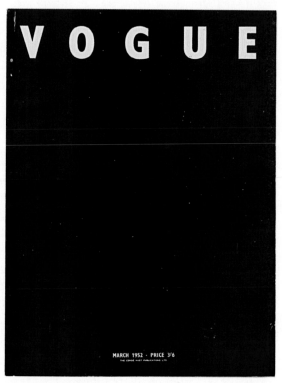

MARCH 1952 · PRICE 3/6
THE CONDÉ NAST PUBLICATIONS LTD

LASTING LEGACY

From HM Queen Rania of Jordan to Kate Moss, Sadiq Khan to Victoria Beckham, in this month's issue prominent voices share their memories and thoughts with us on the life and reign of HM Queen Elizabeth II. From a shared joke with Grace Jones about her Hula-Hoop to a special letter received by Emma Raducanu, Vogue celebrates a unique, personal influence that spanned decades.

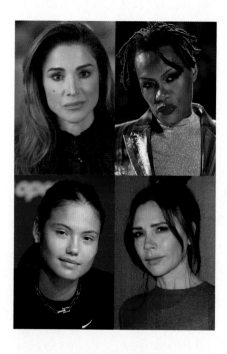

Colleen Harris

Colleen Harris, a former press secretary for HM King Charles III, reflects on her years working with the heir to the throne in the late 1990s and early 2000s, on page 180. One of her favourite memories? "I remember being with [the former] His Royal Highness on the royal train once – a surreal experience in itself – and getting into a passionate conversation with him about shoes. He's much more knowledgeable about fashion than many people realise."

RICHARD MILLE

RM 72-01

In-house skeletonised automatic winding calibre
50-hour power reserve (±10%)
Baseplate and bridges in grade 5 titanium
Patented flyback chronograph
Function indicator and date display
Rotor in platinum
Case in white gold and baguette-cut diamonds

A Racing Machine
On The Wrist

IN-ROOM DINING

Find recipe inspiration and whip up comfort food the fashion set would approve of.

COLD-WEATHER CAPSULE

From timeless investment buys to the very best of the high street, see – and shop – winter wardrobe essentials, as curated by team Vogue.

LIKE WHAT YOU SEE

In a between-seasons wardrobe slump? Find the hottest celebrity trends and street-style inspiration in spades on Vogue.co.uk.

WINTER IS COMING

From PROTECTIVE *skincare to the* PERFECT COAT, *find everything you need to see you through a* COLD SNAP *at Vogue.co.uk*

FACE TIME

The beauty experts bring you pro tips for taking care of your skin in the harsh winter months, and the soothing, plumping products and treatments to try now.

NOT GOING OUT

Vogue's culture writers review the books and TV worth staying in for.

TUDOR

#BORN TODARE

What is it that drives someone to greatness? To take on the unknown, venture into the unseen and dare all? This is the spirit that gave birth to TUDOR. This is the spirit embodied by every TUDOR Watch. Some are born to follow. Others are born to dare.

28 millimetre case

Integrated "five-link" bracelet

Swiss self-winding mechanical calibre T201 with chronometer performance

Five-year transferable guarantee with no registration or periodic maintenance checks required

TUDOR ROYAL

VOGUE

EDWARD ENNINFUL
EDITOR-IN-CHIEF & EUROPEAN EDITORIAL DIRECTOR

GLOBAL NETWORK LEAD & EUROPEAN DEPUTY EDITOR SARAH HARRIS
GLOBAL PRINT STRATEGY LEAD & EUROPEAN CONTENT OPERATIONS DIRECTOR MARK RUSSELL
GLOBAL NETWORK LEAD & EUROPEAN FEATURES DIRECTOR GILES HATTERSLEY
GLOBAL NETWORK LEAD & EUROPEAN BEAUTY & WELLNESS DIRECTOR JESSICA DINER
DEPUTY DIRECTOR, GLOBAL FASHION NETWORK LAURA INGHAM
EUROPEAN DESIGN DIRECTOR JAN-NICO MEYER
GLOBAL CONTRIBUTING FASHION EDITOR KATE PHELAN
GLOBAL DIRECTOR, TALENT & CASTING ROSIE VOGEL-EADES
GLOBAL ENTERTAINMENT DIRECTOR, THE TALENT GROUP DEBORAH ABABIO

FASHION
FASHION DIRECTORS JULIA SARR-JAMOIS, POPPY KAIN
CONTRIBUTING FASHION DIRECTOR VENETIA SCOTT
CONTRIBUTING STYLE DIRECTOR DENA GIANNINI
JEWELLERY & WATCH DIRECTOR RACHEL GARRAHAN
FASHION & ACCESSORIES EDITOR DONNA WALLACE
FASHION CREDITS EDITOR HELEN HIBBIRD
ASSOCIATE FASHION EDITOR ENIOLA DARE
FASHION ASSISTANTS THALIA METALLINOU, HONEY SWEET ELIAS,
JACK O'NEILL, LOIS ADEOSHUN, JULIA STORM
CONTRIBUTING FASHION EDITORS
JACK BORKETT, JULIA BRENARD, BENJAMIN BRUNO,
GRACE CODDINGTON, JANE HOW, JOE McKENNA, CLARE RICHARDSON,
SARAH RICHARDSON, MARIE-AMÉLIE SAUVÉ
CONTRIBUTING WEST COAST EDITOR LAW ROACH
CONTRIBUTING SUSTAINABILITY EDITOR AMBER VALLETTA
CONTRIBUTING EUROPEAN SUSTAINABILITY EDITOR DANA THOMAS
TALENT CASTING MANAGER JANAY BAILEY
CONTRIBUTING CASTING DIRECTOR ASHLEY BROKAW

FASHION FEATURES
COMMERCE DIRECTOR NAOMI SMART
FASHION FEATURES EDITOR LAURA HAWKINS
SHOPPING EDITOR JESSICA GERARDI
FASHION CRITIC ANDERS CHRISTIAN MADSEN
SENIOR COMMERCE WRITER JOY MONTGOMERY
COMMERCE WRITER HENRIK LISCHKE

FEATURES
DEPUTY FEATURES DIRECTOR OLIVIA MARKS
ACTING FEATURES EDITOR KATE LLOYD
ASSOCIATE FEATURES WRITER AMEL MUKHTAR
FEATURES INTERN CHEYENNE DARKO
ENTERTAINMENT DIRECTOR-AT-LARGE JILL DEMLING
CONTRIBUTING EDITORS
ADWOA ABOAH, RIZ AHMED, LAURA BAILEY, SUSAN BENDER WHITFIELD,
MUNROE BERGDORF, SINEAD BURKE, LAURA BURLINGTON,
VASSI CHAMBERLAIN, ALEXA CHUNG, MICHAELA COEL,
RONNIE COOKE NEWHOUSE, JOURDAN DUNN, ALEXANDER GILKES,
AFUA HIRSCH, ELGAR JOHNSON, PARIS LEES, GIANLUCA LONGO,
PATRICK MACKIE, STEVE McQUEEN, JIMMY MOFFAT, KATE MOSS, SARAH
MOWER, ROBIN MUIR, DURO OLOWU, LORRAINE PASCALE, ELLIE PITHERS,
HARRIET QUICK, ELIZABETH SALTZMAN, NONA SUMMERS, LEE SWILLINGHAM,
EMMA WEYMOUTH, CAROL WOOLTON, HIKARI YOKOYAMA

BEAUTY & WELLNESS
SENIOR BEAUTY & WELLNESS EDITOR LAUREN MURDOCH-SMITH
BEAUTY & WELLNESS EDITOR HANNAH COATES
BEAUTY & WELLNESS ASSOCIATE TWIGGY JALLOH
BEAUTY EDITOR-AT-LARGE PAT McGRATH
CONTRIBUTING BEAUTY EDITORS
KATHLEEN BAIRD-MURRAY, FUNMI FETTO, VAL GARLAND, SAM McKNIGHT,
GUIDO PALAU, EUGENE SOULEIMAN, CHARLOTTE TILBURY

CREATIVE
ASSOCIATE ART DIRECTOR EILIDH WILLIAMSON
DESIGNER MONTSE TANÚS
VISUALS DIRECTOR JAMIE SPENCE
VISUALS EDITOR KOFI PAINTSIL
ASSOCIATE VISUALS EDITOR ISABELLA BRUNNER

PRODUCTION/COPY
EUROPEAN PRODUCTION DIRECTOR VICTORIA WILLAN
ART PRODUCTION MANAGER ISABELLA PAPAZ
COPY DIRECTOR HOLLY BRUCE
COPY MANAGER AUGUST STEVENS

CONTENT STRATEGY/OPERATIONS
OPERATIONS MANAGER TIMOTHY HARRISON
**EXECUTIVE ASSISTANT TO VOGUE EUROPEAN
EDITORIAL DIRECTOR** YASMINE HANNI
PERSONAL ASSISTANT ZOE EDMUND-JONES
EDITORIAL BUSINESS MANAGER JESSICA BORGES
ACTING EDITORIAL BUSINESS MANAGER LOUISA McGOVERN
SYNDICATION ENQUIRIES SYNDICATION@CONDENAST.CO.UK

VOGUE DIGITAL
DIGITAL DIRECTOR KERRY McDERMOTT
EXECUTIVE FASHION NEWS & FEATURES EDITOR ALICE NEWBOLD
WEEKEND & PLANNING EDITOR HAYLEY MAITLAND
SENIOR MANAGER, AUDIENCE GROWTH ALYSON LOWE
SENIOR SUSTAINABILITY & FEATURES EDITOR EMILY CHAN
FILM & CULTURE EDITOR RADHIKA SETH
DIGITAL FASHION WRITER ALICE CARY
JUNIOR FASHION EDITOR ALEX KESSLER
AUDIENCE GROWTH EXECUTIVE ELEANOR DAVIES
SENIOR SOCIAL MEDIA MANAGER LEXXI DUFFY
ASSOCIATE SOCIAL MEDIA MANAGER HANNAH DALY

VIDEO
**DIRECTOR, DIGITAL VIDEO PROGRAMMING,
DEVELOPMENT & CREATIVE PRODUCTION** MINNIE J CARVER
PRODUCER GEORGIE BUTZ
VIDEO EDITOR & POST-PRODUCTION CO-ORDINATOR LYDIA BOWDEN
DIGITAL CREATIVE DIRECTOR-AT-LARGE ALEC MAXWELL

CONDE NAST IS COMMITTED
TO GLOBAL ENVIRONMENTAL
SUSTAINABILITY.
SCAN HERE FOR DETAILS

VOGUE GLOBAL
ANNA WINTOUR GLOBAL EDITORIAL DIRECTOR
APAC EDITORIAL DIRECTOR (TAIWAN, INDIA, JAPAN) LESLIE SUN

HEAD OF EDITORIAL CONTENT, FRANCE EUGÉNIE TROCHU
HEAD OF EDITORIAL CONTENT, GERMANY KERSTIN WENG
HEAD OF EDITORIAL CONTENT, INDIA MEGHA KAPOOR
HEAD OF EDITORIAL CONTENT, ITALY FRANCESCA RAGAZZI
HEAD OF EDITORIAL CONTENT, JAPAN TIFFANY GODOY
HEAD OF EDITORIAL CONTENT, MEXICO & LATIN AMERICA KARLA MARTÍNEZ DE SALAS
HEAD OF EDITORIAL CONTENT, SPAIN INÉS LORENZO
EDITOR IN CHIEF, CHINA MARGARET ZHANG

GLOBAL CREATIVE DIRECTOR JUAN COSTA PAZ
GLOBAL EDITOR AT LARGE HAMISH BOWLES
GLOBAL DIGITAL STRATEGY LEAD & US CONTENT STRATEGY EXECUTIVE DIRECTOR ANNA-LISA YABSLEY
GLOBAL NETWORK LEAD & US DEPUTY EDITOR TAYLOR ANTRIM
GLOBAL HEAD OF FASHION NETWORK VIRGINIA SMITH
GLOBAL NETWORK LEAD & US EDITOR, VOGUE.COM CHIOMA NNADI
GLOBAL DIRECTOR, VOGUE RUNWAY NICOLE PHELPS
GLOBAL NETWORK LEAD & US FASHION FEATURES DIRECTOR MARK HOLGATE
GLOBAL NETWORK LEAD & BEAUTY & WELLNESS DIRECTOR CELIA ELLENBERG
GLOBAL DIRECTOR, SOCIAL MEDIA STEFF YOTKA
GLOBAL DESIGN DIRECTOR AURELIE PELLISSIER ROMAN
GLOBAL CONTENT MANAGER TANNY ONSALO
ASSOCIATE APAC (TAIWAN, INDIA, JAPAN) CONTENT OPERATIONS DIRECTOR VAV LIN

JAEGER-LECOULTRE

REVERSO
DUETTO

Jaeger-LeCoultre Boutique, 13 Old Bond Street, Mayfair, London W1S 4SX

VOGUE

VANESSA KINGORI
CHIEF BUSINESS OFFICER, CONDE NAST BRITAIN & VOGUE EUROPEAN BUSINESS ADVISOR

EXECUTIVE ASSISTANT TO CHIEF BUSINESS OFFICER EMMA COX

LEAD BUSINESS REPORTING MANAGER CHLOE HAGGERTY

STYLE
CHIEF BUSINESS OFFICER, STYLE SOPHIE PISANO
VP, BUSINESS PARTNERSHIPS CLAIRE SINGER
LEAD COMMERCIAL DIRECTOR, FASHION & BEAUTY MADELEINE CHURCHILL
COMMERCIAL DIRECTOR, RETAILERS OTTILIE CHICHESTER
COMMERCIAL DIRECTOR, JEWELLERY ANA-KARINA DE PAULA ALLEN
ASSOCIATE COMMERCIAL DIRECTOR, FASHION ALEXIS WILLIAMS
SENIOR ACCOUNT DIRECTOR, FASHION ROYA FARROKHIAN
SENIOR ACCOUNT DIRECTOR, FASHION & JEWELLERY CHARLOTTE PENNINGTON
SENIOR ACCOUNT DIRECTORS, BEAUTY CAROLINE HOOLEY, JESS PURDUE, CAMILLA WILMOT-SMITH
ACCOUNT DIRECTOR, FASHION & JEWELLERY EMILY GOODWIN
SENIOR ACCOUNT MANAGER, BEAUTY CAROLINE SILLEM
ACCOUNT EXECUTIVE, FASHION ELLÉ BUTCHER
ADVERTISING ASSISTANT RACHEL HOLLAND

TRAVEL & LIFESTYLE
CHIEF BUSINESS OFFICER, TRAVEL & LIFESTYLE SIMON LEADSFORD
COMMERCIAL DIRECTOR, TRAVEL NATALIE MOSS-BLUNDELL
COMMERCIAL DIRECTOR, FOOD & BEVERAGES NATASHA CALLIN
SENIOR ACCOUNT DIRECTOR, TRAVEL EMMA HEUSER
ACCOUNT DIRECTORS, TRAVEL KEIRAN COYNE, SOPHIE CHAI
ACCOUNT MANAGER, FOOD & BEVERAGES HANNAH WARING
EVENTS MANAGER SAFFRON ALTMEYER-ENNIS
BUSINESS MANAGER CHARLOTTE TAYLOR

CNX
HEAD OF CNX HELEN ANGLIM
HEAD OF ART & CREATIVE DESIGN, CNX DOM KELLY
CREATIVE DESIGN DIRECTOR, CNX BOATEMA AMANKWAH
LEAD PRODUCTION MANAGER CAMILLA BELLAMACINA
JUNIOR CREATIVE PRODUCER KIRSTY BRADY

CLASSIFIED
CLASSIFIED DIRECTOR SHELAGH CROFTS
CLASSIFIED ADVERTISEMENT MANAGERS VANESSA DAWSON, EMILY VALENTINE
MANAGING SENIOR SALES EXECUTIVE/TRAINER ELENA GREGORI
SENIOR SALES EXECUTIVE/TRAINER ISABEL STUART
SENIOR SALES EXECUTIVES EMMA VAN DEN BURG, CELIA POPE
SALES EXECUTIVES KATY COLWELL, ABIGAIL WILLIAMSON

MARKETING
VP, CONSUMER REVENUE, EUROPE RUSSELL CLEEVE
HEAD OF MARKETING ELLA SIMPSON

PRODUCTION
PRODUCTION DIRECTOR SARAH JENSON
SENIOR PRODUCTION CONTROLLER EMILY BENTLEY
SENIOR PRODUCTION CO-ORDINATOR SAPPHO BARKLA
COMMERCIAL SENIOR PRODUCTION CONTROLLER LOUISE LAWSON
PAPER SENIOR PRODUCTION CONTROLLER MARTIN MACMILLAN

VOGUE BRAND
VICE PRESIDENT, BRAND REVENUE MICHIEL STEUR
SENIOR RETAIL EDITOR HOLLY TOMALIN
SPECIAL PROJECTS & EVENTS MANAGER ELLA NOBAY
SPECIAL PROJECTS & EVENTS MANAGER YASMIN GREAVES
PROJECT CO-ORDINATOR STRATOULA NASIOULA

CULTURE
CHIEF BUSINESS OFFICER, CULTURE NICK SARGENT
LEAD COMMERCIAL DIRECTOR, WATCHES VIKKI THEO
COMMERCIAL DIRECTOR, MEDIA/ENTERTAINMENT SILVIA WEINDLING
COMMERCIAL DIRECTOR, BIZ/FI/TECH CHRISTOPHER WARREN
ASSOCIATE COMMERCIAL DIRECTOR, BIZ/FI/TECH LUCIE BURTON-SALAHUDDIN
COMMERCIAL DIRECTOR, AUTOMOTIVE MELANIE KEYTE
ACCOUNT DIRECTOR, FINANCE JOE TEAL
ACCOUNT DIRECTOR, AUTOMOTIVE NICHOLAS FRENCH
ACCOUNT DIRECTOR, TECHNOLOGY EDDIE ROYLE
ACCOUNT MANAGER, MEDIA/ENTERTAINMENT ROSIE CAMPION
ACCOUNT MANAGER, WATCHES DAWID MATKOWSKI
ACCOUNT EXECUTIVE, WATCHES CHARLOTTE HEARTH
BUSINESS MANAGER ELLEN GARLICK

HOME
CHIEF BUSINESS OFFICER, HOME EMMA REDMAYNE
LEAD COMMERCIAL DIRECTOR, DECORATION SOPHIE CATTO
COMMERCIAL DIRECTOR, TRADE & DESIGN CHRISTOPHER DAUNT
COMMERCIAL DIRECTOR, HOME & PARTNERSHIPS MELINDA CHANDLER
COMMERCIAL DIRECTOR, HOME & RETAIL SAYNA BLACKSHAW
SENIOR ACCOUNT DIRECTORS ALEXANDRA BERNARD LAROCHE, GEORGINA HUTTON, NICHOLE MIKA, OLIVIA McHUGH, MARINA CONNOLLY
ACCOUNT DIRECTOR OLIVIA CAPALDI
SENIOR ACCOUNT MANAGER OLIVIA BARNES
ACCOUNT MANAGER ISABELLA FISH, FIONA McKEON
ACTING ACCOUNT EXECUTIVE FREYA HILL
BUSINESS MANAGER SOPHIA WARNER
GROUP PROPERTY DIRECTOR FIONA FORSYTH

CIRCULATION & INSIGHT
CIRCULATION DIRECTOR RICHARD KINGERLEE
NEWSTRADE MARKETING MANAGER OLIVIA STREATFIELD
SUBSCRIPTIONS DIRECTOR PATRICK FOILLERET
SENIOR CREATIVE DESIGN MANAGER ANTHEA DENNING
DIRECT MARKETING & EVENTS MANAGER LUCY ROGERS-COLTMAN
SUBSCRIPTIONS MARKETING MANAGER EMMA MURPHY
ASSISTANT PROMOTIONS & MARKETING MANAGER CLAUDIA LONG
INSIGHT MANAGER ERIN McQUITTY
RESEARCH EXECUTIVE HOLLY HARLAND

ASSOCIATE PUBLISHER US SHANNON TOLAR TCHKOTOUA
ITALIAN OFFICE MIA SRL

DEPUTY MANAGING DIRECTOR, EUROPE ALBERT READ
VP, HEAD OF REVENUE STRATEGY, WESTERN EUROPE MALCOLM ATTWELLS
FINANCE DIRECTOR DAISY TAM
PEOPLE DIRECTOR, LONDON ROSAMUND BRADLEY

MANAGING DIRECTOR, EUROPE NATALIA GAMERO DEL CASTILLO

PUBLISHED BY THE CONDE NAST PUBLICATIONS LTD,
VOGUE HOUSE, HANOVER SQUARE, LONDON W1S 1JU (020 7499 9080)

GIOVANNI RASPINI

5, South Molton Street - London

LONDON MILAN ROME FLORENCE VENICE MONTE CARLO

Coat, £4,400.
Gloves, from
a selection.
Both ALAIA

"EMBRACE a
full-length
OVERCOAT
that covers all
the BASES *"*

NAOMI SMART,
COMMERCE DIRECTOR

From left: £895, RAEY, *at*
Matchesfashion.com. From £3,490,
PROENZA SCHOULER. *£2,700,*
GUCCI *£1,695,* DRIES VAN
NOTEN. *£3,200,* STELLA
McCARTNEY

Shower DRESSING

Fashion's style FORECAST?
RAIN-READY *Wellingtons are
going down a* STORM

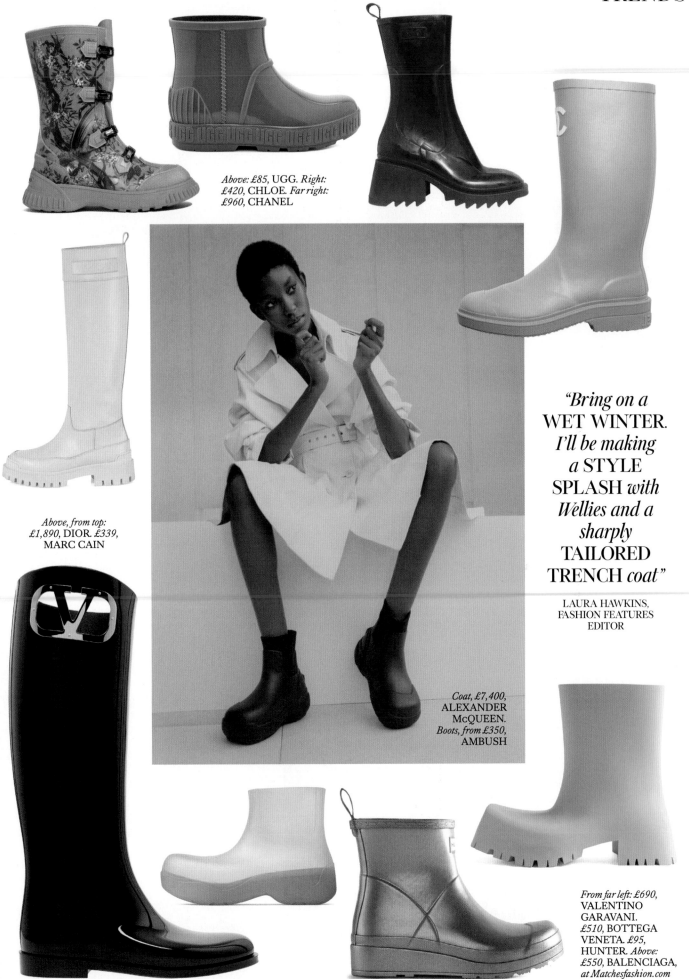

Above: £85, UGG. Right: £420, CHLOE. Far right: £960, CHANEL

Above, from top: £1,890, DIOR. £339, MARC CAIN

"Bring on a WET WINTER. I'll be making a STYLE SPLASH with Wellies and a sharply TAILORED TRENCH coat"

LAURA HAWKINS, FASHION FEATURES EDITOR

Coat, £7,400, ALEXANDER McQUEEN. Boots, from £350, AMBUSH

From far left: £690, VALENTINO GARAVANI. £510, BOTTEGA VENETA. £95, HUNTER. Above: £550, BALENCIAGA, at Matchesfashion.com

BOUCHERON

PARIS SINCE 1858

Easy SLIDER

SLIP-ON *has never looked* **SMARTER.** *The thigh's the* **LIMIT** *for ultra-luxe second-skin* **BOOTS**

Coat, £1,350,
EMPORIO
ARMANI.
Boots, £1,950,
BURBERRY

Right: jacket, from £1,920. Sweater, from £785. Top, from £1,745. Belted skirt, from £1,395. Boots, from £1,750. All GIVENCHY

Above: £2,010, BOTTEGA VENETA, at Net-a-porter. com. Below: from £635, MM MAISON MARGIELA

From far left: £995, NEOUS. £1,605, GIANVITO ROSSI. £1,400, KHAITE, at Net-a-porter. com. £400, MIISTA

> "The most ALLURING way to flaunt these fluid STYLES is without showing SKIN. Keep your body HIDDEN and let your boots seamlessly SLIDE into your pencil skirt"

ALICE CARY,
DIGITAL FASHION WRITER

KURT
GEIGER

One KNIT wonder

Prismatic PATTERN *is topping the* CHARTS. *We're wearing our wildest* WOOLLIES *on a* LOOP

Sweater, from
£1,050, PRADA

"From graphic PRINTS to cosy TEXTURES, this season's standout knitwear is the ultimate WINTER INVESTMENT"

JESSICA GERARDI,
SHOPPING EDITOR

*Sweater, £1,010.
Dress, £1,280.
Boots, £8,130. All*
BOTTEGA
VENETA

*Above, from top: £2,490, BURBERRY.
£795, ROKSANDA, at Net-a-porter.
com. From £650, ZANKOV. £2,700,
LORO PIANA, at Net-a-porter.com.
Top right: £2,520, LOUIS VUITTON.
Right, from left: from a selection, FENDI.
£1,130, SAINT LAURENT BY
ANTHONY VACCARELLO, at
Mytheresa.com. From £1,565, AKRIS*

Paul Smith

Jacket, £5,500. Trousers, £825. Both LOEWE

Jacket, £1,300, ALEX EAGLE. *Poloneck, £265,* N PEAL. *Trousers, from £1,000,* PRADA. *Belt, £430,* MIU MIU

Flight MODE

We're PILOTING *aeronautical proportions. The* BOMBER *jacket takes off with first-class* FINESSE

Clockwise from top left: from £430, ETUDES. *£1,400,* DIOR. *£2,900,* PRADA. *From £1,090,* FABIANA FILIPPI. *£1,000,* ISABEL MARANT. *From £3,490,* GIVENCHY. *£2,290,* BALENCIAGA

Camille x Mango

Ready-to-party pieces for those who know
how to have fun, by *Camille Charrière.*

MANGO

LIVE IN THE OPEN

CANADA GOOSE

Style REDUX

Noughties favourite
ROLAND MOURET *is back –*
and all GROWN UP

When Roland Mouret debuted his skintight, form-flaunting Galaxy dress in the mid-2000s, confident, body-positive women, from A-listers to royalty, were enchanted by its orbit. Winter marks a starry new trajectory for the label, founded more than 20 years ago and acquired in December 2021 by Han Chong, the entrepreneurial Malaysian founder of paycheque-friendly, partywear favourite Self-Portrait.

"The label is like Self-Portrait's big sister," Mouret says from the North London headquarters of Chong's 2013-founded brand, which launched with a line of instant-signature lace brocade dresses and is now synonymous with the sparkle and sequin of occasionwear. Mouret's studio sits side by side with Self-Portrait's, where his designs for the girl that has grown up, such as structural lilac diamanté gowns, fuchsia fit-and-flare dresses and sharply tailored coats, reflect his idiosyncratic focus on sensuality, comfort and colour.

"Our girl isn't borrowing these clothes from her mum," Mouret says. She's at the centre of her own universe. LAURA HAWKINS

Coat, £895. Dress, £895. Both ROLAND MOURET

MY STYLE RULES

Commerce director NAOMI SMART *recounts what she's learnt from more than 10 years as a* VOGUE EDITOR. *Photographs by* DANIKA LAWRENCE

F ashion rules can sometimes sound restrictive, but I think they offer a really good framework for building a working wardrobe that you're going to get the most out of. I've gone through many style phases over the years, but I've never stuck to one particular trend or "look", and that's served me well. Because even through the ebb and flow of trends, I've always gravitated towards foundational pieces that I can slot in alongside new silhouettes and of-the-moment accessories. This means I've still got denim jackets from when I was 16 and oversized charity shop shirts from when I was 20.

I've become much better at editing as I've gotten older, and I'm now stricter about not buying anything unless it's exactly what I'm looking for. Being an editor at *Vogue* has obviously played a huge role in that, and where I used to buy a lot of "it'll do" pieces, and end up owning multiple pairs of jeans even if they weren't the perfect fit, I've now learnt a more concise approach. I also see so many things that won't date well, so only choose pieces where the quality will hold, and I can pass down to my daughter – styles that are so good they'll definitely come round again.

My style rules live under certain categories that I love and always fall back on – double denim, oversized outerwear and '90s minimalist-inspired basics. I also have my go-to stores that I rely on, and Uniqlo is always at the top of my list because once you've found something that works, why change it?
For more information, visit Uniqlo.com

RULE 1
Oversized outerwear

A great coat is probably the most important purchase of the season and so it has to tick a few boxes. When I shop for womenswear, I always buy a couple of sizes up, not just for a more relaxed look, but for practicality too, as it needs to fit over heavy knitwear. It also needs to work 24/7, seven days a week, and finding a coat that works over eveningwear isn't easy. I think it's always worth scanning the menswear department. For example, this season a men's navy, drop-shoulder Balmacaan overcoat has caught my eye. I'll wear it slouched over dresses or teamed with over-the-knee boots – it's sure to be a key player in my wardrobe.

"A great COAT needs to work SEVEN days a week – it's the most important purchase of the SEASON"

Balmacaan coat,
£100, UNIQLO.
Accessories and
jewellery, throughout,
Naomi's own

This page: denim
shirt, £35.
Baggy jeans, £35.
Opposite: corduroy
shirt, £35.
Corduroy trousers,
£35. Belt, £25.
All UNIQLO

RULE 2
Nineties minimalism

Pared-back, understated basics never go out of style, and the '90s-era version of minimalism really encapsulates how I like to approach styling such staples. I've always been obsessed with throwback images of Carolyn Bessette-Kennedy – she pivoted around a neutral palette and effortlessly paired everyday wardrobe essentials, such as a crisp white shirt with a sharp evening maxi skirt. There is a street photograph from the mid-'90s of her walking through the city in brown corduroys and a black sweater, the styling was so simple and great for the weekend. I found the exact same shade in this Uniqlo pair and they look great with precise black accessories.

2

RULE 3
Double denim

My go-to outfit has become double denim, even for the office. It's super quick and easy to pull together, much like a suit, maxi dress or jumpsuit, because the only extras you need to think about are the accessories. As co-ord styles go, I think it's the most classic with everlasting appeal – it's the epitome of smart casual to me, especially when worn with heels. I keep it fresh by pivoting around the cut or wash of the season. This year it's all about the women's baggy jeans, so ask in-store for this exact style. Wear it low on the hip until the hems pool on the floor. Both the jeans and shirt are three sizes up from my usual size. Keep experimenting with sizing until you find that perfect oversized fit.

"As CO-ORD *styles go,* DOUBLE *denim is the most* CLASSIC *with* EVERLASTING *appeal"*

Fashioning the FUTURE

DANA THOMAS
spotlights a new class of MODERN ARTISANS

O n a warm summer evening at Dumfries House – the sustainability education centre in Ayrshire, Scotland, of the former Prince of Wales, now HM King Charles III – eight fashion and textiles students unveiled their work for Modern Artisan, a responsible design and craftmanship incubator organised and supported by Yoox Net-a-Porter and The Prince's Foundation. The capsule collection of 13 looks is the second that Modern Artisan has produced since 2020.

For six months, the group worked on the collection at the Textile Centre, a fashion studio on the 2,000-acre estate, and everything they employed was a hundred per cent responsibly sourced. The materials are made of natural fibres and half the fabrics were surplus or "deadstock". The thread is cotton rather than the ubiquitous polyester, which is petroleum-based, and the notions are eco-minded, such as buttons in mother-of-pearl or biodegradable beetroot. The finished items bear the new Digital ID – a QR code developed by the SMI Fashion

HM King Charles III, Yoox Net-a-Porter CEO Geoffroy Lefebvre and Modern Artisan Zhenqi Weng

Taskforce to detail a garment's production journey. The collection will be available across the Yoox Net-a-Porter sites on 3 November, with 50 per cent of each sale going to The Prince's Foundation. The aim of Modern Artisan, Yoox Net-a-Porter CEO Geoffroy Lefebvre told guests at the presentation, is "to support the next generation of creative talent that will push our industry forward".

As the United Nations states in its Youth in Action initiative, there are 1.8 billion people between the ages of 10 and 24, and according to the Berggruen Institute, an independent think tank in Los Angeles, 41 per cent of globally surveyed young people view the climate crisis as the biggest issue facing the world today. These young people possess a "massive power" to "hold decision-makers accountable", the UN states, and they are employing their skills – sewing included – to accelerate climate action.

Take Xiye Bastida, a 20-year-old Mexican-born, US-based climate activist. Her gift is in organising: she helped stage Greta Thunberg's Fridays for Future school

strikes in New York City. More recently, she cofounded Re-Earth Initiative, a youth-driven global NGO that works to bring climate justice to all. For Dominique Palmer, a 23-year-old climate activist based in London, it's all about engaging communication. To that end, she has helped organise Climate Live, a series of mini-concerts "that harness the power of music to empower people to take action", she said. Both young women will attend Cop27 in Egypt in November to share their pro-climate message with global policymakers.

Similarly, the Modern Artisans hope to express the urgency of climate action through fashion. "We know that people aren't going to stop buying clothes," Isabelle Pennington-Edmead, a 24-year-old British Kittitian, admitted, "so it's good to offer a beautifully crafted, sustainable alternative with a message". Zhenqi Weng, a 26-year-old raised in Treviso, Italy, concurred. "What we learnt here is to make ethical fashion that aligns with our beliefs," he said. "We must all think about the planet in everything we do."

FLANNELS
WELCOME TO NEW LUXURY

FLANNELS.COM

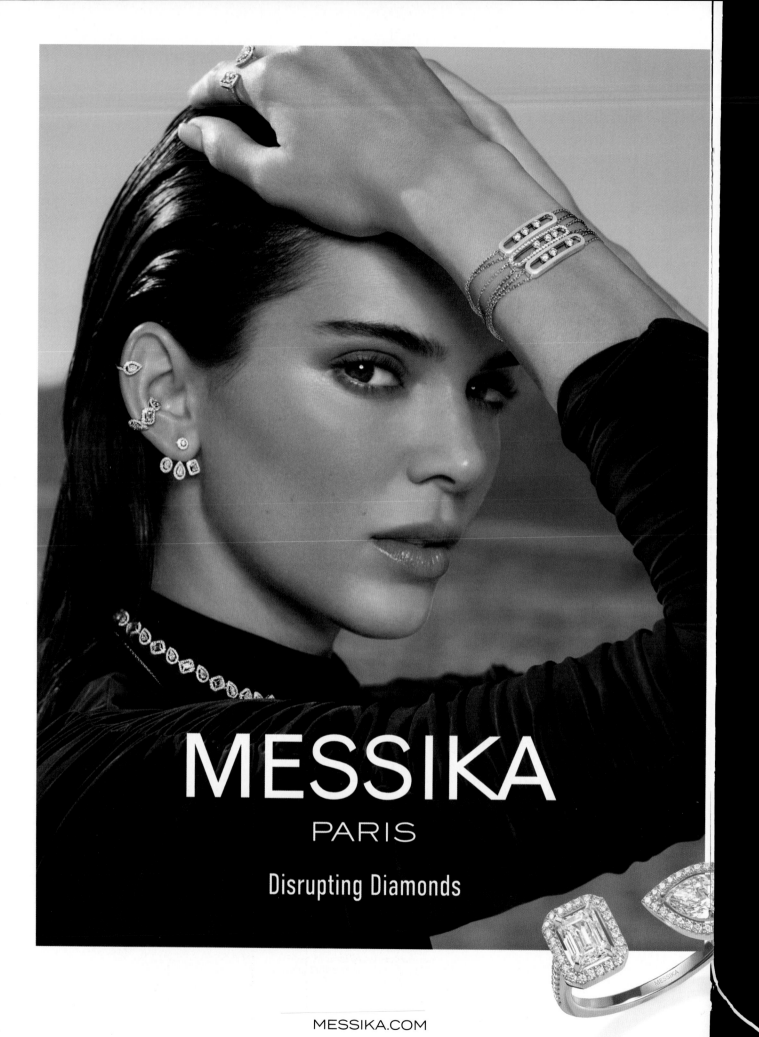

MESSIKA

PARIS

Disrupting Diamonds

MESSIKA.COM

1.

3.

2.

4.

5.

Perfect TIMING

Chic, precise – and WITH *added* STOPWATCH *details – these chronograph watches are* RIGHT *on time, says* RACHEL GARRAHAN

6.

7.

1. Gold, OMEGA. 2. Steel, £8,300, ZENITH & WATCHES OF SWITZERLAND. 3. Steel, £4,220, TUDOR. 4. Rose gold, diamond and steel, £15,300, CHOPARD. 5. Steel, mother-of-pearl and diamond, £520, TISSOT. 6. Aluminium, rubber and titanium, £3,950, BULGARI. 7. Steel, £7,250, BREITLING. 8. Platinum, VACHERON CONSTANTIN. Prices on request unless otherwise stated. For stockists, see Vogue Information

8.

CRAFTED *to* LAST

From top: bracelet, £690.
Bangle, £1,090. Ring,
£690. Earrings, £690.
All PANDORA

PANDORA *has*
introduced new
STYLES *to its*
DIAMOND
jewellery range,
just in time for
GIFTING *season*

PANDORA LAUNCHED ITS first-ever diamond jewellery collection, Diamonds by Pandora, last year. Following the success of its early designs – which included minimalist necklaces, rings, earrings and bracelets – Pandora has welcomed several new styles to the line-up. The fresh additions feature the same delicate teardrop motif as the initial release, seen across curb-chain pendants, understated rings, double-layer necklaces, bangles and stud earrings.

The collection explores the wondrous qualities of sustainable lab-grown diamonds – or "exquisitely beautiful, lab-created diamonds", as Pandora describes them. Rather than working with mined stones, Pandora offers exclusively lab-grown diamonds, meaning they are available at an accessible price point. Prices start from £250 and the diamonds range from 0.15 to one carat. Jewellery pieces are available in sterling silver and 14-carat gold, while the higher-carat diamonds are also available in white gold.

Steering clear of trends, Pandora focused on timelessness. The strong, instantly recognisable teardrop emblem seen throughout the range has been met with great response from Pandora customers. The reasonable price point has also attracted younger consumers, who can trust Pandora with their first diamond purchase. Another unique selling point? The creation process of lab-grown diamonds makes it Pandora's first-ever carbon-neutral collection, a milestone feat for the brand, which was originally founded in 1982 by Per Enevoldsen and his wife, Winnie.

Lab-grown diamonds are identical to traditionally mined stones and possess the same unique qualities. Keen to replicate the flair of mined stones, Pandora set a standard for every diamond made, which is known as the four Cs: cut, clarity, colour and craft. Every lab-grown stone is individually crafted by artisans who keep the four Cs in mind at every stage of production and are "obsessed with breathing fire and beauty into every diamond".

Explore the collection online at Pandora.net
and in selected Pandora stores

BREAKING THE SURFACE

From Syrian war zone to the Rio Olympics, MARIA HUNSTIG
*meets the miraculous Mardinis – and the sisters who play them in
new film The Swimmers. Photographs by* TOM KLEINSCHMIDT.
Styling by JULIA BRENARD

*From left: Yusra Mardini
wears viscose dress,*
BOTTEGA VENETA.
Necklace, MILLY GRACE.
*Sara Mardini wears crêpe
shirtdress,* PROENZA
SCHOULER. *Trousers,*
TIBI. *Silver earrings,*
ALIGHIERI. *Nathalie
Issa wears viscose dress,*
STELLA McCARTNEY.
Gold-plated double ring,
TILLY SVEAAS. *Manal
Issa wears swimsuit,*
HERMES. *Trousers,* TIBI

O n a sunny Berlin afternoon, at a lido next to the river Spree, sisters Sara and Yusra Mardini are joking around with Manal and Nathalie Issa, the actors (also sisters) who will portray the refugees turned Olympic swimmer and campaigner in this winter's *The Swimmers*. Here to be photographed for *Vogue*, it's hard to believe the four have hardly ever met in person. And almost impossible to imagine what it took them to get here.

The Mardini sisters' story is well told, yet never fails to leave you speechless. Yusra and Sara, who grew up close to Damascus, were gifted swimmers, coached by a passionate father. Yet, in the summer of 2015, aged 17 and 20, the two had to flee the bombs of the Syrian civil war, leaving behind their parents and younger sister. Via Lebanon and Turkey, they were smuggled from Izmir towards Greece on a desperately overcrowded dinghy, whose motor broke down mid crossing as it began to sink under the weight of its passengers. It was the sisters' courage

and exceptional swimming skills that saw them, and two others, jump into the deep waters to lessen the load until, after several hours, the group reached the island of Lesbos, saving the lives of 18 people. (In the biopic, this crossing is brought to life with jaw-dropping brilliance by director Sally El Hosaini.)

From Greece, the Mardinis took a land route across the Balkans, partly by foot, and ultimately arrived in Berlin. Yusra couldn't wait to train again and found a swimming club and coach who helped her achieve her most cherished dream: swimming at the Olympics. In 2016 she competed in Rio de Janeiro, part of the Games' first Refugee Olympic Team, winning one of her heats in butterfly. Later that year, she was listed by *Time* as one of "The 30 Most Influential Teens of 2016". She met Barack Obama and Pope Francis and, in 2017, was appointed the youngest ever UNHCR Goodwill Ambassador, aged 19.

"After the Olympics, I realised that it's not just my story anymore. I realised that my responsibility is to >

This page, from left:
Yusra wears silk/wool
dress, SALVATORE
FERRAGAMO. *Gold and*
diamond ring, MATILDE
JEWELLERY. *Sara wears*
dress, TIBI. *Silver bracelets,*
TILLY SVEAAS.
Earrings, as before.
Opposite: Manal and
Nathalie wear swimsuit
and dress, as before.
For stockists, all pages,
see Vogue Information.
Hair: PEGGY KURKA.
Make-up: JULIA BARDE.
Production: VERS
BERLIN. *Digital artwork:*
FABIAN BOLLIG.
With thanks to HOTEL
DE ROME *and*
ARENA BERLIN

raise awareness and bring hope to millions of refugees around the world and speak for all of those who do not have a voice," she tells me, emphatically. From the shy, worried teenager depicted in the movie, Yusra has clearly developed a warm and confident presence.

Meanwhile, Sara took a less starry but no less remarkable path. Described by her sister as "the wild child", a few years ago she returned to Lesbos with an NGO to help other boat refugees by rescuing them from the water and supporting them with translation. In 2018, she was arrested. Greek authorities accused her and other helpers of numerous crimes, including smuggling, espionage and fraud. Sara, now 27, was remanded in custody (first in Lesbos, then in Athens) for more than 100 days before she was released on bail and could return to Berlin, where the rest of her family now live.

A trial against her began last November, though she was not allowed to enter Greece to defend herself. If found guilty, Sara faces a combined sentence of up to 20 years. She has repeatedly claimed her innocence; NGOs such as Human Rights Watch consider her charges "absurd" and possibly "politically motivated"; a European Parliament study called the Lesbos trial "the largest case of criminalisation of solidarity in Europe".

The past four years have been hard on Sara. She had to pause her studies and work projects. What helped? "The amount of people that came together and spoke up for me when my freedom was taken away," she says. It's overwhelming for her, but she remains a people person, ever keen to make the others on set laugh. "That's exactly what I'm standing up for. I want people to uplift each other. We have to work for a better future, all of us together."

The Swimmers is not a documentary. It does not, for example, contain Sara's most recent trials, ending as she returns to the Mediterranean to volunteer. From producers Working Title Films and Netflix, and director El Hosaini, the film-makers' aim was not purely to tell the Mardinis' story with unyielding realism. It had to encapsulate the greater sense of what millions of refugees go through every day. "They believe the film is not only about them," says Manal, who plays Sara, "but about everyone who doesn't have a home anymore."

At the centre of the film sit a pair of naturalistic performances that cut to the heart. The team initially tried to cast Syrian actresses to portray the Mardinis, but the need for paperwork to travel freely for filming was prohibitive. When they decided to widen the search to neighbouring countries, Manal, a French Lebanese actress who recently impressed in 2021's *Memory Box*, was one of the first names that came to El Hosaini's mind. Yet Manal wasn't instantly interested. She didn't want to be part of "another stereotypical movie about the Syrian refugee crisis", she tells me vivaciously over Zoom a few days after the shoot. (Manal is no stranger to activism herself: in 2018 she hit the Cannes red carpet with a "Stop the Attack on Gaza" sign in hand.) "Not everybody is able to speak about refugees the way they want to be spoken about." But El Hosaini's approach and nuanced portrayal of sisterhood convinced her – even to learn swimming.

"We go through really TOUGH STUFF *while crossing to* EUROPE. *And no, we don't come here because of the* LUXURIES. *We come because we want to live in* PEACE*"*

It was Manal who suggested her younger sister, Nathalie, as a candidate to play Yusra. Again, this took some persuasion. "I refused to do a self-tape, twice, because I was really scared of swimming and water, and because I really wanted to focus on my studies," Nathalie explains, gesticulating wildly, as is her style. Eventually curiosity got the better of her. She got the role and embarked on two months of intense swimming and muscle training, spending hours in the pool six days a week. "I have surprised myself a lot," she continues, adding she loved her training time with "the real" Sven Spannekrebs, Yusra's coach.

The Issas bring so much of themselves to their roles: as sisters, from their own experience of fleeing war (they first left Lebanon for France in 2006) and the continual struggle to define where "home" is for them. They do not depict the film's heroines as victims. Nor is Syria shown as if it's only ever been a war zone. There's lightness and sarcasm, both of which were crucial to cast and crew. "When I act in Europe, I often find my characters to be very serious," says Manal. "But that's not how we deal with things. You can have the worst problem in your life and someone comes to see you and you laugh."

Yusra agrees: "The main point is to show that refugees are normal. We have dreams. We want to achieve things in life. We go through really tough stuff while crossing and coming to Europe. And no, we don't come here because of the luxuries. We come here because we want to just have a fair chance in life. We want to live in peace."

She's planning to study film and production, while Sara is interested in working on her German so she can apply to fashion school in Berlin. Manal wants to explore directing and Nathalie just finished her studies and dreams of writing a book. Watching them on set, full of empathy and promise, their drive impresses the most.

"We learnt a lot," says Sara, thoughtfully, of the trials of their young lives. "I would never have it any other way. I would do the same journey, and would do it with my sister, and would risk everything as we did because we found safety at the end."

The Swimmers will be released in cinemas on 11 November, and on Netflix from 23 November

La vie est belle

THE ICONIC EAU DE PARFUM,
NOW REFILLABLE

LANCÔME PARIS

*The best way to connect
is simply to disconnect.*

THE RESIDENCE
by *Cenizaro*

FOREVER YOURS

Cenizaro Hotels & Resorts
Bintan | Maldives | Marrakech | Mauritius | Tunis | Zanzibar

cenizaro.com

La Maison Arabe
MARRAKECH
by Cenizaro

THE RESIDENCE
by Cenizaro

VOGUE
TRAVEL

THE BIG
CHILL

*Sensational CITY breaks, WINTER on the
Riviera & Europe's last WILDERNESS*

Bethlen Estates in Transylvania. Below: the Caretaker's House bedroom and kitchen; Lake Tarnița

WHEN *in* ROMANIA

Eclectic, EERIE *and oh so charming,* TRANSYLVANIA *is having its moment, finds* LUKE ABRAHAMS

T ransylvania. The name alone conjures up thoughts of literary nostalgia: dark fairy tales, Gothic castles, occasional vampires. But, beyond stories of a bloodthirsty count, for too long many travellers have known too little about the rural wonders of Romania. Hidden from the world by the icy plumes of mist that top its share of the Carpathian Mountains, it has remained a scandalously overlooked time capsule; a secret sonnet to Europe's great lost wilderness.

That's beginning to change though. A new wave of travellers has begun to trickle into the region. Tired of Instagram tourism, these holidayers are searching for adventures that have all the natural, historic beauty of, say, a trip to the Dolomites or the lakes of Croatia, but with a sense of the unknown, and far fewer tourists to compete with.

Within a few minutes of landing in the unofficial capital city, Cluj-Napoca, I'm glad I followed their lead. As I drive out into the countryside, modernity fades and a pastoral landscape reveals itself. This is a place of higgledy-piggledy rolling hills, wildflower meadows and ancient oak forests. Wood smoke rises from the chimneys of charming Saxon villages. Brown bears, lynx, wolves, deer and chamois roam the hiking trails. And horse-drawn carriages, loaded with working men, trundle down narrow Sylvan lanes.

It takes three hours to arrive at Bethlen Estates, my home for the next two nights. It's a cluster of pretty cottages where visitors can enjoy the slow-go pace of rural life – and learn about Transylvania's

Clockwise from far left: Depner House at Bethlen Estates; Cluj-Napoca; the region's vast countryside

turbulent history while they're at it. The area was passed between Hungary and Romania until the end of the Second World War. It remained behind the Iron Curtain until 1989, when Nicolae Ceaușescu's regime fell. During that time, lands were stolen, castles ransacked and some families ended up in Russian internment camps or fled to Hungary or Austria. One such family was that of Count Miklos of Bethlen, who had grown up in a castle – once at the centre of his estate – set above the Sleepy Hollow-like village of Cris.

He spent years sneaking over the border from Austria to revisit his ancestral homeland. "My husband never cut ties with the place or his roots," his widow, and now castle matriarch, Countess Gladys Bethlen tells me, a cigarette in one hand and a wicker basket in the other. She's giving me a tour of the building, a place she confesses she's not visited in years because it's too painful. "The mission was always to restore my husband's family's home to bring some form of life and normality and presence back to the village," she says.

Once considered one of the finest Renaissance fortresses in Transylvania, much of the building is still in disrepair, but in recent years, Bethlen and her son Nikolaus have worked to renovate many of the other ancestral properties on the family's estate, turning them into pit stops for travellers. The result is a unique holiday experience – a quiet escape built for reflective nomads in surroundings that look like the backdrop of a Netflix Christmas movie.

The village of Cris is all about the simple life – only 800 or so people live here. There's no baker, no farmer, no caretaker. A feeling of no-fuss luxuriousness cocoons many of her restored residences. "That's what everybody wants! Simplistic elegance… to the point, no fuss, luxury… to hide away from the world and disappear after all this Covid and this terrible war," Gladys insists.

Her headliner is the four-bedroomed Caretaker's House, a picture of soft linens, library-chic and rooms with views of dewy pastures. There's also Saxon Cottage Depner House, pretty in blue limewash, which has reclaimed beams on its low ceilings and shelves stocked with a medley of curated books, old photographs and fine china.

Food is whatever the chef can find on the day, served in the Kitchen Barn. More spaces, the countess promises, will open soon.

While Bethlen is a place of stillness, the rest of Transylvania cries out for exploration. The countryside is dotted with imposing medieval and 19th-century architecture. Bran, just outside the mighty Carpathians, is world-famous for its starring role in the myth of Count Dracula. Peleş, an hour or so away, is even more ornate: think neo-Renaissance design topped off with great big spires, glistening tiles and storied portraiture. Meanwhile, up north, you'll find Sighişoara, the small Unesco-protected medieval city full of colourful houses, ancient churches, artisan boutiques and cobbled streets. (Rumour has it, it's is also one of the most haunted on the planet.)

If you tire of stripped-back pomp and idyllic pastures, there are places to find a glimpse of everyday Transylvanian life. In Cluj you'll find a thriving cultural scene. The Interest Centre brings the best contemporary art out there to the locals, and the National Art Museum is brimming with works from the likes of Ion Andreescu to Nicolae Grigorescu and Stefan Luchian. If you're into jazz and blues, Sibiu is dotted with atmospheric speakeasies to disappear in.

To me, the whole of Transylvania has the allure of a mumble-jumble speakeasy: it's off-grid that you'll find its charms. Whether you're here to find retreat in a half-restored aristocratic estate, to dip your toe into kooky Eastern European theatre or to hike through meadows filled with tuberose, white narcissus and violet sage, there's a romanticised chaos to it all. It's a place to get lost in, rather than seen in. And, that's very much part of its growing appeal.

Rooms from £178 per night. Bethlenestates.com

95

SUITE DREAMS

The best BOLTHOLES *in the Middle East, chosen by* TALIB CHOUDHRY

Habitas AlUla, *Ashar Valley, Saudi Arabia*

Located in a desert dotted with Nabatean ruins and contemporary art installations, Habitas AlUla is the kingdom's first proper boutique hotel. Each guest villa has a tented veranda, and the setting is breathtaking, with sunset yoga, hikes and stargazing on offer to showcase its mercurial beauty. *Rooms from £349 per night. Ourhabitas.com*

Souq Waqif Boutique Hotels, *Doha, Qatar*

Doha's waterside Souq Waqif has been artfully restored in preparation for the World Cup, but Qatari fishermen and spice merchants can still be found selling their wares to locals. Nestled throughout the souq, eight properties boast luxe decor and a calmness that belies the bustle beyond their carved wooden doors. Rooms with colonnaded balconies provide the perfect spot to sip Arabic coffee as the sun sets over the Corniche. *Rooms from £97 per night. Tivolihotels.com*

Nuzul Al Salam Hotel, *Muharraq, Bahrain*

Lined with grand, faded mansions, the Bahrain Pearling Path became a Unesco World Heritage Site in 2012 and Nuzul Al Salam is the new jewel in its crown. Built in 1947, Fathallah House has been transformed into a six-room hotel that preserves the essence of a Bahraini home. Styled by interior designer Ammar Basheir, the suites are inspired by the Epic of Gilgamesh, blending locally sourced artworks and vintage details with contemporary furniture and Lebanese tapestries. *Rooms from £249 per night. Joulan@ shaikhebrahimcenter.org*

Arthaus Beirut, *Lebanon*

Set in the city's lively Gemmayze district, this hotel is made up of four Ottoman-era stone buildings, restored by married hoteliers Nabil and Zoe Debs. The Beirut outpost plays host to a creative crowd, who flock to exhibitions in the courtyard gallery, sip cocktails in the arch-ceilinged bar, or lounge by the outdoor pool. *Rooms from £252 per night. Arthaus.international*

XVA Art Hotel, *Dubai, United Arab Emirates*

Tucked away in the narrow alleyways of Dubai's Al Fahidi historical neighbourhood, XVA is as much an art gallery as it is a hotel, and attracts those who seek a contrast to the high-octane glamour of new Dubai. The 13 white-washed rooms channel rustic romance without falling into *Arabian Nights* pastiche, thanks to the elegant vision of founder Mona Hauser. *Rooms from £83 per night. Xvahotel.com*

ISLAND LIVING

Start 2023's holiday planning now with a LUXURY VILLA *in* GREECE's *picturesque Cyclades*

With their combination of tasteful decor, extraordinary facilities and fantastic locations, each property within The Greek Villas's portfolio has been designed to meet your every need, meaning you'll never want to leave

WHITEWASHED BUILDINGS, VIBRANT bougainvillea and turquoise waters – there's nowhere quite like the picture-perfect Greek islands for a relaxing getaway. When it comes to accommodation, look to The Greek Villas, which boasts a premium portfolio of luxury rentals all over Greece, including two of the prettiest islands of the Cyclades, Paros and Antiparos, with their winding streets and sun-drenched harbours. Stunning views, exceptional facilities, tasteful decor and carefully chosen locations make the villas truly special places to stay, while a 24/7 concierge service, tailor-made itineraries and bespoke recommendations ensure your trip will go off without a hitch.

Take the Neymar II villa in Paros, with its infinity pool overlooking the sea and a vast, sunny terrace nestled among olive trees. Or the spacious Hampton villa in Antiparos, which sleeps 16, built from locally sourced stone and perched atop a hill with unbeatable views of the Aegean Sea. Each property is unique, yet shares the style, luxuriousness and first-class service that sets The Greek Villas apart, and ensures your island escape will be truly unforgettable.

To discover more online and book your stay, visit Thegreekvillas.com

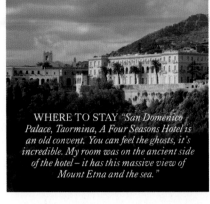

WHERE TO STAY *"San Domenico Palace, Taormina, A Four Seasons Hotel is an old convent. You can feel the ghosts, it's incredible. My room was on the ancient side of the hotel – it has this massive view of Mount Etna and the sea."*

TRAVEL MISTAKE TO AVOID *"I brought eight suitcases to Italy, while my friends all brought these tiny suitcases with one killer outfit in. I've learnt from them to keep packing to just a few items and then you don't have all this luggage to take everywhere. It ended up being a huge imposition!"*

From left: SHISEIDO *Sports BB Compact SPF50+, £34.* SISLEY PARIS *Super Stick Solaire Teinté SPF 50+, £82*

BEAUTY ESSENTIALS *"If I get sunscreen in my eyes then my whole day is ruined! But Shiseido and Sisley do these products that never get in your eyes, even if you sweat. I was told about them by some surfers I met in Hawaii."*

Dress, £1,800, DOLCE & GABBANA, at Browns fashion.com

WHAT TO WEAR *"Dolce & Gabbana always do me right. I wore a lot of their dresses in Sicily, as well as Alberta Ferretti, a couple of Valentino pieces... I have a flowy beachy dress from them that I saw J Lo wearing."*

Sunglasses, £230, VICTORIA BECKHAM

BEST SUNGLASSES *"I have a pair of big, black Victoria Beckhams. People always ask me where they are from."*

THE *ITALIAN* JOB

After months SPENT *filming on the island, actor* JENNIFER COOLIDGE *offers a* SLICE *of Sicily to* KATE LLOYD

"Want me to tell you how you really get to know Italians?" asks Jennifer Coolidge, with a pause for dramatic effect. Earlier this year, the 61-year-old actor spent five glorious months living in Sicily. She was there to film series two of *The White Lotus*, Mike White's dark comedy about moneyed holidaymakers being horrendous, having picked up an Emmy for her appearance in the first series. But she's not here to talk about that, she's here to share her guide to the rugged Italian island, a place she fell deeply in love with during filming. "It was my first time there," she gushes. "I experienced beauty that I have never seen before." The actor filled her downtime by hiking, swimming, "staring at the sea", indulging in large chocolate desserts ("I didn't hold back!") and, of course, meeting the locals. "You've got to go out with them late at night," she says. "They really have a blast. The film business starts early, but I would sacrifice the morning just to join them."

TRUMAN CAPOTE LOCAL COLOR

WHAT TO READ *"Local Color by Truman Capote. He lived in Taormina with his partner, Jack Dunphy. His house, Fontana Vecchia, is still there."*

THE VIEW *"In Taormina, I would climb up to a little church called Chiesa Madonna della Rocca. It has a magnificent view of the sea. My hiking outfit? Always a pink and black Diane von Furstenberg skirt."*

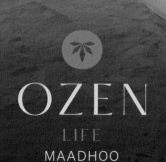

REFINED ELEGANCE

OZEN
LIFE
MAADHOO

ON THE TOWN
The latest COSMOPOLITAN *openings suggest it's* TIME *to reconsider the* CITY *break, says* OLIVIA MARKS

PARIS

Nestled among the boutiques and book shops of Saint-Germain, Hotel Dame Des Arts – with a rooftop bar offering unbeatable views of the city – will make for the perfect bolthole for an autumnal trip to Paris's Left Bank when it opens this November. Designed by Raphael Navot, whose diverse portfolio spans nightclubs to Loro Piana's new interiors offering, the 109-room, 1950s-built hotel is a masterclass in understated luxury. The restaurant, which opens on to a courtyard, will see French classics fused with flavours from the North Pacific, and will be soundtracked by DJ Jez Pereira, while a gym and treatment room offer a dose of R&R after a day's shopping and sightseeing. *Rooms from £280 per night. Damedesarts.com*

ATHENS

It was only in 2020 that creative director and photographer Eftihia Stefanidi brought Shila, a boutique hotel and members club, to Athens. Two years later and her newly opened second property, Mona, is very much a sister space, acting as both hub for the city's art crowd and a stylish place to stay. Located in downtown Psirri (it's just a short car ride to the port of Piraeus, from where ferries depart to Hydra and Spetses), Mona occupies an eight-storey mid-century factory, giving it an edgier, but no less bohemian vibe. Alongside 20 beautifully appointed, laid-back rooms you'll find a living room, kitchen – which hosts regular supper clubs – and a basement venue with some of the buzziest live events Athens has to offer. *Rooms from £224 per night. Mona-athens.com*

NASHVILLE

With new outposts from Soho House and 1 Hotel – and now a direct flight from London Heathrow – Nashville has become a fresh contender on the city-beak map. Even more so now that Four Seasons has joined the line-up, taking the Tennessee capital's famed Southern hospitality up another notch with a $400 million 40-storey glass tower, comprising 235 rooms featuring floor-to-ceiling windows and sleek interiors that make the most of the state's native black walnut. For those making a musical pilgrimage, the hotel is situated in the city's SoBro neighbourhood, just minutes from the must-see attractions. Also on offer? The opportunity to collaborate with a local musician, who'll help you write and record your own song. Or, if whiskey's your bag, learn to blend your own at a local distillery. And, naturally, the hotel itself is a huge draw, thanks to an infinity pool atop an expansive roof terrace as well as a notable spa. *Rooms from £569 per night. Fourseasons.com*

TRAVEL special

NEW YORK

LAURA INGHAM, deputy director, Global Fashion Network

When you could experience the timeless elegance of the Casa Cipriani hotel (*right*), why would you stay anywhere else? It has unparalleled waterside views and is a firm favourite with *Vogue* models and editors alike. It was the perfect venue for our June cover shoot with Gisele Bündchen. And, while the team came for the incredible setting, they were charmed by the warm service, which made it difficult to leave.

Above: sunglasses, £270, TOM FORD. *Bag, £465,* MICHAEL MICHAEL KORS

LAURA HAWKINS, fashion features editor

Tucked on a narrow street in Brera's Design District, the waistcoat-clad waiters at Torre di Pisa (*right*) serve up an exceptional parmesan-piled carbonara and an expertly al dente *orecchiette* with a green vegetable sauce. You'll always spot an A-lister at a nearby table at the if-you-know-you-know trattoria. I never leave without sampling the tiramisu – the sugar and caffeine boost is most welcome when filing show copy after dinner.

CAPITAL STYLE

Four VOGUE *editors share their Fashion Month* HIGHLIGHTS

The Punch Room at The London Edition. Below: Deborah Ababio and Sarah Harris with the Vogue team's Mercedes for London Fashion Week

LONDON

MILAN

Left: trainers, £270, HERNO. *Above: hoodie, £310,* MARINA RINALDI BY SARA BATTAGLIA

Above, from left: blazer, £3,200, BRUNELLO CUCINELLI. *Boots, £450,* PAUL SMITH

ROSIE VOGEL-EADES, global director, talent & casting

The revamped Punch Room at The London Edition is the place to go for modern cocktails. Put down your Skinny Bitch and head there for some of the most interesting cocktails you'll ever have.

PARIS

Jacket, £255, MARC CAIN. *Left: suitcase, £6,700,* HERMÈS

DONNA WALLACE, fashion & accessories editor

There's vintage and there is Parisian vintage. Within minutes of entering the Thanx God I'm A VIP (*far left*) boutique on Rue de Lancry, you quickly appreciate the difference. Expect proper fashion finds and a well-curated collection. Meanwhile, The Broken Arm, a hybrid shopping/eating destination on Rue Perrée, is the place to go for a sophisticated edit of the labels you love (and ones you've not discovered yet) alongside an elegant restaurant.

ALPINE
RESIDENCES

Your unforgettable mountain getaway

PRESTIGIOUS HOTELS & RESIDENCES WITH 5* FACILITIES

COURCHEVEL | LES GETS | VAL D'ISÈRE
www.alpine-residences.fr
+33 (0)4 80 94 95 96 - booking@alpine-residences.fr

RIVIERA *REVISITED*

Bid WINTER*'s harsh realities adieu on the* COTE D'AZUR, *says* HAYLEY MAITLAND

Before it became a summer playground for the indolently glamorous, the French Riviera had a different reputation: the place where the beau monde would decamp each winter to partake in health cures and escape the frigid weather in northern Europe. In his 1766 volume *Travels Through France and Italy*, Tobias Smollett touted the region as an open-air sanatorium where the December sun is "as warm as it is in May in England", while Queen Victoria joined the flocks of "winter swallows" pursuing "climate therapy" in Nice at the end of the 19th century.

But by the 1920s, a transformation had begun. "Six years ago, Cannes resembled a winter resort enveloped, for the summer, in slip covers, with only a few of the local shops and one hotel open," *Vogue* marvelled in September 1931. "Now the place is teeming with life in summer, far more so than in winter... The harbour is filled with yachts and speedboats, and the Croisette bristles with the branches of well-known Paris houses."

Almost a century later and the Côte d'Azur is going back to its roots, with The Maybourne Riviera leading the way. Launched at the end of 2021 by the group behind Claridge's, the strikingly modern hotel, built into a cliff above Roquebrune-Cap-Martin, will be staying open all winter, with tailored packages available for those keen to detox before or after party season. On the agenda? A workout regime developed by FaceGym, a skincare programme from Augustinus Bader, and hiking and swimming along the Promenade Le Corbusier, whose fragrant pine woods and hidden sea coves are at their best from September onwards, not least because they're less clogged by superyachts.

Instead, winter on the Riviera is all about chic serenity. You may even discover a creative reset. "There's a long history of artists from Monet to Matisse visiting the Riviera for its light," says general manager Boris Messmer, "and it's at its most vivid at this time of year." Guests can follow the impressionists' lead by painting en plein air (palettes from Green & Stone can be provided on arrival, along with maps of local beauty spots). Prefer the role of observer? Eileen Gray's masterpiece, villa E-1027, is only a few miles away, as is Le Corbusier's Cabanon.

As for cuisine: Roquebrune-Cap-Martin's microclimate means there's an abundance of fresh produce here all year round. "You can go to the farmer's market in November and see a variety of fig that you would never find anywhere else," explains Messmer. Among the gastronomical highlights guests can enjoy this winter? Making preserves with a traditional confiturier in Menton; joining local fishermen for the morning catch in the Bay of Roquebrune; and attending the Fête du Citron, an annual citrus festival that draws more than 200,000 people to the region. Will the off-season become the on-season once more? *Rooms from £656 per night. Maybourneriviera.com*

Right: relaxed scenes from The Maybourne Riviera hotel in Roquebrune-Cap-Martin, France. Below: Vogue, January 1932

VOGUE

+ FREE GIFTS
+ FREE DIGITAL EDITIONS
+ FREE HOME DELIVERY
*FOR ONLY £28**

VOGUE

NOV
£3.99

LIMITED EDITION COVERS

HER MAJESTY
THE QUEEN

1926–2022

HERLUM

LONDON

HERLUM HAND & BODY WASH
AND HAND & BODY LOTION

FREE GIFTS*
RRP £22

HERLUM

LONDON

Sandalwood & Grapefruit
HAND & BODY LOTION

Made in England
with Brazilian murumuru butter
NET WT. 50ml℮ 1.69 fl.oz.

HERLUM

LONDON

Sandalwood & Grapefruit
HAND & BODY WASH

Made in England
with Brazilian murumuru butter
NET WT. 50ml℮ 1.69 fl.oz.

SUBSCRIBE NOW AND RECEIVE THIS HERLUM HAND & BODY WASH AND HAND & BODY LOTION, RRP £22, FREE*
Take a sensory journey and experience the richness of Brazilian ingredients with Herlum. Made in England, this natural duo is enriched with Amazonian murumuru butter, known for its lauric and oleic acid properties, which leaves skin feeling soft and perfumed. The unique scent stems from upcycled flowers, uniting woody and spicy notes. Available at Cultbeauty.co.uk

VISIT **WWW.VOGUE.CO.UK/SUBSCRIBE/CVO22179**
CALL **01858 438 819 REF CVO22179** OR SCAN THE QR CODE

STONE SETTING

For jeweller ANNA JEWSBURY*'s London* REBUILD, *her idiosyncratic* HALLMARK *is clear to see, says* AIMEE FARRELL. *Photographs by* DEAN HEARNE. *Styling by* JULIA BRENARD

Above: Anna Jewsbury in her central London home. Hair: SHARON ROBINSON. *Make-up:* PAMELA COCHRANE. *Nails:* ROBBIE TOMKINS

In the thoughtfully composed life of Anna Jewsbury, the art of creating a home is as much about reduction as accumulation. "I take a bit of a mathematical approach," says the 36-year-old founder of the cult London jewellery and homeware line Completedworks. "For me, whether it's an earring or an entire room, it's always about stripping back to the elements so that only what truly matters remains."

It's an ethos that permeates every aspect of the handsome three-storey Georgian home that Jewsbury shares with her husband – the British Iraqi author and development expert Hassan Damluji, who is a cofounder of think tank Global Nation – and their two young children, Rafi, four, and Maia, one. Occupying a quiet corner plot in London's Marylebone, the three-bedroomed space is set inside a former pub – as, coincidentally, is her nearby studio. Situated a stone's throw from their former flat, when the pair first viewed the property, in July 2020, it had sat unloved since being redeveloped into a dual residence in 2002. Yet despite the garish decor – lime-green curtains, crimson carpets – and the proliferation of fire exit signs, they were smitten. "We could immediately see how it would function for family

life," says Jewsbury of the generously proportioned 1820s interior, which includes a cavernous basement that serves as a family room, art studio and home cinema.

While Damluji focused on the interior structure, reconfiguring the ground floor by shifting the stairwell and the now light-filled stainless-steel kitchen, Jewsbury turned her attention to the mood of each room and the objects that would best conjure it. Cleverly, the couple lived in the space – carpets and all – for a time, fully familiarising themselves before embarking on any work. The result is a deliberately, deeply personal home.

For Jewsbury, interior decoration is simply another mode of transmitting her artistic vision. "I wanted this space to be a true expression of me," she says, "so that someone could walk into our home and see my personality on display at every turn." With a taste for the clean-lined, the raw and the sculptural, that sense of character translates into an interior that's minimally adorned and sparsely elegant. Much like her understated yet artful jewellery designs, which are beloved by everyone from Adwoa Aboah to Jodie Comer, every decorative object and piece of >

furniture is an effort to push the limits of tradition, instilling classical motifs with a subtle air of subversion that skirts surrealism.

This complex notion of beauty comes to fruition most fully in the living room, which has the rarefied air of a gallery. Encased in Bauwerk lime-wash paint, which lends a naturalistic and understated feel, the room is grounded by original columns and oak-panel floors, which offset a series of painted plinths sourced from an art gallery. On the wall hangs a giant, gorgeous canvas depicting the expressive visages of the young Irish artist Sian Costello's friends. "The use of colour is so romantic," says Jewsbury, who has paired the painting with the restrained charcoal drawings by the sculptor and land artist David Nash, whose work she discovered while exploring the Yorkshire Sculpture Park. More conscious contrasts abound in the placement of Faye Toogood's elemental and curvaceous black Roly-Poly chair alongside an angular pair of blocky, crate-style seats by Dutch designer Gerrit Rietveld. Aptly conceived for a jewellery store interior, she picked them up on eBay for a song. "I'd love to move into making furniture at some point – that would be such fun," says Jewsbury, who is currently in the throes of developing a handbag line, launching next year. She is not the only creative force at work here, though: painterly canvases in an assortment of styles created by her husband are dotted throughout the house.

In 2017, Completedworks collaborated with the multidisciplinary artist Ekaterina Bazhenova Yamasaki on a debut line of ceramics. The resulting collection of textural, globular vases and jewellery, titled Fold, explored ideas of drapery in art and the process of clay folding, borrowing its squidgy, work-in-progress look from everyday objects, including hair scrunchies. An opportunity to upscale and create free from the practical constraints of jewellery design, the project has grown in scope in the intervening years to incorporate

Left: Jewsbury stands beside an artwork by Helen Frankenthaler. Below: the book-filled study

"When it comes to DESIGNING jewellery, nothing is there unless it NEEDS to be. It's the same with the HOUSE – everything has its PLACE and PURPOSE"

everything from mugs and bowls to coasters and candlesticks, executed in a rainbow of recycled glass and brushed brass – some paint splattered Pollock-style or embellished with childlike doodles that nod to the liberated hand of the artist Cy Twombly. "Even without flowers, I love how they sit as sculptures," says Jewsbury, gesturing to the series of vessels and containers displayed on the mid-century teak cabinet she inherited from her paternal grandparents, along with the dining-room table. "The primitive nature of clay makes it so satisfying. When you're rolling and kneading you don't even need a result in mind, you can let your hands go wherever they want and just see where you end up."

At times, the spheres of ceramics and jewellery completely collide in this highly creative home laboratory. Take the diminutive "Squeezed" vessel on the sideboard, which is adorned at the neck with a string of the brand's signature pearls. Such jewel-like touches ornament the space elsewhere too. In the hallway hangs a micro mirror cast in lilac resin that's modelled after Completedworks "Scrunch" earrings, and one of Jewsbury's most beloved additions is the rather extraordinary mauve 1960s Murano glass chandelier that decorates the stairwell, which she found at the nearby Alfies Antiques Market. "Purple makes me happy," says the designer, whose affinity for the tone evolved out of lockdown.

Jewsbury's obsession with objects and materiality can be traced back to her childhood growing up in a modern 1980s house in Holmfirth, close to the wilds of the West Yorkshire moors. It instilled in her an appreciation for what she calls "hostile beauty". Born to an English father, who worked as a chemistry lecturer, and a Filipino mother, who worked in marketing and as a television presenter, she filled their home with a wonderfully diverse array of rattan family furniture, porcelain and curiosities. "Coming from two different worlds there is a certain tension imbued in my design," explains Jewsbury of her own eclectic tastes, which span from Tadao Ando to classic Georgian architecture. "It's hard to totally pinpoint your influences, but there's certainly a respect for emptiness in Eastern culture that has stayed with me. It's about taking away from design, rather than adding to it." It's equally telling that Jewsbury studied mathematics and philosophy at the University of Oxford, before setting up her business in 2013. This complex intermingling of free-thinking and problem-solving, imagination and logic, continues to drive her as artistic director today. "It sounds silly, but with maths and philosophy it's all about trying to find new ways to understand the world and to create a beautiful argument," she says. "When it comes to designing jewellery, nothing is there unless it needs to be. It's the same with the house – everything has its place and its purpose."

This compulsion to create and recast her environment began early. As a child, she'd forge bracelets from beach-combed shells and beads, while her mother would spend time talking her through the contents of her jewellery box, inspiring in her an understanding of the ritualistic power of decorative objects. That power, which compelled Jewsbury to carve the very first pillar-shaped Completedworks ring from reclaimed marble all those years ago, has now hewn her own home, her way.

"A twist on the tennis bracelet, this style by ethical brand MINTY features sparkling stones set in colourful layers of ceramic." Bracelet, £5,990

"I'm swapping my classic robe for this burnt-orange towelling number by FRAMA, the perfect colour contrast to my sea-foam green bathroom." Poncho, from £120

"These lavender-hued wine glasses by ESTELLE COLORED GLASS are handblown in Poland." Glasses, £70 for a set of two, at Liberty

"I'll be bringing a tropical touch to my table with this pitcher by Portuguese kings of kitsch BORDALLO PINHEIRO." Jug, £140, at Liberty

"There's no excuse not to raise a glass when you're chilling fizz in this glossy ice bucket from THE LACQUER COMPANY." Ice bucket, £350

"Sumptuously soothing for dry skin, NATURA BISSE's Diamond Extreme [£335] is intensely nourishing, giving a glow even in colder months."

"I'm embracing modernist accessories with PRADA's signature green-and-black jacquard handbag." Bag, £2,100

LIFE & STYLE
Elevated statement pieces, selected by JULIA SARR-JAMOIS

DMR

DAVID·M·ROBINSON
JEWELLERY & WATCHES

LIVERPOOL   LONDON   MANCHESTER   ALTRINCHAM

DAVIDMROBINSON.CO.UK

5 DAYS OF VOGUE BEAUTY

In Partnership With

Augustinus Bader

EAU THERMALE
Avène
LABORATOIRE DERMATOLOGIQUE

CODE8

BIO SCULPTURE   VIDA GLOW

30 OCTOBER - 3 NOVEMBER

Join us at Vogue House for 5 days of inspiration and indulgence. Learn from industry experts in a series of masterclasses and immerse yourself in the best of beauty in our experiential rooms. Tickets on sale now.

Vogue.co.uk @BritishVogue

DEAR #METOO

In 2017, a single HASHTAG ricocheted around the world, unseated STAID powers and REWROTE the status QUO. Only, did it? Five years on, EVA WISEMAN reflects on what's REALLY changed for women

Right: #MeToo campaign founder Tarana Burke; the Women's March on Washington, 21 January 2017. Below: Harvey Weinstein arriving at the Manhattan Criminal Court in February '20

O ne January morning in 2017, I took my two-year-old daughter to the Women's March. For her birthday that year she had received exclusively children's books about "strong women"; she'd used them as tables for tea parties, and she didn't march that day, so much as plod. It was London, the day after Trump's inauguration, and across the world an estimated 4.5 million of us stomped through streets with banners, babies, those awful pink hats and a sense of urgency. Something was gestating. Nine months later came #MeToo.

It was five years ago that actor Alyssa Milano invited anyone who'd been sexually harassed or assaulted to tweet with a phrase first coined by activist Tarana Burke. "Me too," they replied, under stories about manipulative bosses and bad boyfriends, strangers on buses and dark teenage dates. By October 2018, there'd been 19 million #MeToo tweets; it became a scream, a hum, a brand, a punchline. Industries wobbled, little kings toppled. People talked about "the patriarchy" without rolling their eyes. In schools, offices, homes, women had conversations that both validated and wounded them. Men said they couldn't say anything anymore, often in newspaper columns or on prime-time TV.

As I lay in bed this spring, scrolling clips of the Depp v Heard trial, I thought of 2017, with its weird and fizzing hope. What had changed since then? The old rules on sex and power had been dismantled, but when would we see the new structures that formed in their place?

Model Karen Elson watched #MeToo unfold with a kind of bruised relief – she'd been silent about harassment since she was 16. At the end of the summer, I'd reached out to a handful of women, asking what they thought had changed in these five years – and Karen replied in answers that were largely sighs. The fashion industry had been cracked open by #MeToo because it's an industry that "enables bad behaviour – it's been fetishised and glamourised as part of the job". That no model agencies, for instance, boycotted

Victoria's Secret after their #MeToo allegations stopped the commodification of women in its tracks, revealed to her that "money was more important than safety. My hope is that we can continue to make fashion a safer business, and one that empowers those in it." Elson was not surprised when the backlash to #MeToo arrived, because, "When the status quo gets threatened, the scales tip."

As my daughter has grown up, the strong-woman picture books have made way for feminist T-shirts and lady superheroes, and the knowledge that girls are powerful. An empowering pop song was playing this July when I read the news that the highest number of rapes had been recorded by UK police. "Who run the world? Girls," sang Beyoncé. "Who run the world?" I kept reading, that charging and conviction rates remain among the lowest since records began.

Women who'd been empowered to speak up quickly learnt where that power ran out. "Can I see?" my kid asked, looking at the news site over my shoulder. "Nope," I said. When Amber Heard lost her case, feminist campaigners across the world warned of the repercussions – victims of domestic abuse would face the possibility that if they told their stories today they might be sued by their abusers. And for all the think pieces, training sessions, apologies and "cancellations", many #MeToo-ed men have quietly returned to work, or embarked on comeback tours. This year, when Louis CK won a Grammy, one of his sexual misconduct victims said it was proof that "nobody cares" about the #MeToo movement anymore. At times, I've felt the same. Doesn't a movement have to… move?

I emailed Amia Srinivasan, the philosopher and author of *The Right to Sex*. Did she follow the Depp trial (at which he sued over Heard's allegations, which he has always denied)? No. The focus on high-profile alleged sexual harassers and alleged abusers, Amia says, is a Catch-22. "It's what gave the social media campaign its electric energy, but it also places limits on its political possibilities," she explains. Alleged domestic violence and sexual harassment

*It continues – the standing
UP and speaking OUT,
and doing it AGAIN,
and doing it LOUDER*

*Clockwise from
above: Amber
Heard in court,
April 2022;
Carey Mulligan
and Zoe Kazan
star in She Said;
Missoni a/w '18*

are not the preserve of Hollywood billionaires, they're a "mundane and ubiquitous phenomena, ones that harm poor women most of all". A real movement against sexual abuse, she says, would focus on the material realities that make women vulnerable to it. "It would demand an end to Tory austerity and [an end to] the defunding of the NHS, an end to wage depression, and the availability of affordable housing, universal childcare and universal basic income. It is one that would actually be transformative."

How far did it go, that pink-hatted march? Did we take two steps forward but another back? Writing about #MeToo five years on feels a bit like the lights have come on at a party and I'm suddenly forced to acknowledge the broken glass underfoot. Sobering, uncomfortable, but somewhere, isn't that music still playing? The more people I talk to, the more I lean towards the belief that, while sexual harassment and abuse continue to be systemic problems, #MeToo has inspired communities to try and solve them.

On film sets they've introduced intimacy coordinators, to maintain respect during sex scenes, choreographing them as they would fights, dances or "stunts", emails Daisy Edgar-Jones, star of *Normal People*. "Where you are trying to simulate something in the most realistic way possible but are vulnerable and potentially at risk, it is so important to have someone there to guide and protect you. I now feel able to ask for what I need in scenes involving intimacy, and also sit comfortably in knowing that 'no' can be a full sentence."

Off set, in clubs, in bed, the rest of us have become our own intimacy coordinators, newly seeing our lives as fights or dances. Released this month the film *She Said*, starring Carey Mulligan and Zoe Kazan, tells the story of Jodi Kantor and Megan Twohey, the Pulitzer-winning reporters who unmasked Harvey Weinstein. What's changed in the five years since they exposed sexual abuse as endemic rather than exceptional, I asked them. They said their goal hadn't changed. "We're not after men. We're after the truth."

The backlash undoubtedly made the fight a little bloodier. Although the ripples from the Heard case make for grim reading, the breeze can go the other way too – it proves an interplay between public consciousness and the law. Like, for instance, new legislation in the UK (and a growing number of US states) that tackles the misuse of non-disclosure agreements in the workplace, including those that may be used to cover up sexual harassment, racial discrimination and assault. I was interested to read that Tarana Burke, asked earlier this year about the future of the #MeToo, insisted it's a movement with joy at its centre. In films, survivors are depicted as angry or sad, or set upon paths of revenge. But: "There's a lot of joy in survival." Joy in survival. Joy in community, and organising, building on decades of collective work against sexual abuse. What #MeToo has done is push us to confront the structures that facilitate and obscure abuse, and power itself – those who have it, those who don't, and what horrors that relationship can enable.

Karen Elson's therapist, discussing the PTSD she's left with from her early experiences in the industry, advised her to give up modelling. She considered it, but, "I realised that instead of quitting I needed to ask myself, 'How could I remain in fashion and not have it break me?' Part of that is using my voice for change." It continues, she's saying – the standing up and speaking out, and doing it again, and doing it louder.

There's plenty the movement has yet to achieve, including further reckonings with what justice should look like, and providing real security for survivors. But its impact is unmistakable. Its slow, lumbering footprint. #MeToo was never meant to give the answers, it was meant as a call, both to action, and like a song, across countries, streets, offices – a reminder to push for change. Five years on one thing is clear: #MeToo was just the beginning. Real change takes time, it moves at a two-year-old's pace, more of a plod than a march. It's worth pointing out – we got home eventually.

The art of the interview

In the third instalment of British Vogue and YouTube's new VOGUE VISIONARIES series, radio broadcaster LAUREN LAVERNE and journalist, comedian and YouTube Creator AMELIA DIMOLDENBERG share what makes their interview STYLES stand out

T o have the freedom to have your own show and vision is amazing," Amelia Dimoldenberg, comedian, journalist and creator of *Chicken Shop Date*, tells broadcaster Lauren Laverne in the third episode in British *Vogue* and YouTube's second Vogue Visionaries series. Following two enlightening conversations – with YouTube Creator NikkieTutorials and make-up artist Val Garland, and Nile Rodgers and Rina Sawayama – Dimoldenberg and Laverne met to discuss their jobs as two of today's most successful interviewers, swapping anecdotes and career advice, as well as reflecting on how they've carved out distinctive voices.

Beginning her career in the public eye as a teenager in the band Kenickie, Laverne moved into television before finding her home in radio. Since 2018, she has been the presenter of the legendary programme *Desert Island Discs*, where her recent guests have included Adele and Kate Moss. Dimoldenberg, meanwhile, first had the idea for her wildly popular YouTube series *Chicken Shop Date* – in which she takes on a deadpan persona to pose questions to musicians, actors and other well-known personalities in a chicken shop – at school. It started life as a print feature for a youth-led magazine, before Dimoldenberg decided the unique format would make first-rate viewing too.

"YouTube was always going to be the platform [to host the videos on] because it's so accessible," says Dimoldenberg. "I could connect with a whole range of different people and get it out there to the masses."

Opposite: Amelia Dimoldenberg and Lauren Laverne in conversation for Vogue Visionaries's third instalment

Furthermore, she says, "The comments are where I do a lot of my research. I'll get a sense of what people think about a certain person and that's a great way to carve questions." In one of Dimoldenberg's favourite and most-watched videos she interviewed Louis Theroux. "He was such a hero of mine," she says, smiling. "A lot of my awkward interview style comes directly from him." In that episode, Theroux recalls a rap he once wrote – "Jiggle Jiggle" – which then became a viral sensation. One thing that taught her as an interviewer was the importance of digging deep. "If I hadn't done in-depth research," says Dimoldenberg, "then I wouldn't have known he did that rap in one of his documentaries over 20 years ago."

What makes her YouTube interviews stand out, she thinks, is how they show another side of a personality, while the ideal interviewee for Laverne is someone who has "nothing to prove. It's always lovely to get people when they've had the success they want to have and they can just enjoy it."

In terms of the success of their own shows, Dimoldenberg credits the fact that they "have a very clear format. I think that as a viewer people can really connect with something that's so simple," she continues. Ultimately, Dimoldenberg has three tips for getting a project off the ground: "Believe in your idea, be persistent and annoy people to the point where they end up saying yes."

To watch the film, visit British Vogue's YouTube channel

PREP *TALK*

It's time to SWOT UP *on studious*
STYLE. *Edited by* HOLLY TOMALIN.
Photograph by KENNY WHITTLE

BEST IN CLASS
This season your wardrobe essentials get a preppy overhaul
with revamped classics taking centre stage. Case in point:
the latest collaboration between Palace Skateboards and
Gucci. Paying homage to the influence of the former on
youth culture, the collection plays with the power of the logo
while pushing the boundaries of the latter's timeless design.

Loafers, £865, PALACE GUCCI
COLLECTION, *at Vault.gucci.com and
Palace Skateboards, 26 Brewer Street, W1*

SUNSPEL

ENGLAND 1860

EDIE CAMPBELL FOR SUNSPEL

SUNSPEL.COM

CHECKLIST

Bag, £1,600,
SAINT LAURENT BY
ANTHONY VACCARELLO

Sunglasses,
£149,
HOLLAND
COOPER

Jacket, £350,
MICHAEL
MICHAEL KORS

Bag, £4,715,
CHANEL

Blouse, £100,
UNIQLO

Boots,
£1,250,
SERGIO
ROSSI

Bag, £1,300,
GIORGIO ARMANI

Skirt, £595,
MARGARET
HOWELL

Sweater,
£1,355,
LORO
PIANA

Necklace, £878, DAINTY
DAGGER, at Fashion
Crossover London

Vogue, September 2018

CHECKLIST

Trench coat,
£1,790,
BURBERRY,
at Flannels

CODE8 Iconoclast
Eyeshadow
Palette, £45

Blazer,
£120, MANGO

Bracelet, £6,900,
ASPREY

Jumper,
£290,
PAUL
SMITH

Bag, £4,600,
FENDI

Trousers, £260,
TOMMY
HILFIGER
COLLECTION

Loafers, £325, RUSSELL
& BROMLEY

VIDA

@VIDA_GLOW | VIDAGLOW.COM

NATURAL MARINE COLLAGEN

VIDA GLOW

NET WT 3 g

ORIGINAL

ORAL POWD

GLOW

Improve wrinkles and fine lines.
The future of beauty is *ingestible.*

AVAILABLE AT *Harrods*

BEAUTY &
WELLNESS

EDITED BY JESSICA DINER

Now & AGAIN

When it comes to wellbeing, TRADITIONAL *tricks work alongside* HI-TECH *treatments for truly* HOLISTIC *care*

EASTERN STANDARD

I t would be remiss to say that Traditional Chinese Medicine is having a revival, when it's been there all along. But in our current times, when stress levels soar daily and the journey to score an appointment with a GP takes far longer than the appointment itself lasts, it's more popular than ever.

From cupping and gua sha to reflexology and acupressure, TCM-led treatments are a wellbeing mainstay. "It's been around for thousands of years and dealt with all the weird and wonderful symptoms human beings have experienced," says acupuncturist Ross J Barr. "Nothing remains in circulation for that amount of time unless it works."

Whether it's migraines, poor sleep, fertility issues or simply feeling a bit off, treatments such as acupuncture take around 45 minutes and a couple of sessions can really help. Unlike Western medicine, which tends to treat the symptom, "Chinese medicine seeks to understand the root causes, and holistically rebalance," says TCM expert Ada Ooi. "It recognises the inseparable relationship of the body, mind, spirit and nature, and also has a long-term preventative effect for the whole of wellbeing, so individuals can feel better and live longer."

One of the key concepts behind TCM is qi, otherwise known as the "energy force" that keeps us going. When we are out of sorts, our qi is disturbed, blood can stagnate and organ health can deplete. Practitioners will often look at the tongue or feel the pulse, temperature or limbs to gain an understanding of which organ is off-balance, and treat accordingly by stimulating points on the body's meridian system.

"If you're stressed or irritable, this could be linked to the liver; lack of self-expression can directly impact the heart's function, while chronic stress, worry and anxiety can damage stomach function," explains Ooi, who offers an array of treatments at her clinic, including gua sha and cupping to help relieve stagnated tension in the body. Alongside Barr and Ooi, other excellent practitioners to book in with include Marie Reynolds, Renata Nunes and Sarah Bradden. Trust us, it works. HANNAH COATES

Clockwise from top left: MARIE REYNOLDS *Liver Rescue,* £23.50. BED OF NAILS *Acupressure Mat,* £70. 001 SKINCARE *MicroSculptor No1 The Pick Gua Sha,* £60. VIE HEALING *Calm You Ear Seeds,* £29. ROSS J BARR *Adrenal Calm Supplements,* £15

SMART WORKOUTS

At the start of the pandemic – with gyms closed and home exercise booming – the fitness industry had to adapt quickly to a new way of working out. Fast-forward to today and it's busy evolving again. "Technology has found its way into the gym in a number of ways, post-lockdown," explains A-list trainer and educator Luke Worthington. "There has been a rise in smart exercise equipment that automatically adjusts its settings and resistance to track and monitor progress when a user either inserts a smart key or scans their phone. We are also seeing a rise in private training studios that now have a 'Zoom room'," he continues, "a workout station fully kitted out with cameras and mics, allowing trainers to deliver sessions in person and also stream online. It is also no longer unusual to see clients working out in a gym with a smartphone on a tripod, being coached by a trainer who could be anywhere in the world."

Future is the latest fitness app to capitalise on the trainer-trainee digital relationship, providing a more accessible, affordable version of at-home workout equipment. Think of Future like an at-home beauty services app, where you find a trainer that best suits your needs and goals and, once matched, you'll have a FaceTime meeting followed by a weekly workout schedule with personalised video instructions to ensure you exercise correctly. Your trainer will monitor your metrics by syncing with an Apple Watch. Similarly, Fitalike, the fitness version of a dating app, matches users with like-minded trainers to help achieve fitness goals as well as building a new fitness community and inspiring motivation.

Where home workout devices are concerned, Hydrowave, the rowing machine that offers live and on-demand classes with instructors "on" famous landmark rivers, from the Thames to Loch Ness, has now introduced the Hydrow Wave Rower. It's a lighter and more compact version of the original but still has the patented computer-controlled dynamic resistance that mimics the real feel of water. Hydrow has even seen revenue grow more than three times from 2020 to 2021, despite gyms fully reopening.

If virtual boxing has more appeal, Boxx+, which launches in January 2023, comes in the form of Punch Pods, Punch Bag and an app. The Punch Pods fit inside your boxing gloves, much like wireless earbuds, to measure metrics in real time, which then feeds into a live leaderboard. It's not restricted to home-use, so you can also use the Pods in a gym class and continue to gather your stats.

After all, there's no denying the power of an IRL workout, motivated by those around you. Just ask Peloton, the popular at-home workout bike brand. "We've seen strong demand from members to attend classes in reality," explains Peloton's VP of content international, Pete Flamman. "We knew from before Covid that members love taking classes in real life with their favourite instructors and meeting up with new friends from the Peloton leaderboard." The most significant move was the creation of Peloton Guide, its first connected strength product. "Peloton Guide is an AI-enabled device that connects to televisions, providing members instant access to a suite of expert instructors and the Peloton content library. Peloton Guide makes it easy to check your form through Self-Mode and to keep yourself accountable as you work out."

With regular exercise also comes the need for effective recovery, which means sleep and downtime need to be optimised. Therabody, the brand behind the muscle massage tool, Theragun, has launched SmartGoogles, a hi-tech mask that has a SmartRelax mode to physically lower your heart rate, helping to reduce stress and anxiety. The device combines targeted vibration, heat and massage to ease facial tension to enhance sleep quality and recovery. The workout of the future is in your hands. LAUREN MURDOCH-SMITH

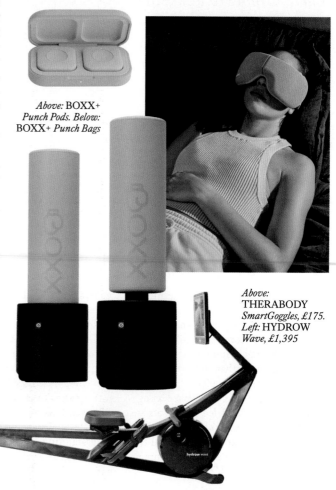

Above: BOXX+ *Punch Pods. Below:* BOXX+ *Punch Bags*

Above: THERABODY *SmartGoggles, £175. Left:* HYDROW *Wave, £1,395*

THE SHROOM BOOM

Mushrooms are the latest buzz in superfoods and now easily available in a variety of forms, whether that's powder, blended with CBD in drops or simply ingested. Research suggests that certain mushrooms have an impact on cognitive health, including relieving stress and preventing brain ageing, as well as providing proteins, minerals and vitamins. Cannabotech's The Relax Drops, £79, help promote a healthier stress response, as the blend of lion's mane, cordyceps and reishi mushrooms help regulate neurotransmitters, while Dirtea has a range of organic coffee, hot chocolate and powder blends that uses different mushrooms to deliver countless benefits, such as Cordyceps Mushroom Powder, £30, for energy, performance and endurance. Make way for the mushrooms. LM-S

ESTEE LAUDER LUXURY FRAGRANCE OASIS DAWN EAU DE PARFUM, £138
Is this a chypre? Or a floral? The truth is: it's both. Combining a base of earthy vetiver – which is synonymous with the chypre fragrance family – with the freshest of orange flower, this is the type of scent that wraps you up in a warm, welcoming hug.

HERMES HERMESSENCE VIOLETTE VOLYNKA EAU DE TOILETTE, £197
Concocted by Christine Nagel, the brilliant director of creation and olfactory heritage at Hermès Parfums, this blend of powdery violet and strong leather might not seem like a match made in perfumery heaven on paper, but in reality its unique infusion spells utter perfection.

TOM FORD PRIVATE BLEND BOIS MAROCAIN EAU DE PARFUM, £195
The Tom Ford Private Blend collection has long paid homage to the olfactive treasures of wood (Santal Blush and Ebène Fumé are odes to sandalwood and palo santo respectively) and now – in this deeply enigmatic, smoky blend – a celebration of the evergreen thuya tree joins the ranks.

MAISON FRANCIS KURKDJIAN 724 EAU DE PARFUM, £335
Inspired by perfumer Francis Kurkdjian and his urban travels (he has lived in New York, Sydney, Tokyo, Seoul, Shanghai and London), this is a scent for the city, as jasmine, sweet pea, sandalwood and musk mix to form a creamy, moreish concoction.

LOEWE EARTH EAU DE PARFUM, £89
Loewe adds to its Botanical Rainbow collection with this floral, musky scent that celebrates all that lives both below and above the soil: from the notes of mimosa and violet to the hints of truffle, this is autumn in a bottle.

HIGHER GROUND

The FRESHEST *incoming* FRAGRANCES *draw from the* earth *and* BEYOND *for both inspiration and* INGREDIENTS. *Breathe them in, says* JESSICA DINER

30 years of commitment. United to help end breast cancer.

The Estée Lauder Companies supports research, education, and access to medical services to continue improving the lives of the global breast cancer community.

#TimeToEndBreastCancer

Learn more and join us
ELCompanies.com/BreastCancerCampaign

ESTĒE LAUDER COMPANIES
BREAST CANCER CAMPAIGN

Line in THE SAND

JARED LETO *has entered the* BEAUTY *game, but his desert-inspired* DEBUT *is more than a* MIRAGE, *finds* LIAM HESS

Y ou would think we'd be immune to the famous founder story at this point, yet I was still surprised to receive Twentynine Palms, an 11-piece range of gender-neutral skincare, bodycare and haircare products from Jared Leto. I had questions. "Twentynine Palms, like the town at the entrance to Joshua Tree National Park?" (Yes.) And, "Is this eye cream actually £77?" (Also yes.)

"I know I'm a student here, but I think that's the best place to be," Leto says of his entry into a very crowded space when I interrupt his Tuscany holiday via FaceTime in late August. The Oscar-winning actor, Gucci muse and Thirty Seconds to Mars frontman is sporting a scruffy beard and a dressing gown, chiselled chest on view, but it's his skin that draws the eye: at 50, Leto has the porcelain-smooth complexion of a Renaissance cherub. "I've never been really interested in beauty products," he insists, "but I'm interested in the idea of taking care of ourselves in the most natural way possible."

Leto is known for going all in on anything he does and his wellness-oriented way of life is no exception: he is a vegan who abstains from both alcohol and caffeine, and when he discovered the "rugged beauty" of the desert while directing a 2016 documentary series about rock climbing, his interest in the sport snowballed into a full-blown obsession. Leto bought a home in Nevada to further immerse himself in the Mojave Desert, and his new brand's refillable violet-hued glass, aluminium and post-consumer recycled plastic bottles nod to its purple skies at twilight. The formulations follow a similar script. "Because of this challenging, unforgiving environment, these ingredients have to be incredibly resilient to survive," Leto says, relaying the restorative benefits of the line's desert botanicals.

Leto's willingness to learn and his dedication to both clean formulas and clean living is what persuaded Kate Forbes to join Twentynine Palms after years of heading up innovation for Aesop. "If I could adhere to some of Jared's strict guidelines, I think I'd be much healthier," says Forbes, laughing. "He is a hundred per cent committed to anything that he decides that he wants to do," confirms Jimmy Chin, the codirector of the Oscar-winning rock climbing documentary *Free Solo*, who met Leto six years ago.

That commitment will soon take Twentynine Palms beyond beauty, Leto tells me with such enthusiasm he briefly drops his iPhone. He is planning a partnership with High Desert Test Sites, the ambitious Coachella Valley-adjacent artist residency, as well as limited-edition home and design objects in collaboration with a rotating list of multidisciplinary creators. Fragrances that build on earthy aromatics (smoky Japanese vetiver, eucalyptus, myrrh) will come next. It's a convincing performance in which Leto plays the part of wellness apostle (maybe it's the beard). "It's just the beginning," he suggests.

From top: TWENTYNINE PALMS *Moonlight Mesa Hand Cream, £35. Rock Rose Clay Mask, £47. Desert Tumbleweed Cleansing Shampoo, £44. Santa Ana Salve Facial Moisturiser, £68*

PARTY PREP

Excited for party season? You might be persuaded after seeing these new limited-edition make-up launches. Charlotte Tilbury's Hypnotising Pop Shots, £25, which come in seven shades, are perfect to dress up the eyes, with embellished packaging to match. Violette_FR's Bisou Blush, £37, comes in three shades, with in-built brush, making it the perfect on-the-go party companion, with make-up artist Violette also turning her hand to beautiful party palettes in her additional role as creative director of make-up for Guerlain. The Ombre G Eyeshadow limited-edition Butterfly palettes, £62, are highly pigmented, with four different textured finishes: matte, satin, metallic and iridescent. In further eye palette elevation, each of the eye shadows in Chanel's Les 4 Ombres eye shadows, £67, are embossed with the house's signature tweed design and come in their own woven pouches. For skin, look to Westman Atelier's Vital Skincare Complexion Drops, £62, which will help keep skin looking glowy, even after you've removed your make-up, with the added skincare ingredients of tsubaki oil, ginseng and pomegranate extract.

Beauty MUSINGS

It's time to UPGRADE *your at-home* BLOW-DRY *and* MAKE-UP *supplies, says* LAUREN MURDOCH-SMITH

SALON SAVIOURS

Upgrade your at-home hair armoury with these updates, designed with a salon-worthy blow-dry in mind. Hershesons's hairdryer, £295, looks different and is different. Lightweight and quiet, but supremely powerful, its compact design means it's great both at home and on the go. Sam McKnight Happy Endings Hair Balm, £28, will nourish your hair as well as style it. Pro-vitamin B5, keratin and shea butter smooth, polish and hydrate for the ultimate finish to your blow-dry. Virtue Frizz Block Smoothing Spray, £42, does what it says on the can: it blocks hair from becoming frizzy. Apply on damp or dry hair and it creates a lightweight veil to protect from humidity for 72 hours. Larry King Wild & Unruly Curl Enhancer, £26, took five years to perfect. The cream has been developed with avocado and jojoba to bring back curls' natural waves and texture.

NAILED IT

Subtle metallics will elevate manicures come winter. Both Hermès's 90 Gris Eétain, £42, and OPI's Go Big Or Go Chrome, £14, will add a different spin on your usual go-to winter nail colours. Also try Essie's Expressie FX top coats, £8, to add a metallic finish or a sheer flash of chrome.

VOGUE

SKIN-CARE
special

GLOW
GETTERS

The GUIDE *to your best* SKIN *yet.*
Edited by FUNMI FETTO.
Photograph by MATT HEALY

The light TOUCH

There are NEW *skin-tech* INNOVATIONS *that are promising big things for your* SKIN, *but, as* HANNAH COATES *discovers, it's* EVERYTHING *but the* NEEDLE

H ow do the world's most radiant faces get their skin like that? Most of us assume it's down to Botox, filler or some other injectable treatment. But while tweakments such as these are now mainstream (the market is predicted to grow at an annual rate of 12 to 14 per cent over the next five years), increasingly there are a wealth of other unsung treatment options that can create more lifted, firmer and healthier-looking skin, no needles required.

No one is better proof than the Oscar-winning actor Julianne Moore, who I recently interviewed for Vogue.co.uk. At 61, she has the plump, glowy skin that dreams are made of, and for this, she explained, she relies upon radiofrequency (an energy-based treatment that uses radio waves to boost collagen and elastin). "I use my face for a living," she said. "I need to make sure that I look like me and that my face is mobile – radiofrequency is the way to do it." You name the celebrity and you can reasonably expect they also incorporate a number of noninvasive treatments in their skincare routines.

One facialist Moore sees regularly is London-based Teresa Tarmey. Known for her cutting-edge facials, Tarmey's Tribella Facial combines three popular non-injectable techniques to improve skin quality at every age. During the treatment, radiofrequency is combined with fractional radiofrequency, a micro-needling technique in which radio waves are pulsed through needles to address skin texture and boost collagen production. After that, Tarmey deploys intense pulsed light to target pigmentation and thread veins. This combination is a particular favourite among aestheticians right now. "I swear by fractional radiofrequency for its excellent results and effectiveness at treating textural irregularities, scarring, wrinkles and pigmentation," Tarmey tells me. "We see dramatic improvements in skin texture and lines are also reduced."

For facial aesthetic doctor Maryam Zamani, lasers are a key tool in the quest for skin rejuvenation. "It's treatments such as these that are going to give you the best bang for your buck," she says. "If you're looking for textural changes, fractional, non-ablative lasers are the way to go." One she's most excited about right now? Moxi by Sciton, a gentle but effective laser that is great for tackling sun damage, uneven skin tone, texture and general signs of ageing. Facialist Debbie Thomas is also a fan of lasers and enthuses that they are "by far the most effective way to boost the health of the skin". Her newest machine in her London clinic is the AdvaTx, which has two settings – yellow laser technology and a unique, deeply penetrating wavelength – that can be used separately or combined, depending on the individual's skin concerns. "The yellow laser setting – ideal for fairer skin tones – works really well on all types of redness, but unlike other lasers it does this with very little heat. Adding heat to inflammatory conditions, such as eczema or rosacea, can make them worse," she explains. "The other setting on the machine – for rejuvenation, with can be used on all skin tones – offers deep heating within the skin, which is excellent for collagen stimulation and shrinking overactive oil glands." Thomas has already witnessed great results on adult acne, scarring, enlarged pores and dullness.

If it's jowls, laxity and gravity your skin is faced with, then ultrasound treatments are the gold standard. The best known is Ultherapy, a nonsurgical, noninvasive alternative to the facelift that can tighten, contour and firm the neck, jawline and face. It works by delivering micro-focused ultrasound energy deep into the skin to stimulate a thermal effect, which ultimately boosts collagen and elastin production. It's slightly uncomfortable, but, say experts, worth it: "It takes three to six months to see the final result, but as soon as you see the tightening happening… I do it for myself every couple of years," says Zamani. A more comfortable ultrasound alternative to Ultherapy, one that also boosts collagen production in the dermis and helps to lift and firm, is the FDA-approved Sofwave. Sophie Shotter of Illuminate Skin Clinic (in London and Kent) is one of the first to introduce this treatment to the UK. "You can see the effects straight away, with best results after six months," she explains. "It can also lift the delicate eye area, as well as the brow."

Will these treatments ever totally replace the more ubiquitous Botox and dermal filler? Highly unlikely, but, argues Zamani, they don't need to be mutually exclusive: "Everything has its place," she says. "I don't think you're going to get the results on dynamic lines with Ultherapy as you would with Botox, but what you can get is a complementary ability between the two – and I think that's really important. It's not one or the other."

AT-HOME HELPERS

Above: THE LIGHT SALON *Boost LED Collar, £195. Right:* NUFACE *Trinity Facial Toning Device, £329*

From left: TERESA TARMEY *Lactic Acid Treatment, £38.* AVÈNE *XeraCalm AD Lipid-replenishing Cream, £18.50.* FACEGYM *Hydrating Active Roller, £55*

RODIAL
*Snake
Jelly Face
Mask, £12*

RODIAL
Vit C Pads, £45

RODIAL *Snake
Serum O2, £75*

RODIAL
*Dragon's
Blood
Sculpting
Gel, £85*

The skin
YOU'RE IN

Having provided innovative, results-focused SKINCARE *for
more than* 20 YEARS, RODIAL *knows a thing or two about
how to get your* COMPLEXION *looking its very best*

LOOKING FOR SKINCARE that delivers results, and fast? Rodial
is all about performance-driven, highly effective products that provide
benefits you can really see, both immediately and long-term.

Take the brand's hero products. The Dragon's Blood Sculpting
Gel helps skin appear firmer and more plumped thanks to actives
such as Collageneer and Volufiline, which stimulate collagen
production. Containing the brand's unique dragon's blood complex
and moisture-retaining glycerine, it dramatically boosts hydration
in a light gel-cream formula that sinks weightlessly into the skin.

The Vit C Brightening Cleansing Pads, too, are brilliant, infused
with a blend of brightening vitamin C, exfoliating fruit AHA acids
and pore-tightening salicylic acid, transforming dull complexions
in an instant. Or there's the Snake Serum O2, a revitalising formula
with peptides that mimic the effect of viper venom to freeze and
smooth the complexion. A unique oxygen-delivery system and
hyaluronic acid boost moisture, while a blurring complex evens the
appearance of fine lines, making it a perfect precursor to make-up.

And for an immediate skin boost, the Snake Jelly Face Mask
improves suppleness and elasticity. Designed with cooling hydrogel
technology, this easy-to-use mask results in hydrated and healthy-
looking skin right away. These products? They're iconic for a reason.
Discover more at Rodial.com

Silk slip dress, SAINT LAURENT BY ANTHONY VACCARELLO

Turning PRO

What happens when there's no SIMPLE skincare fix? KATHLEEN BAIRD-MURRAY consults the EXPERTS on a trio of conditions when one size does not fit ALL

ECZEMA

If you have eczema you'll be all too familiar with those cracked, dry and scaly patches of skin that show up a bright red on paler skin tones or an ashy, almost grey on darker skin. Left untreated, eczema becomes scalier, itchier, thicker and more hyperpigmented.

THE GP "There are two primary causes of eczema: a leaky gut – increased intestinal permeability – which creates a low-grade inflammation in reaction to food particles leaking through your gut wall, and/or abnormal gut flora, or dysbiosis, which is when the trillions of bugs in your gut become out of balance, driving inflammation. This is caused by a high-sugar, refined-carb, low-fibre, processed diet," says general physician Sabine Donnai, whose hi-tech diagnostic clinic in London, Viavi, prides itself on a holistic approach. "But there are other culprits, such as chemicals and other substances in creams, lotions and detergents, as well as household cleaning products." Her advice is to look at the whole, rather than treat the surface. "The creams, antibiotics and other topical solutions are really just short-term solutions. You wouldn't address every yellowing leaf of the plant if the problem is that the roots need more water!"

THE DERMATOLOGIST "There are three pillars for eczema we try to tackle," says consultant dermatologist Emma Wedgeworth. "Firstly, strengthen the skin barrier using moisturisers that can replenish. Secondly, we look at the abnormality in the skin's immune system, treating itchy patches with medicated creams – there are more targeted creams, called phosphodiesterase inhibitors, currently in development in the US, which dampen inflammation. If these don't work, we use light therapy, as well as immunosuppressants in the form of injections and tablets."

THE FACIALIST Pietro Simone, who has a clinic in London at Flemings Mayfair Hotel, says, "Avoid glycolic acid, colourants, fragrances, mineral oils, unstable vitamin C and retinol."

THE NUTRITIONIST "Detoxification is key, as systemic toxic levels make eczema worse," says Lucy Miller, a registered, clinically qualified nutritional therapist based in Bath and London. "A whole-food, anti-inflammatory, low-allergenic diet that contains lots of pre and probiotic foods, fibre and good fats is vital. It needs to be low in processed foods, sugar, refined carbohydrates and alcohol to help balance blood sugar, all of which helps to control inflammation, balance hormones and improve immunity."

Clockwise from top left: AVENE *XeraCalm AD Lipid-replenishing Cream,* £18.50. PURE PEONY *High Factor Peony Root Skin Remedy,* £8. LA ROCHE-POSAY *Cicaplast Baume,* £15. EPIONCE *Renewal Calming Cream,* £65. CLINISOOTHE+ *Skin Purifier Spray,* £15

From top:
DERMATOLOGY
M *Unstable Psoriasis
Cream, £42.*
PIETRO SIMONE
*Skin Alert Unguent,
£65.* IS CLINICAL
*Sheald Recovery
Balm, £60.*
CERAVE *SA
Smoothing
Cream, £20*

PSORIASIS

This is an autoimmune condition that causes an excess turnover of skin cells that can build up into thickened plaques. There is no quick fix, but treated correctly it can be managed well, with minimal flareups.

THE GP "Take away the things that cause the problem and add those that ameliorate it. In the vast majority of cases, this will naturally heal psoriasis," says Donnai. She advises her patients to focus on eight things. 1. Eat a whole-food diet. 2. Remove any food sensitivities such as gluten and dairy. 3. Test for heavy-metal toxicity (mercury and other metals can trigger or exacerbate psoriasis). 4. Fix your gut ("Studies suggest intestinal permeability, or leaky gut, can contribute to psoriasis"). 5. Use the right supplements. 6. Exercise regularly. 7. Sleep for eight hours every night. 8. Practice deep relaxation.

THE DERMATOLOGIST "Psoriasis can be associated with lifestyle, with sufferers having higher rates of smoking, alcohol and higher BMIs, so sometimes making a change of this nature can help," says Wedgeworth. Psoriasis also looks different according to ethnicity, with more redness in whiter skins and more associated problems with pigmentation in darker skins. Depending on its severity, Wedgeworth will start treatment with vitamin D creams, moving on to light therapy, "which dampens it down".

THE FACIALIST "Less is more. Keep it simple," says Katharine Mackenzie Paterson, founder of KMP Skin. "Avoid heavily fragranced products and use occlusive creams to help reduce the roughness. LED – such as Dermalux Flex – can also be fantastic for psoriasis."

THE NUTRITIONIST "A high level of zonulin, a protein that controls the size of the gap junctions in the gut, which can indicate if you have a leaky gut, is often associated with psoriasis, so ask for a blood test to measure it," says Miller. Her vitamin and mineral recommendations include vitamin A, B and D, omega-3 and quercetin. Plenty of soluble fibre will also help control blood sugar and reduce inflammation.

Clockwise from top left: CYSPERA *Intensive
System, £224.* PCA SKIN *Acne Gel Advanced
Treatment, £64.* SKINBETTER SCIENCE
Even Tone Correcting Serum, £140. ULTRA
VIOLETTE *Daydream Screen SPF50, £38*

PIGMENTATION

Those annoying patches on your jawline, the minor acne spot that turns into a stubborn darker splodge, that sunspot that gets in the way of an otherwise even complexion… Sounds familiar?

THE GP "I've seen a few clients who have had cosmetic treatments who have then developed hyperpigmentation as a result of not adhering to the advice of avoiding sun exposure for a period of time," says Donnai. "Sun exposure is the most common cause of pigmentation." Donnai advises the first approach is to decrease the risk of further damage with factor 50 skin protection and at-home skincare protocols that include vitamin C and retinol.

THE DERMATOLOGIST Wedgeworth recommends products with niacinamide and vitamin C, but also prescribes retinol, hydroquinone, "the gold standard", or melasma tablets. "It's important to establish what type of pigmentation you have," she says, as not all treatments are equal – for example, lasers can be great for a sunspot, but can make other types of pigmentation worse.

THE FACIALIST "To quell pigmentation and excess melanin in the skin," says Dija Ayodele, aesthetician and founder of West Room Aesthetics, a skincare destination for women of colour, "darker skin tones should be prepped before any facial treatments with a tyrosinase-inhibiting serum. Otherwise, the melanin cells will go into overdrive and produce melanin in a very patchy way. Caucasian skin tends to be absolutely fine to go in for a same-day treatment, but most practitioners will want to prep the skin even a little bit, as it gives better results."

THE NUTRITIONIST "Some pigmentation is hormone related and this can be addressed with nutrition," says Miller. "I'd approach it with a hormone-balancing nutrition protocol – decided on with a professional nutritionist – as well as focusing on a diet rich in antioxidants and polyphenols to help reduce free radicals, lower inflammation and support skin turnover."

GET YOUR GLOW ON

NOBLE PANACEA's *new Vitamin C Booster offers effective* **DAILY DOSES** *of the radiance-boosting* **POWERHOUSE**

Anyone with even a passing interest in skincare knows that vitamin C is a true beauty hero. A powerful antioxidant renowned for its abilities to brighten, clarify, fortify and protect skin, it's your go-to ingredient for a healthy, youthful radiance. What it's also known for, however, is its sensitivity to light and air, meaning it can quickly lose its efficacious potential when oxidised. That's why Noble Panacea's new Vitamin C Booster is the perfect way to get the best out of this powerhouse glow-booster, without compromising on any of its amazing benefits.

Noble Panacea's unique Organic Super Molecular Vessel technology (OSMV) was developed by the brand's founder, Nobel laureate Sir Fraser Stoddart. Ten-thousand times smaller than a skin cell and built from biodegradable, renewable materials, the innovative, groundbreaking technology perfectly houses and protects active ingredients to ensure optimal freshness,

stability and efficacy for the very best results for your skin. What's more, the new Vitamin C Booster comes in Noble Panacea's Active Daily Dose packaging, ensuring precise, box-fresh doses adding up to an intensive four-week treatment programme. Mix with your favourite serum for the best results.

The latest addition to Noble Panacea's The Exceptional collection, the Vitamin C Booster is packed with an impressive 20 per cent pure L-ascorbic acid, encapsulated within the OSMV for peak freshness and all-day micro-dosed delivery. It works to reduce the effects of photoaging and protect against environmental aggressors, resulting in brighter, more radiant skin. The product also features eight additional sources of vitamin C, including camu camu, acerola and kakadu plum, alongside clarifying upcycled white pine bark and radiance-boosting mullein flower extract to ensure an incomparable glow and bright future ahead.

And with plastic-free starch-based boxes, refill options and 100 per cent recyclable Active Daily Dose packaging, it really is the best way to get your vitamin C fix, every single day.

To discover more, visit Noblepanacea.com

From top left: NOBLE PANACEA *Vitamin C Booster, £124. Noble Panacea brand ambassador Jodie Comer*

The KEY to improving your SKIN*'s*
HEALTH is with a NOURISHING,
state-of-the-art FORMULA

RAISE
your skin's
BARRIER

O
ften sensitive skin requires a compromise
when it comes to skincare and it's usually
between efficacy and luxury that restricts
your choice when finding products that
work with delicate skin. Sensai, the Japanese
skincare brand who are experts in sensitive
skin, have developed a final skincare step
that offers an effective yet luxurious solution.
The Comforting Barrier Mask is specifically
designed to deal with delicate skin that often
feels irritated, dry and sometimes rough in
texture. Koishimaru Silk Royal CB complex
is the key to the formula's barrier-repairing
power. It immediately works to preserve
moisture – breaking the cycle of dry, exposed
and vulnerable skin, which can lead to it
feeling fragile, irritated and showing redness
– and helps stimulate the skin's natural
production of hyaluronic acid.

Skin is made up of two barrier layers,
with the first acting as the protector of the
lower layer, ultimately protecting the cells
and sealing the gaps beneath the surface. If
these barriers are compromised they can
become sensitive, but by using the
Comforting Barrier Mask as a final step in
your skincare routine, the cream melts into
skin, helping its natural ability to retain
moisture, and instantly hydrates to restore
calm. Designed to be left on, the mask works
throughout the day and night to preserve
and protect skin (and its moisture function)
and can also be used to target dry areas,
resulting in a soft, plumped complexion.

To complement the Comforting Barrier
Mask, you can diagnose what your skin
needs using Sensai's Silk Skin Checker, a
virtual skin-analysis tool. The AI technology
will recommend products based on the skin
score it comes up with after taking your
photograph, analysing and highlighting the
areas that might need attention (such as
dark circles or texture) and then offering a
personalised skincare programme for you.
It's time to strengthen your skin and make
it healthier, inside and out.
*To find out more, visit Sensai-cosmetics.com
and follow @sensaibeauty on Instagram*

SENSAI *Comforting
Barrier Mask, £139*

TONERS, *reinvented*

With a new, completely REDEVELOPED *iteration,* TONERS *are making a* COMEBACK. *But do we really* NEED *them?* TWIGGY JALLOH *finds out*

Toners, once considered a crucial step in a cleansing routine, have been off the skincare radar for years. Arguably, their downfall was driven by a shift in what consumers were (and were not) willing to accept in their skincare products. Most toners, famed for their astringent properties that supposedly removed any cleansing residue and balanced the skin, were chock-full of drying alcohol. Thankfully, there is now a coterie of toners that is much kinder to skin than its predecessors. But the question still remains: do we need it?

"Contrary to popular belief, toners are an essential part of any beauty routine," shares Marie-Hélène Lair, director of responsible innovation at Clarins. "The key purpose of a toner is to remove any dirt or impurities that may have been left on your skin after cleansing. A toner helps to balance the natural pH level in the skin to promote a healthier-looking complexion and prepare the skin for a serum and moisturiser." While many may argue that this is exactly the same function of toners of old, now it's different. "Toners have evolved over time, regarding ingredients and formulation, and consumers now also have opportunities to find the preferred consistency or texture, whether it's water, a texturised jelly or milk,"

says Paula Cziryak, vice president of research and innovation skin development at L'Oréal. "Either way," she asserts, "toners are still the foundation for maintaining skin's natural balance."

Additionally, this new slew has been created to counter a plethora of skincare issues. The focus is now not just on balancing and pore refining but also on plumping, hydrating, soothing and resurfacing. Toners have become efficacious, time-efficient multitaskers. Launches from progressive beauty brands such as Fenty Beauty are an example of this. Case in point, Fat Water Hydrating Milky Toner Essence. It is what Rihanna – the singer, actor, businesswoman and founder of Fenty Beauty – described as the "perfect toner essence hybrid that gives you a fast, fat splash of hydration for soft, smooth skin".

Other brands are also taking this hybrid approach. Charlotte Tilbury's toner not only refines but also brightens. Aesop's focuses on both hydrating and balancing. Freya & Bailey's offering works on evening out skin tone. Clarins, in particular, are doing a lot of innovative work in this area. Their extensive skincare research is discovering all the ways our balance can be disturbed by factors such as temperature changes and aggressive cleansing. Hence their range of toners, explains Lair, are being developed to "guarantee a balanced microbiota – a unique ecosystem that helps to keep the skin barrier healthy – and therefore more radiant, smooth and even skin". Still questioning a toner's place in your skincare routine? Thought not.

Radiance, bottled

The EVERLASTING YOUTH FLUID *foundation from* CLARINS
blends the brand's skincare and make-up EXPERTISE

WHAT DOES BEAUTIFUL skin look like to you? For many of us it's all about radiance: a lit-from-within glow that signifies wellness, vitality and youth. But with time that natural radiance can start to fade, which is why Clarins's Everlasting Youth Fluid foundation is all about restoring it – both instantly and day after day with lasting skincare benefits. A creamy yet lightweight medium-coverage formula, the foundation combines more than 60 years of Clarins's unbeatable skincare expertise with the brand's make-up knowledge. The star ingredient, chicory extract, boosts collagen synthesis to firm skin and help target the appearance of wrinkles, while improving skin luminosity and tone over time. It also contains a Skin Tone Optimising Complex, created by Clarins to provide instant radiance via a combination of pigments, pink pearls and soft-focus powders that prevent dullness, even skin tone, blur imperfections and boost glow. Everlasting Youth Fluid foundation is also formulated with plumping konjac micro-pearls and nourishing argan oil, leaving skin fuller, firmer and more glowing right away.

In fact, whatever you want from your foundation, Clarins has a skincare-powered formula for you. For fuller coverage, look to the Everlasting foundation, which contains bamboo powder and naturally derived silica to mattify and perfect the skin, as well as organic quinoa to hydrate and reinforce the skin's barrier function. For lighter coverage, there's Skin Illusion foundation, whose lightweight, serum-like texture is formulated with a Light Optimising Complex to instantly revive radiance and red jania extract to boost cell renewal and remove dead skin cells. All three contain Clarins's unique Anti-Pollution Complex to protect skin from environmental aggressors, leaving you ready to face the day.

Discover the full complexion range at Clarins.co.uk or enjoy your complimentary foundation sample in store

From right:
TYPOLOGY *Calming Scalp Treatment Bisabolol 1% & Cotton Extract, £24.* ARKIVE *The Root-ine Scalp Serum, £14.* OUAI *Scalp Serum, £46*

Above: DR BARBARA STURM *Scalp Serum, from £25.* Below: GUERLAIN *Abeille Royale Scalp & Hair Youth Oil-in-Serum, £92*

SCALP

Looking after your scalp is just as important – if not more – as looking after your hair, because if you keep your scalp healthy you'll have healthier hair. While scalp serums are increasing in popularity within haircare ranges, a growing number of skincare brands are also recognising the scalp as an extension of your face – and it shouldn't be treated any differently. Sensitive scalps, just like the skin on your face, can be calmed and balanced. A good scalp serum not only soothes but can help improve flakiness and encourage healthy hair growth.

BODY

Slathering on body lotions should be part of your daily skincare routine and with the variety of textures, such as serums, creams or oils, you can now find one suited to your preference. But start with regular, weekly exfoliation – if not a liquid exfoliant, a physical option that isn't overly abrasive. This will help lift away dead skin cells and make way for healthy, fresh new ones, and it will make your moisturiser work harder. For best results, apply your daily moisturiser directly after showering, when your skin is still damp (it will work more effectively). Don't forget to also moisturise after exfoliating – it's a key step in keeping skin smooth and hydrated, especially if you're a regular user of self-tan.

Below: VOYA *Buoyancy Luxury Body Butter, £38. From right:* TATA HARPER SKINCARE *Resurfacing Body Serum, £139.* PAULA'S CHOICE *5% Niacinamide Body Serum, £36*

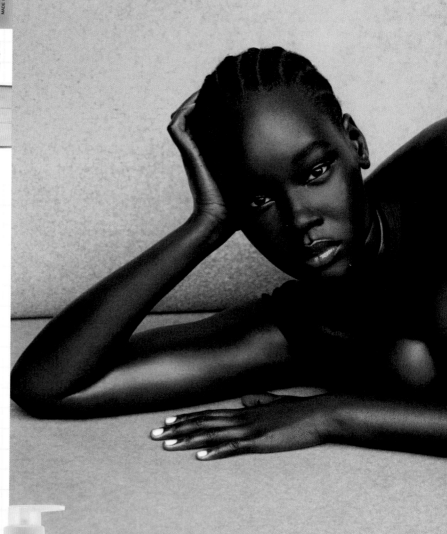

From right:
LEGOLOGY *Peach-lite Super Lift For The Derrière, £55.* SUSANNE KAUFMANN *Hyaluron Body Gel, £49*

111SKIN *Celestial Black Diamond Body Cream, £125*

LEGS & FEET

After the summer months, legs and feet need extra care. Heels can take a particular hit after a season of sandals and the winter months are the perfect time to restore hydration. Thick but high-absorbency foot and heel blends of intense moisturising ingredients, such as shea butter and oils such a jojoba, will help soften dry and hard skin. Using leg and foot scrubs beforehand will make moisturisers work more efficiently.

Left: CAUDALIE *Vinosculpt Lift & Firm Body Cream,* £27. *Below:* BAMFORD *Geranium Hand Balm,* £23

From left: U BEAUTY *The Sculpt Arm Compound,* £94. HERMES *Les Mains Hermès Complete Hand Care,* £88

TOP *to* TOE

Beginning with your SCALP *and ending with your* FEET, *there's now a product that's been developed specifically to* TREAT *and* NOURISH *every part of your* BODY, *says* LAUREN MURDOCH-SMITH

ARMS & HANDS

To improve tone and hydrate skin on your arms, use a nourishing cream with antioxidants and moisturising ingredients such as shea butter. For smoother texture, look out for skin-sloughing ingredients such as lactic acid, as this helps with exfoliation. Hands are a key area for premature ageing, so applying extra hydration not only protects them, it also leaves them smoother and softer. Massaging arms and hands while applying creams will increase circulation while helping skin stay firm.

SISLEY PARIS *Neck Cream The Enriched Formula,* £128. *Right:* NECESSAIRE *The Neck Serum,* £60

Above: BEAUTY PIE *Uber Youth Neck & Chest Super Lift Serum-spray, from* £17.50. *Below:* CLARINS *Super Restorative Décolleté & Neck Concentrate,* £60

Satin dress, ETRO

THIS WORKS *Perfect Legs 100% Natural Scrub,* £25

Clockwise from above: L'OCCITANE *Shea Butter Foot Cream,* £22. AMELIORATE *Intensive Foot Therapy,* £16. MARGARET DABBS *Firming Leg Serum,* £45. AUGUSTINUS BADER *The Body Oil, from* £25

NECK

Just like your scalp, the skin around your neck and décolletage is simply a continuation of the skin on your face, therefore the best way to look after it is to treat it with as much care. Investing in a cream specifically formulated to look after the thinner skin on your neck – which naturally has less collagen – is something to consider. To help with firming, look for one with high levels of peptides. Active ingredients such as niacinamide are also key. They help reduce age spots, which are common on the neck and chest area (a result of being left out of the daily SPF application), so remember to also extend the cream past your neck and down to your décolletage.

Boum-Boum Milk
(3-in-1 cream spray)

VIOLETTE_FR

200 ml   6.76 fl oz

Boum-Boum Milk
(3-in-1 cream spray)

VIOLETTE_FR

Red-carpet TREATMENT

As CELEBRITIES *continue to move into the world of* COSMETICS, FUNMI FETTO *spotlights six VIP* BEAUTY *brands worth the* HYPE

T he news that yet another celebrity is launching yet another beauty line is usually met with a cynical reaction grounded in two central questions, the first being: "Does the world need yet another celebrity beauty brand?" Perhaps not. That said, what the beauty consumer will always want is efficacious skincare. And these days, perhaps surprising to some, there is a wave of excellent celebrity-backed products that, unlike their predecessors, go beyond the coattails of their founder's fame and deliver exactly that. "The market for celebrity skincare products," explains June Jensen-Mills, head of UK beauty at the trend forecasting NPD Group, "has witnessed a shift in the past few years. Previously celebrities were more likely to simply endorse a product or become 'the face'. Now they not only are investing time and effort into creating a line that appeals directly to their fans and followers, there is a greater emphasis on formulation, ingredients and delivering top-quality products for all consumers. They do this with an eye on longevity in the market."

While the rate of celebrity beauty launches is unlikely to slow down any time soon – and why would it when the global skincare market is estimated to be worth more than £155 billion by 2025 – the renewed focus on exacting formulations means perhaps the predisposed answer to the second central question around celebrity beauty brands ("Is it any good?") is not a foregone conclusion. Here are six of the best celebrity-backed products to have on your radar.

Selena Gomez

From top: RARE BEAUTY *Stay Vulnerable Liquid Eyeshadow in Nearly Mauve, £19. Positive Light Tinted Moisturiser, £26*

RARE BEAUTY

Selena Gomez's mindful brand was created to combat unrealistic beauty standards, celebrate individual looks and shape conversations around the concept of beauty and its relationship with mental health, something the actor and singer has been vocal about. One per cent of the sales from Rare Beauty goes towards increasing mental health resources and the actual products are also considered. Dermatologically tested and suitable for sensitive skin, everything – from the lipsticks and eyeshadows to moisturisers and skin-smoothing mist – have been created with a skincare lens.

PLEASING

PLEASING
*Acid Drops
Lucid Overnight
Serum, £37*

Pleasing, the line developed with a mission to blur boundaries, operates quite differently to most other celebrity brands. Firstly, if you weren't paying attention you'd have no idea the actor and singer Harry Styles was behind it. There is also no rhyme or rhythm as to how, when or what products are released. Regardless, while ultimately the products are created to "excite the senses and blur the boundaries", the formulations are results-driven. Case in point, the Acid Drops Lucid Overnight Serum. It incorporates sustainably sourced hibiscus acid, from a cooperative in Burkina Faso, to resurface and brighten the skin brilliantly. >

Harry Styles

KEYS SOULCARE *Let Me Glow Illuminating Serum, £25*

KEYS SOULCARE

Inspired by the physical and emotional impact of battling skin issues in the public eye, singer-songwriter Alicia Keys sought a holistic approach to skincare. Her answer was Keys Soulcare, which she launched in 2021 with dermatologist Renée Snyder. The latest release, Let Me Glow Illuminating Serum, is a perfect example of the brand's ethos. Not only does it include antioxidants and brightening ingredients, such as niacinamide, it comes with one of Keys's now famous affirmations: "I give myself permission to glow."

Alicia Keys

ROSE INC

It has been a while since a chic, earth-friendly, inclusive brand has garnered so much attention, but Rosie Huntington-Whiteley has managed to pull it off with Rose Inc. She joined forces with Amyris – a Californian-based biotech company – to create products that pushed the boundaries of "clean" beauty, delivering noncomedogenic products, be it blushers or cleansers, that are not only good for the environment but also super advanced in their formulations.

Rosie Huntington-Whiteley

ROSE INC *Skin Clarity Gentle Exfoliating Cleanser, £29*

Pharrell Williams

HUMANRACE

In 2020, when Pharrell Williams, the musician, producer and all-round cultural entrepreneur and tastemaker, launched his skincare line, Humanrace, the products sold out in under 24 hours – and with good reason. Created in conjunction with the esteemed doctor Elena Jones, Pharrell's own personal dermatologist, it came out of the gates with solid skincare formulation credentials. As did the recent expansion into suncare: a sublime refillable line for all skin tones that Williams hopes will remind everyone of the importance of SPF, regardless of season.

HUMANRACE *Routine Pack, £95*

S'ABLE LABS

The lotions and masks Sabrina Elba had seen her mother blend growing up made the actor and model want to incorporate her Somalian roots into a beauty brand – and she, in conjunction with her husband, fellow actor Idris Elba, has done exactly that. The small-but-mighty curation launched this year features high-performance products with consciously sourced ingredients. The Black Seed Toner is full of vitamin C, E and ferulic acid, there's a radiance-boosting Baobab Moisturiser, which features niacinamide, and the Qasil Cleanser and newly launched mask use qasil, a traditional Somalian beauty staple that protects skin from extreme conditions.

Idris & Sabrina Elba

From left: **S'ABLE LABS** *Qasil Cleanser, £28. Qasil Exfoliating Mask, £28*

Clockwise from top left: FOREO
*Luna 4 Body, £129. Luna 4,
£239. Luna 4 Plus, £349*

SKINCARE, SUPERCHARGED

The new LUNA 4 *range from*
FOREO *offers superior cleansing
for both* FACE *and* BODY *at
the* TOUCH *of a button*

more hygienic than nylon bristles, helping to ensure a truly thorough cleanse, while low-frequency pulsations mean the device can be used as a skin-rejuvenating massage tool as well. Raj Arora, GP and aesthetic doctor, says, "An effective cleansing step is necessary to ensure deeper penetration of active skincare products and will also result in fewer breakouts. All of my clients are advised to use one and they never go back to cleansing in any other way!"

And thanks to the new Luna 4 Body, you can now supercharge your skincare from head to toe. With a velvety-soft design that adapts to your body's individual curves, the game-changing device creates a smoother skin texture thanks to its ability to tackle clogged pores, ingrown hairs and keratosis pilaris with its gentle exfoliating action. The massaging effect of the T-Sonic technology also helps to temporarily dilate pores, so that your skin is perfectly prepped to absorb the creams you apply afterwards, promoting a super-soft finish. The Luna 4 Body also acts on cellulite, boosting microcirculation to distribute fat deposits, as well as maintaining healthy blood circulation so that your body can produce more collagen.

Effective, hygienic, easy-to-use and a chic addition to your bathroom shelf, the Luna is the world's best-selling soft silicone facial-cleansing device for good reason, and the new Luna 4 only serves to make the experience better still. Combining the very best and latest technology with Foreo's skincare know-how, the Luna range supercharges your daily routine without having to add extra steps. And with options for both face and body, you can enjoy a superior cleanse all over. Because skincare shouldn't stop at your neck; skincare means everywhere.

*Explore the complete Luna range online at
Foreo.com and at selected retailers*

L ooking to turbocharge your daily skincare regime? Foreo's award-winning Luna cleansing devices offer a deeper and more effective cleanse from the comfort of your own home, using ultra-hygienic silicone touch points and relaxing T-Sonic pulsations to remove 99 per cent of dirt, oil and make-up residue with ease, making clogged pores and breakouts a thing of the past. And now the Luna 4 facial-cleansing device is joined by the Luna 4 Body, Foreo's first body-cleansing device, designed to visibly soften and smooth skin from the neck down.

The Luna 4 offers your most effective, but gentle, cleanse yet, with three cleansing modes – Gentle, Regular and Deep – and 16 T-Sonic pulsation intensities to choose from. The silicone touch points are 35 times

BALMY NIGHTS

DR HAUSCHKA's *new cleanser is the* PERFECT BALANCE *between cleansing and* CARING *for your* SKIN

H

ow to cleanse with intention? You might not realise it, but finding the right formula is key. Washing your face might seem like a straightforward step in your skincare routine, but it's actually the perfect time to indulge in rituals, such as facial massage, and to reconnect with yourself.

Dr Hauschka's new Cleansing Balm is just the formula, thanks to its balm-to-milk texture, which quickly removes impurities and light make-up, leaving skin feeling soft, supple and thoroughly clean. Formulated to preserve the skin's unique oil-moisture balance, its hero is Rügen chalk, an anti-inflammatory ingredient that essentially lifts impurities and excess oil from the skin without stripping the skin barrier. Other ingredients in the vegan formula include apricot kernel oil, birch and precious oils, which work together to protect against the environment, revitalise, moisturise and generally boost the skin. Put simply, it's the perfect starting point to prepare skin for ensuing serums and moisturisers.

Of course, cleansing with intention is about much more than just physically cleaning the skin: it's also about how earth-friendly the formula you use is. A little of Dr Hauschka's Cleansing Balm goes a long

way, plus it is a low-water formulation, meaning that the amount of packaging required is reduced. The packaging that is used is all totally recyclable too – from the aluminium tube the formula is housed in (which is easily drained when you come to finish the Balm) to the folded box it arrives in, which is also made of 100 per cent recycled material. Add to that the mineral oil-free printing inks and a QR code to replace the information insert and you've got a cleanser with excellent sustainability credentials.

To discover more, visit Drhauschka.co.uk

DR HAUSCHKA *Cleansing Balm, £23*

DR HAUSCHKA *Soothing Cleansing Milk, £26*

DR HAUSCHKA *Cleansing Cream, £16.5*

Above & BEYOND

Protective, restorative SKINCARE *abounds, as* TWIGGY JALLOH *lines up the most* SHELF-ASSURED *formulas. Photograph by* ADAM GOODISON

Top row, from left: SENSAI *Comforting Barrier Mask,* £139. FARMACY *Beauty Honey Potion Plus Ceramide Hydration Mask,* £53. BIOEFFECT *EGF Serum,* £129. DIOR *Cica Recover Balm,* £40. DECLEOR *Neroli Bigarade Hydrating Night Balm,* £50.50. *Bottom row, from left:* DR JART+ *Cicapair Tiger Grass Sleepair Intensive Mask,* £33. LANCOME *Advanced Génifique Night Cream,* £65. REN CLEAN SKINCARE *Evercalm Overnight Recovery Balm,* £45. DERMALOGICA *Barrier Repair,* £45. BIOSSANCE *Squalane & Omega Repair Cream,* £45. GLOSSIER *After Baume,* £25

SHISEIDO
*Ultimune
Power Infusing
Concentrate,
from £32*

SHISEIDO *Benefiance
Wrinkle Smoothing
Cream, from £81*

SHISEIDO *Vital
Perfection Uplifting
and Firming
Cream, from £107*

TRULY
scientific
SKINCARE

**SHISEIDO *has been
shaping the* FUTURE *of
skincare for* 150 YEARS
with GROUNDBREAKING
*products that really deliver***

BEHIND EVERY GREAT skincare product is some really great science. And that's particularly true in the case of Shiseido, which is celebrating 150 years of pioneering innovation, patented technologies and incredible results with products that truly bring out the best in all skin types. Born in 1872 in Tokyo's Ginza district, Shiseido has drawn upon breakthrough science from Japan to shape the future of skincare for a century and a half. Alongside its high-performance products, scientific supremacy and impressive heritage, the brand has maintained the holistic aspect of skincare, ensuring your daily routine is a true sensorial experience, revealing your most vibrant and youthful self.

Of course, those 150 years have seen some truly groundbreaking skincare creations come to life. Vital Perfection is Shiseido's most advanced lifting and firming collection, visibly lifting the skin in just one week, while firming and brightening in just four weeks*. It calls upon Shiseido's unique Kurenai-TruLift technology to promote skin resistance and elasticity (demonstrated via in-vitro data), ReNeura Technology++ to fight the signs of ageing and the botanicals-infused VP8 complex to improve skin tone and brightness. Then there's Benefiance, a range designed to tackle early signs of ageing by reducing the appearance of wrinkles in just two weeks**. Key ingredient ReNeura Technology+ reawakens skin sensors for faster, more efficient results, while an innovative Kombu-Bounce complex targets the skin's internal mechanism of wrinkle formation to reduce the appearance of lines for a smoother, more youthful-looking complexion.

And then, of course, there's Ultimune Power Infusing Concentrate, Shiseido's number one serum with double anti-ageing technology. Suitable for all skin types and ages, it features ImuGenerationRED Technology to turbocharge skin's resilience and boost microcirculation, swapping a dull, lacklustre complexion for more radiant skin in just three days***.

To discover more about Shiseido's 150 years, visit Shiseido.co.uk

2.

3.

Kate
Somerville

HydraKate™
Recharging Serum
Sérum revigorant

4.

cannabinoid
face serum
by Cellular Goods

SUPER SERUMS

SUPERCHARGED
skincare SAVIOURS *for*
the EVERYDAY. *Edited*
by HOLLY TOMALIN

Vogue, November 2021

7.

5.

VICHY
LABORATOIRES

V

MINÉRAL
89

BOOSTER QUOTIDIEN
FORTIFIANT ET REPULPANT
FORTIFYING AND PLUMPING
DAILY BOOSTER

6.

EVE LOM

RADIANCE REPAIR RETINOL SERUM
SÉRUM RÉGÉNÉRATION
ET ÉCLAT AU RÉTINOL

BIO·PERFORMANCE

SHISEIDO

Infill Serum
Sérum Comblant

Night / Nuit

1. OLE HENRIKSEN *Banana Bright
Vitamin C Serum,* £56. *2.* KATE
SOMERVILLE *HydraKate Recharging
Serum,* £67. *3.* SKINCEUTICALS *HA
Intensifier,* £90. *4.* CELLULAR GOODS
Rejuvenating Cannabinoid Face Serum, £99.
5. VICHY *Mineral 89 Hyaluronic Acid
Hydrating Serum,* £26. *6.* EVE LOM
Radiance Repair Retinol Serum, £145.
7. SHISEIDO *Bio-performance Skin
Filler Serums,* £231

A new LIGHT

Make GOLDEN HOUR *last 24 hours with these* RADIANT WONDERS. *Edited by* HOLLY TOMALIN

1. EVIDENS DE BEAUTE *The Special Mask, £170, at Fenwick.*
2. REVIVE *Glow Elixir, £100, at Harvey Nichols. 3.* SUNDAY RILEY *CEO Afterglow Brightening Vitamin C Cream, £60.*
4. L'OREAL PARIS *Age Perfect Golden Age Rosy Oil-serum, £20.*
5. REN CLEAN SKINCARE *Ready Steady Glow Daily AHA Tonic, £28. 6.* VIDA GLOW *Radiance Advanced Repair, £49.*
7. NOBLE PANACEA *Prime Radiance Serum, £235, at Harrods*

Vogue, April 2020

If the STYLE lures ME in, the substance keeps ME interested

Next-gen
SKIN SAVIOURS

KATHLEEN BAIRD-MURRAY *explores* SISLEY
PARIS*'s revolutionary* SKINCARE *line-up.*
Photograph by BENJAMIN MADGWICK

WHEN YOU'RE SENT as many beauty products to try as I am, you quickly notice the ones you return to time after time. And Sisley Paris's Sisleÿa L'Integral Anti-Age moisturiser is one I always use until the pot runs dry. If the texture, fragrance and timeless packaging lures me in – the "style", if you like – it's the substance beneath that keeps me interested. In 2015, as the world discovered the significance of epigenetics – the way in which our lifestyles can radically affect and change what was thought to be fixed firmly in place by genetics and environment – Sisley's Sisleÿa L'Integral was launched. Building on this new research, L'Integral's raison d'etre was to target all three types of ageing, genetic, behavioural and environmental, which affect the life cycle of skin cells. The basic principles that apply to all Sisley products were still there – harnessing the most efficacious plant extracts in conjunction with pioneering scientific discoveries – but with the new L'Integral Anti-Age collection there would be a newer set of formulations that would maintain our skin's condition to the best of its potential.

With this new approach came three complete action creams and three targeted treatment serums. The former includes the Sisleÿa L'Integral Anti-Age Face Cream, £365, in two textures, and the Sisleÿa L'Integral Anti-Age Eye & Lip Contour Cream, £160, while the latter includes an Anti-Wrinkle Concentrated Serum, £375, a Firming Concentrated Serum, £375, and an Anti-Dark Spot & Radiance Serum, £375. Additionally, there's a four-week programme called La Cure, £800, intended to give a boost to skin that looks and feels like it needs one. Designed to capitalise on the 28 days it takes for your skin to renew, it is centred around the mitochondria. While my L'Integral Anti-Age moisturiser takes care of all my needs and is like a complete daily treatment in one, I'm looking forward to trying La Cure this winter. Will I still use other moisturisers? Of course – it's my job to try. But I like to think of my skincare as a wardrobe and L'Integral is one of those little black dresses I'll wear time and time again. *To discover more, visit Sisley-paris.com or your nearest Sisley counter for a complimentary treatment*

Sisley Paris's Sisleÿa L'Integral Anti-Age collection of creams and serums start from £160

Perricone MD

HIGH POTENCY HYALURONIC INTENSIVE HYDRATING SERUM

A lightweight, deeply nourishing serum formulated to strengthen your skins moisture barrier whilst visibly smoothing, firming and plumping.

The results speak for themselves. In clinical and consumer testing: 97% saw improved skin hydration for 72 hours,* 86% saw softened fine lines and wrinkles** and 85% felt firmer, more supple skin.**

From £79. Available at John Lewis and NET-A-PORTER

GOODBYE, DARK CIRCLES

Chronolux, the powerful skin-repair technology behind Estée Lauder's famed Advanced Night Repair serum, is now a feature of the Supercharged Gel-Creme, £52. The formula works to fight free-radical damage – one of the reasons we can develop dark circles – and boasts a two-week difference in their appearance.

THE SPRITZ

If you haven't jumped on the misting skincare trend yet, its worth reconsidering. Pai's Century Flower mist, £39, calms and the lotus root and hyaluronic acid in the formula will help appease irritated skin. For dry skin, Shane Cooper's Hyaluronic Mist, £60, is great sprayed throughout the day. It'll also help make-up stay put.

GRAB A LIFT

Chanel Le Lift Pro Concentré Contours, £144, Crème Volume, £155, and Massage Tool, £70, have been developed to be used in tandem to contour, plump, lift and smooth the skin. The unscented skincare contains a rare honey from Costa Rica, which has a highly active enzymatic ingredient from melipona bees that works to support skin against anti-ageing. The magnetic facial tool, which separates and connects together, helps lift the "youth triangle", the area between the top of your cheekbones and the tip of your chin.

PEEL FACTOR

If you're a fan of the Clarins cult favourite Beauty Flash Balm, then you'll love the latest addition to the family. Beauty Flash Peel, £38, is a gentle chemical peel that can be used up to three times a week to resurface and bring back radiance to skin that's looking and feeling dull. The AHA glycolic acid and BHA salicylic acid work together to exfoliate and clear pores.

Skincare MUSINGS

With new LAUNCHES *and clever* REFORMULATIONS, *winter skincare never looked so* GOOD, *says* LAUREN MURDOCH-SMITH

BALMY ARMY

There's a whole new army of lip balms launching to ensure lips are protected this season. Sisley Paris's iconic pink, potted lip balm has been reformulated and is now even more concentrated with kokum and mango butter, plum kernel, sweet white lupin and wheat germ oil. De Mamiel Lip Rx – one many have been on the waitlist for – is rich in rose wax and even has pomegranate to plump. Byredo's three scented lip balms, Camomille d'Anjou, Bergamotte de Bahia and Thé à la Menthe d' Agadir, not only smell divine, of course, but are highly hydrating, with jojoba seed oil and shea butter. Also try Laneige's Lip Mask at night and Armani and Honest Beauty's tinted balms in the day. *Clockwise from above left: Honest Tinted Lip Balm, £10. Armani Beauty Neo Nude Ecstasy Balm, £29. Laneige Original Lip Sleeping Mask, £19. De Mamiel Lip Rx, £28. Byredo Bergamotte de Bahia, £40. Sisley Paris Nutritive Lip Balm, £59*

GOING FOR GOLD

The latest technology in La Prairie's Pure Gold Nocturnal Balm, £773, has been developed to help strengthen skin overnight. So while you are sleeping, the balm works hard to trigger the skin's replenishing process using their Pure Gold Diffusion System. It also releases gold particles onto the skin for immediate radiance.

GADGET UPGRADE

Foreo, the brand that brings sonic technology to skincare, have given their bestselling Luna cleansing device an upgrade. Adapting the silicone cleansing "touch points" so that they're even softer allows the gadget to glide across the skin more easily. The thinking behind this upgrade is to also benefit the preservation of the natural elasticity in your skin. Combined with deep and gentle cleansing modes, the latest iteration of the Luna cleansing device won't disappoint. *Foreo Luna 4, £239*

"Skin care with added glow"

LANT INNOVATION
hicory extract boosts
llagen synthesis
firm the skin.

CLARINS
PARIS
Everlasting
Youth Fluid
Teint Lumière & Fermeté
SPF 15 / PA+++
Illuminating & Firming
Foundation

CLARINS

Everlasting Youth Fluid
Powered by Clarins age-defying skin care expertise.
A buildable, lightweight foundation to firm, plump and illuminate skin. Formulated with chicory extract to enhance luminosity and help leave skin fuller and firmer.

Skin care with added glow.

Visit in-store to enjoy your complimentary sample.

CLARINS.COM

ASPINAL

LONDON

FASHION & FEATURES

HM Queen Elizabeth II photographed in 1975

The Pleasure of HER COMPANY

In glittering REGALIA or at elegant EASE, the women of the house of WINDSOR have long SHONE through the PAGES of Vogue, thanks to a line of GIFTED photographers. ROBIN MUIR looks back on some of their FINEST moments

R evisiting back issues to look through readers' eyes at the events of four reigns, it is the details of modes and manners, the nuances of royal fashion, that endure. As *Vogue* was 10 years older than Her Majesty Queen Elizabeth II, her history was often *Vogue*'s history too. The magazine commissioned the greatest writers and illustrators of the day to record royal lives as they unfolded, but surely it's the achievements of its photographers that have best defined the Crown.

Perhaps one figure more than any other propelled royal photography into the modern age. In 1939, Cecil Beaton was summoned to the Palace to take his first pictures of the then Queen Elizabeth, later the Queen Mother. The photographs were a dazzling departure, an alchemical balance of benign approachability and majestic detachment. A new era in royal portraiture had begun.

Beaton first shot her daughter, then Princess Elizabeth, 80 years ago in 1942, at the height of the war. Later, as it drew to a close, he felt able to revive the glamour of earlier royal portraits, placing her in a pink-spangled crinoline – her mother's dress altered to fit – against a fairy-tale backdrop. He did not neglect the "other princess", Margaret, four years her junior; beautiful, with, as Beaton rapturously wrote, "ice-cream pink cheeks… the eyes are of a piercing blue, catlike and fierce, very pristine, very youthful".

Beaton's last portrait of the Queen was made in 1968 and by then his position, jealously guarded for so long, was in peril. Lord Snowdon, who had been a star photographer at *Vogue* since the '50s, had married the Queen's younger sister, Princess Margaret, in 1960. When she told Beaton that her new husband had no intention of giving up his day job, he shuddered further. And so it would turn out. For *Vogue,* Snowdon photographed Lady Diana Spencer before her engagement was announced (the magazine was presumed to have inside knowledge), discerning in the 19-year-old an innate poise and sophistication, long before it would be the chief commodity of Diana, Princess of Wales.

Eventually, she would appear on four *Vogue* covers, her life all but played out in pictures, becoming a global fashion icon and a celebrity with notions of style that all but obliterated her aristocratic roots. As *Vogue* observed in its obituary, "Clothes were her vocabulary." After her death in 1997, she left a vacuum *Vogue* found difficult to fill, even as the nation's long-serving monarch celebrated her milestone anniversaries. Not perhaps until the arrival of the Duchess of Cambridge, the daughter-in-law Diana never met.

In 2016, the then duchess, now Princess of Wales, appeared on *Vogue*'s centenary cover, a photograph taken en plein air, which suggested she might take a more understated approach to duty and service. In 2017, Prince Harry announced his engagement to Meghan Markle, who would go on to guest-edit *Vogue*'s fastest-ever selling issue in 2019, highlighting her charity and activism work. Now the Duke and Duchess of Sussex, they made the decision to step away from royal duties, while remaining, as the duke's late grandmother put it, "much loved members of the family".

Vogue celebrated Queen Elizabeth II's Platinum Jubilee in April this year, as she celebrated her 96th birthday – a coda, as it would turn out, to a reign the magazine had charted since 1952. She leaves a legacy to which all who follow, royal women and royal men alike, will be justifiably measured.

The Crown in Vogue by Robin Muir and Josephine Ross (Conran Octopus, £30) is out now

CROWNING GLORY
Queen Elizabeth II & The Duke of Edinburgh (1953) by Cecil Beaton

Cecil Beaton was given a ringside seat at the Coronation, reporting back to *Vogue* from Westminster Abbey in vivid detail. He was lucky to be there.
The Duke of Edinburgh lobbied for a friend of his, Baron Nahum, to be official photographer, but the new Queen's mother fought Beaton's corner
– and won. Philip disliked Beaton's fluttery manner and this would be the only occasion he would consent to sit for him on his own. >

STUFF OF DREAMS
The Princess of Wales & The Queen (1981) by Lichfield

She had started her journey that summer's day as Lady Diana Spencer, with her father in the Glass Coach en route to St Paul's Cathedral, and ended it at Buckingham Palace in the open-topped 1902 State Landau as the Princess of Wales. "Theirs is a triumphant journey," *Vogue* proclaimed. With an empathy that would mark her out from then on, the princess, watched over by her new mother-in-law, the Queen, comforts her youngest bridesmaid, Clementine Hambro, in a defining image of a magical day.

AT EASE
The Duchess of Cambridge (2016) by Josh Olins

The then duchess – now Princess of Wales – had agreed to a cover shoot to celebrate *Vogue*'s centenary. A misty January morning clearing into bright blue skies heralded a day of unexpected informality. It became obvious that Olins was to portray the woman, not the figurehead, in an unhurried picture of an easygoing subject. Her Royal Highness wore a vintage hat from Beyond Retro.

COURT & SPARK
Princess Margaret (1951) by Cecil Beaton

The princess was known for radiating a natural glamour. For her 21st birthday portrait, she wore a creation by Christian Dior, which might have raised a few eyebrows in austere post-war Britain. "She was a real fairy-tale princess," the great couturier wrote later, "delicate, graceful and exquisite." To *Vogue,* the princess was "probably the first member of the house of Windsor to understand how positive an injection of glamour and style can be to those who look on".

HEIR OF DISTINCTION
Princess Elizabeth (1934)
by Marcus Adams

Aged nine, and third in line to the throne, this portrait eventually ran in *Vogue* on the eve of her father's Coronation in 1937, which would elevate her to heir presumptive. Adams, a favourite for photographing royal children, was entranced by the princess. She was beautifully behaved, he noted, but like all children sometimes needed distraction. On this occasion, a ball was repeatedly thrown against the studio wall to keep her attentive.

ALWAYS IN VOGUE
Queen Elizabeth, The Queen Mother (1980)
by Norman Parkinson

Parkinson replaced Cecil Beaton in the Queen Mother's affections. His approach was less formal, investing his royal portraits with a thoughtful sense of fun. This droll and knowing picture was taken for the Queen Mother's 80th birthday – his sitter appreciated Parkinson's inexhaustible reservoir of charm and his old-world courtesies.

PICTURE OF ELEGANCE
The Duchess of Cornwall (2022)
by Jamie Hawkesworth

Earlier this year, in a message celebrating her Platinum Jubilee, Queen Elizabeth wrote these simple words: "It is my sincere wish that, when that time comes, Camilla will be known as Queen Consort." Her Majesty has been married to the new King for 17 years, a working member of the Royal Family for just as long and, since the summer, a Royal Lady of the Most Noble Order of the Garter, the most senior order of chivalry in Britain, and solely in the gift of the monarch. On the eve of her 75th birthday, the then duchess was photographed for *Vogue*, wearing a dress from her own wardrobe, in the Garden Room of Clarence House. >

WINDSOR OF CHANGE
The Duchess of Sussex (2019)
by Peter Lindbergh

The duchess guest-edited that year's September issue, which featured game-changers, activists, artists, politicians and campaigners set to reshape society in positive ways. It became the fastest-selling issue in the magazine's history. Meghan had recently been appointed royal patron of Smart Works, a charity aiming to provide clothes and coaching and, as *Vogue* put it, "a large dose of self-belief" to unemployed women in need, and in so doing change their lives. She is seen here working at one of their centres. Despite stepping away from royal duties several months later, she remains the charity's patron.

THE ROYAL WE
Princesses Beatrice & Eugenie (2018)
by Sean Thomas

With two brace of Norfolk terriers, the princesses – in their first significant *Vogue* appearance – outlined their desire "to shine light and love in the world". This has taken many forms, not least multiple charitable roles and patronages. Both now married with children, the sisters remain extremely close, having endured a childhood in the glare of the media spotlight, telling *Vogue*, "We're the only other person in each other's lives who can know exactly what the other is going through."

GRACEFUL WINNER
Princess Anne (1973)
by Norman Parkinson

BBC Sports Personality of the Year, 1971, and Olympian, part of the GB three-day eventing squad at the 1976 Montreal games, the Queen's only daughter was regarded as an unstuffy and thoroughly modern princess. She was also the first member of the Royal Family to be photographed for the cover of *Vogue* (in 1971, also by Norman Parkinson). This cover and a special six-page portfolio were taken to celebrate the wedding of Her Royal Highness to fellow Olympic equestrian Captain Mark Phillips. The princess's diamond and sapphire engagement ring was made by Garrard.

RULE BRITANNIA
Queen Elizabeth II (1972)
by Lichfield

As first cousin once removed to the Queen, Lord Lichfield's proximity to the family allowed for a more personal perspective on royal events, unaffected by protocol or official constraint. Here on HMY *Britannia* in the Indian Ocean on a leg of the Queen's South-East Asian tour, he captures her on the bridge laughing at him. A successful image rather against the odds as he was being ducked in water at the time as part of a nautical Crossing the Line tradition. "I did have the wit to take a waterproof camera with me," he recalled later.

PORTRAIT MODE
Diana, Princess of Wales (1991)
by Snowdon

Like Lichfield, Lord Snowdon's closeness to the Royal Family – he was, of course, once married to Queen Elizabeth's sister – made for some disarmingly natural pictures. He first took Diana's portrait for *Vogue* in 1981 (the magazine – with some inside knowledge – trumping news of her engagement to the Prince of Wales by a month) and was quick to detect in her the self-possession and elegance that would serve her so well.

POWER OF THREE
The Queen, Queen Elizabeth, The Queen Mother &
Princess Margaret (1980)
by Norman Parkinson

Perhaps only Parkinson with his effortless (if forceful) personal charisma could have pulled off this outlandish picture. Taken to celebrate the Queen Mother's 80th birthday, he cajoled the three most senior female members of the Royal Family into matching bright blue sateen capes. (He had previously cajoled royal dressmaker Hardy Amies into creating them.) "I feel it may make a timeless, fashion-free picture, which will ensure its place of importance in the future," was Parkinson's view of his picture. Sadly, not everyone shared his optimism – several observers compared the royal figures to a high-gloss all-girl singing trio.

In GRIEF *and gratitude,* VOGUE *salutes* LEADER, *family woman and* FRIEND, *the late* QUEEN ELIZABETH II, *with a special collection of personal* TRIBUTES, *accompanied by images captured by* TOM CRAIG *on the day of Her Majesty's funeral*

STEWART PARVIN

In the 20 years that I designed clothes for Her Majesty Queen Elizabeth II, it usually began with a loose brief. Rather than use fabrics from my collection, I'd go to a separate source that guaranteed no one else would have them. I'd lock myself in my room with a huge amount of samples, and sketch and sketch – normally two or three ideas for each fabric. I'd send them off to Angela Kelly, the Queen's dresser, who'd select what she liked with notes. Then I'd create the dresses for fittings.

For instance, for a state visit to Bermuda, they wanted coral and lilac to represent the national colours. We made the most amazing corally-pink evening dress – a beautiful floral embroidery with a chiffon knot-waisted skirt – and another coat and dress trimmed in that colour combination. It's very subtly representational.

From me, she'd like a bold print that was actually quite youthful: frequently floral, sometimes geometric, and often quite outrageous. We'd tone them down with a block-colour coat, but while the overall appearance was one single colour, there'd be something beautiful underneath, sometimes in the coat's lining too, for when she did occasionally take it off or the wind flipped it up.

My favourite might be the very first I made for her: a blue cobweb-lace evening dress for a state banquet in Jamaica. All the power failed on the island, and the Queen came down in her beautiful tiara, diamond necklace, and this shimmering dress that twinkled by candlelight. She wore it on quite a few memorable occasions. Nothing the Queen ever wore was worn only once – it wasn't what people think. It wasn't fast fashion. It was proper couture and was readjusted and altered as she changed. It was really sustainable.

The Queen was always amazing. She put you at ease as soon as you saw her. She was the most positive person. Fitting her was just like any normal fitting. She was also an enduring icon. Her steadfast style evolved hugely from her being a princess to the end of her reign. I think it's a lesson to all of us that we should carry on, keep trying and never let the standards down.

When I got my MVO, I was completely surprised. I wasn't expecting it. It was wonderful. When I went to receive the honour from the Queen, she chose to wear one of my suits. That was an extra bonus.

KATE MOSS

I first met the Queen when I was at primary school and she visited Croydon. I gave her a poesy and curtsied, but couldn't really concentrate on the moment as I had borrowed my dad's camera and thought I had broken it. I was scared I was going to get in trouble. Then, around 20 years later, I was invited to the Palace. I wore a royal-blue outfit and so did the Queen! My distinct memory of that occasion is "what a fashion faux pas". The Queen was so gracious, it was such an honour to meet her. I always have and always will be in awe of her.

EMMA RADUCANU

My strongest memory of the Queen will always be, right after the US Open final, when she had written me a letter. It was a note of congratulations, and it was amazing to know that she had been watching my matches and supporting me. That was a very special moment and will live with me forever. She was a solid presence to look up to. She dedicated her life to her duties and will be deeply missed.

PAT McGRATH

The Queen's lifetime of duty, devotion and service will always be a great inspiration to me and countless others. Receiving letters from Buckingham Palace notifying me of my MBE on the Her Majesty's New Year's Honours list in 2014, and later a damehood in 2020 for services to fashion, beauty and diversity, were both humbling and surreal. They remain two of my fondest and most cherished memories.

She was a brilliant leader with an unparalleled work ethic and deep commitment to duty. Thank you, Your Majesty, for the incredible legacy you have left behind.

HER MAJESTY QUEEN RANIA OF JORDAN

When I first met Her Majesty, I'd been in my role less than a year. She had reigned for half-a-century – in my eyes, she was walking history. And yet, her calm dignity put me at ease. She managed to be both elegant and approachable, an icon in sensible shoes, helping those around her to feel steadier and more secure.

Her life was exceptional, yet her presence somehow offered a sense of normalcy. From her signature bright outfits to her playful humour, she stayed vibrant into her nineties, showing us all how to navigate hard times – even heartbreak – with faith and resilience. Forget the fairy tales, Queen Elizabeth was a strong, hard-working leader who never wavered in her duty. I looked up to her, learnt from her and will miss her.   >

VICTORIA BECKHAM

The loss of Her Majesty Queen Elizabeth II is a profound one, both on a personal and global level. She will be remembered not least for her steadfast loyalty and lifelong service, but for her incredible kindness, grace and compassion, which have served as a safety blanket when we needed it most.

A moment I will never forget was meeting Her Majesty at the Royal Command Performance in 1997 with the Spice Girls. I was nervous, but the Queen was courteous, gracious and kind, and I'll always be grateful for that special memory. The ultimate icon in every way and the epitome of elegance, she will live on in our hearts and minds forever.

CHARLOTTE TILBURY

The Queen has been a constant source of personal inspiration all my life. Receiving my MBE and celebrating her Platinum Jubilee are two of my proudest days ever. One thing that stands out is how much she understood the power of colour, and the power of a bold statement lipstick – I created my shade Legendary Queen in homage to her! The way she set bright red and cerise pinks against her radiant complexion and that gorgeous white hair made her beautiful blue eyes sparkle and twinkle even more. In June, it was a privilege to get a glimpse of her on the balcony at Buckingham Palace as we sang the National Anthem at her Platinum Jubilee Pageant. She looked as magical and captivating as ever in that bright green dress coat and hat, paired with the perfect pink lip. I'm smiling as I think of it. I will hold all these memories close as I try to imagine a world without her. Thank you, Ma'am.

ADJOA ANDOH

Let's talk about Ghana, 1961. There's a photograph of the Queen dancing with Kwame Nkrumah, four years after the country's independence. It makes me think of my Ghanaian dad and my English mum dancing together at the same time – the Queen was doing something radical in that era. She brought nations together. I actually met her for the only time earlier this year, at The Platinum Jubilee Celebration: A Gallop Through History performance. It had rained all afternoon and was chilly. Despite the Queen's mobility issues, she stayed for the entire evening. Afterwards, we were all told to line up and wave as she drove past. Then, unexpectedly, Alan Titchmarsh walked over to me. "Follow me," he said. That's where I met the Queen! There was something so engaging and charismatic about this 96-year-old beautiful woman, so tiny and twinkly. She was delighted by life. I looked at her and thought, "I hope that I have that much curiosity, engagement and fun about me when I'm your age."

STEVIE WONDER

The time I met the Queen was at the Diamond Jubilee in 2012. I said to her, "I'm a Taurus," to which she replied, "I know. We both are." I didn't know she knew that! On that day, I was focused on celebrating her. I wanted to be a part of the joy of the occasion, but I wish I had been able to have a conversation about change. It wouldn't have been a stubborn one. I'm happy that I was invited to spread love that day, and I'm happy that God blessed the Queen with 96 years of life. Like I say in my song "If It's Magic", why can't life be everlasting?

ANDREA TANNER

Fortnum & Mason, where I work as archivist, treasures its lifelong relationship with Queen Elizabeth. We made clothes for her and her sister when they were children, and welcomed her many times as a young woman, when she undertook her Christmas shopping in person. Our first warrant from her in 1954 reflected her love of our Earl Grey tea and our handmade chocolates, which at that time were made on the top floor of our Piccadilly home.

In 2012, she visited us to open our Diamond Jubilee Tea Salon, alongside the then Duchesses of Cornwall and Cambridge. To our delight, she was dressed from head to foot in our own eau de nil, which demonstrated both her sense of fun and her love of Fortnum's. The hamper we gave her in thanks contained a very special selection of her favourite chocolates, and a goodly supply of dog treats. >

DAVID OYELOWO

Born in the UK but raised in Nigeria, I saw the legacy of colonialism. However, I was able to separate the complexities of such from the Queen as a person, who represented kindness, stability and faith – values of great importance to my family. I still have a photograph of the time that my late mother met the Queen because she took so much pride in it – the impact of Her Majesty's passing was seismic to my family, but also to me as someone in close proximity to the Royal Family via my role as an ambassador and beneficiary of The Prince's Trust. She is irreplaceable. There's no question about that.

STELLA McCARTNEY

I first met Her Majesty with my father when he opened LIPA, the Liverpool performing arts school, and I just remember being so proud of him. The Queen had come specifically to cut the ribbon on his old school, which was going to fall into decay had he not of saved it and created the institute. I met Her Majesty again when I visited the Palace and received my MBE. I was so conscious not to forget what she said to me because I'm known to forget many a magnificent moment. But with Her Majesty, I remember vividly. She said, "You seem like a very busy woman," which I found so surprising. It was the last thing that I ever thought she would say to me! And I replied, "Not as busy as you, Ma'am," and then we smiled.

JULIE ANDREWS

Her Majesty and I were fairly close in age. As I grew up, she was always there ahead of me, setting an example of grace and dignity that I tried so hard to emulate. I noted how her parents stayed in London during the war. I followed her as she joined the Royal Auxiliary Territorial Service and learnt how to drive a van and fix an engine. I watched her Coronation on TV and began to sense how much hard work was in her future.

I started performing when I was 12 years old. I would often travel up to London with my mother, for performances and rehearsals. We would drive along the Mall and if the Royal Standard was flying, my mother would turn to me, with a smile, and say, "Oh, good, she's *in*." It might sound odd but I felt so much safer knowing that Her Majesty was in residence. I remember, one day, asking my mother: "Do you think I would ever get to have tea with the Queen? "And, she said: "Well, if you're very good, and work very hard, it might be possible."

Throughout my life there were times when my path crossed with the Queen's. I did a Royal Command Performance in 1948 and she was in the box. In 1958, she came to see me in *My Fair Lady* and greeted the company backstage. Then, in 2000, came a staggering message from the British ambassador in New York, where I was working. Her Majesty hoped to bestow upon me the honour of Dame Commander of the British Empire. Would I accept?

I remember that special day so clearly. At Buckingham Palace, in the grand ballroom, an orchestra was playing songs from the musicals. Her Majesty entered the room through tall double doors and she was flanked by ladies and gentlemen of the court. When my name was announced and after I had curtsied before her, she said, "I've been waiting a long time to see you here." I was almost speechless.

In the days since the loss of our Queen, memories of my own past have come flooding back to me. Seeing the many flags placed along the Mall for her funeral, I was vividly reminded of her Coronation. I remembered how the Royal Family supported us through the darkness of war and the celebrations when it ended. Our Queen worked so very hard and faced so many challenges. Yet she remained steadfast. She united us all with her presence, gave us a sense of identity and made us proud to be British. I mourn her greatly.

BELLA FREUD

I remember my father telling me he was going to paint the Queen, and that she would give him 10 sittings. Some of my portraits had taken a year and I wondered how he would manage. He had amazing powers of persuasion, but there was no getting around this with HM. The Queen was originally going to come to his studio, which was an incredibly exciting concept, but the paparazzi got wind of it and the location changed to a room in St James's Palace. When I invited my father to my registry office wedding on 14 December 2001, it happened to coincide with the Queen's last sitting. I decided we should both keep our respective commitments and was secretly relieved to be married without the intense presence of my father. He did come to the party later and danced all night with Kate Moss.

GRACE JONES

I remember her saying when she came backstage to meet everyone involved in her Diamond Jubilee, "You changed."

Meaning that I had changed my costume. She thought I would still be wearing my Hula-Hoop! Really that was a moment. Forever that will always bring a big silent laugh whenever I think of it. >

SADIQ KHAN

One of my fondest childhood memories was lining the streets with fellow Londoners as Her Majesty's Silver Jubilee procession wound its way past our estate in Tooting. I was there with family, friends and neighbours waiting eagerly by the roadside, Union Jack flags in hand and paper crowns on our heads. I'll never forget that day, nor what it meant to swear my oath of allegiance to the Queen as an MP, or my pride at becoming a member of her Privy Council. Throughout Her Majesty's life, she was a shining force that bound us all together. The Queen leaves an extraordinary legacy that will endure in our hearts for generations to come.

ZANDRA RHODES

I had the pleasure of meeting Her Majesty numerous times throughout her reign. The most notable for me was the Christmas of 1998. It was an honour that year to have been asked to design the quaint pink fairy for the top of the Buckingham Palace Christmas tree. The tree featured ornaments from hundreds of notable names who had tried their hand at embroidery and sewing. Her Majesty was so polite – standing with me to admire all the creations and complimenting the skills of all who were involved. I remember most vividly her elegant and fashionable dogtooth suit jacket, which she matched with her favourite pearls.

Queen Elizabeth II was an icon and a wonderful leader whom cared for her country and its people wholeheartedly. She will be missed greatly.

TWIGGY

I met the Queen a few times – at gatherings, film premieres and at garden parties at the Palace. It was always exciting. I'm a big royalist. She was an amazing woman and so loved by the country. Nothing seemed to sway her. It was a real honour for me to get my damehood. I come from an ordinary working-class family and it was incredible, what happened to me in the '60s and what's happened since. That was a fabulous day.

I was also reminded of a time when I was six, when I did this painting of the Queen at school. I think it was titled "The Queen Going for a Walk". I drew her with her crown, a long dress and a pageboy holding it up. I remember my teacher sent it into a competition and I won. I didn't get the painting back, though, and I don't have it now. I always joke that I wonder if she ever put it up in Buckingham Palace?

NAOMI CAMPBELL

In remembrance of Her Majesty, who not only gave us lifelong service, but was a beautiful daughter, wife, mother, grandmother, great-grandmother and, of course, the late patron of The Queen's Commonwealth Trust, which I know she held so close to her heart. It was such an honour being chosen as QCT's global ambassador, and in my role this past year with them nothing has been more special than to have the work of young leaders recognised and their experiences shared. By telling these stories of strength, we are able to come together more as a nation against adversity and ensure we support each other around the globe.

HELEN MIRREN

The first time I met Her Majesty was at a polo match – the only one I've been to in my life. I was taken into a tent with around 200 people inside, drinking tea and eating cucumber sandwiches. It was me and Chloë Sevigny who were being taken to meet the Queen. She was very gracious and waiting patiently for us. Of course, one never forgets. It's imprinted on your memory. She was very sweet and there was a sparkle in her eye. I was with her for about two seconds. This was long before I played her and before I was made a dame. Prince Charles, as he was then, did the honours on that occasion, actually. After meeting the Queen, I was left with the impression that it was an extraordinary and consistent performance. Her character, personality, her humanness fed into that performance, but it was still a performance. There were two different people – Her Majesty and Elizabeth Windsor. When playing her, I thought about her as the latter. In the end, I'm an Elizabethan. My first memory is from when I was at primary school, all dressed up for a pageant to celebrate the Queen's Coronation. My life has been bookended by her and I've been very fortunate for that.

HM King Charles, then Prince of Wales, photographed with his mother, the Queen, in 2016

KINGDOM COME

As KING CHARLES III *begins his reign,*
His Majesty's former press secretary COLLEEN HARRIS
offers an INSIDE GLIMPSE *of what's to come.*
Photograph by NICK KNIGHT

I

t's funny to recall now that I first met His Majesty King Charles III, then Prince of Wales, in an echoing Piccadilly outpost of the British Museum, where I worked as a press officer during the 1980s. He loves anthropology, having studied it at Cambridge, and he had come to see the Asante gold on a private visit. Many years later, in a twist of fate, His Royal Highness would hire me as his press secretary – the first Black member of the Royal Household – after a complete hash of an interview in a terribly grand room at St James's Palace, where I nervously spilt tea all over myself and Prince Charles politely ignored it. In fact, I expect he found it hilarious. Over the five years that I worked with him, he often laughed with me about just such "mistakes" made by myself and others.

Truthfully, I joined his team at a difficult moment. Diana, Princess of Wales, had died the year before, and the public felt angry with him no matter what he did. There is no defined constitutional role for the Prince of Wales, and he realised it would be decades before he became king, decades that he insisted on using productively. He already felt passionate about topics considered niche in 1998 and essential in 2022, including sustainability and diversity, and set about addressing them – whether that meant raising organic crops on his Highgrove estate or conducting youth outreach through The Prince's Trust. He also cared enormously about Princes William and Harry. You hear that members of the Royal Family are different – that their parenting style is cold and distant – but I witnessed first-hand the affection and closeness between His Royal Highness and his sons.

In many ways, it reminded me of my childhood. I came from a different background from the aristocratic young ladies who worked for me at the Palace, girls with *Horse & Hound* and *Country Life* subscriptions, who'd been part of that world far longer than I had. While my presence at St James's ruffled some feathers, I never questioned my right to be there. My parents had emigrated from Guyana, a former colony, in the '50s to work for the NHS, and both displayed pride for their Queen. The majority of Brits can remember one verse of the National Anthem – in the Caribbean, most people can sing it all. I still have the memorabilia that my mother bought in honour of Charles and Diana's wedding in 1981. My family instilled a sense of duty in me and expected me to do my part for my country – and, critically, for the UK to support me in return.

I sometimes wonder whether I should have asked myself more questions about the Royal Family's colonialist history before I made my way beneath the arches of St James's for the first time, but I was focused on doing a good job for both the prince and my parents. Before I became press secretary for His Royal Highness, I had worked in public relations for London museums, followed by more than two decades in various state departments. In every role, I had been a novelty. When I first joined government communications, I became the only Black person working in PR across the entire British government. I remember once arriving late to a meeting, and a senior civil servant asked me to fetch more milk for the tea, assuming I worked in catering. It wasn't an isolated incident.

What I did do at the Palace, though, is push for change from within – and, happily, I had the full support of the Prince of Wales. Right away, he gave me a senior title and made me a member of the Royal Household, granting me a certain status and ensuring I met and had the approval of the Queen, whom he adored. One of our first projects together was honouring the 50th anniversary of the Windrush migration, based on Trevor and Mike Phillips's book, which brought the story of the 492 people who travelled from the Caribbean to the public's attention. It set the tone for so much of our work together, with the now King forever searching for ways to elevate those who had been marginalised.

King Charles may no longer be able to speak as freely, but his principles – and his sense of devotion and generosity – will serve him well in the years ahead. His Coronation will take place in a different world from the one the Queen inherited in 1952, and the realm will only change further as time goes by. The Asante gold that he came to see at the British Museum all those years ago may well be returned to Ghana, and while the Commonwealth may help to foster international cooperation, it is also a legacy of the Empire – one that many justifiably struggle to accept. Yet, it speaks volumes that, when Barbados became a republic in 2021, it was Prince Charles who joined Prime Minister Mia Mottley in Bridgetown for the celebrations. It is a first step in a complicated road that the King will have to navigate – balancing reverence for Her Majesty's legacy with an openness to creating a better future for all people. I, for one, believe he's more than up to the task.

LEAGUES AHEAD

Whether it's designer TEAM-UPS *or* GO-FASTER
stripes, the latest SPORTSWEAR *strategies
are a* WIN-WIN. *Let the* GAMES *begin.
Photographs by* CAMPBELL ADDY.
Styling by GABRIELLA KAREFA-JOHNSON

On your marks, get set, glow! Bottega Veneta's sporty shades command attention on the track.

Opposite: headband and bra top, NIKE. *Sunglasses,* BOTTEGA VENETA. *Silver chain necklace,* TIFFANY & CO. *Whistle earring (worn on necklace),* COACH.

A match made in heaven? Gucci and Adidas's team-up scores points in sports-luxe style.

This page: velvet gown with train, jersey and canvas corset, and velvet bonnet, GUCCI. *Leather shoes,* VERSACE

Team colours: Balenciaga
and Matty Bovan's
bright stripes make for a
winning combination.

*Jersey T-shirt, red
detachable parka (worn as
skirt), and spandex boots,*
BALENCIAGA. *Yellow
jacket (tied at waist),*
ADIDAS CUSTOMISED
BY MATTY BOVAN.
Hoop earrings,
PAULA MENDOZA

With an assist from choreographer Abdourahman Njie, Maty and Nyagua kick things up a gear.

From left: Maty wears T-shirt, PUMA & DUA LIPA. Leather shorts, LOEWE. Key pendant (on necklace), BALENCIAGA. Necklace and whistle, as before. Nyagua wears jacket and orange shorts, PUMA & DUA LIPA. Embroidered leather and silk skirt, PRADA. Both wear trainers, COMME DES GARCONS & NIKE PREMIER, at Dover Street Market. Socks, stylist's own

Sports strips take a
luxurious away trip,
when imagined by Loewe,
Prada and Puma.

*From left: Maty and
Nyagua wear clothes and
accessories, as before.
Ring, Nyagua's own*

Dress for success! Louis
Vuitton's rugby shirt
and ruffled gown are
worthy of a victory lap.

*Cotton shirt, embellished
dress, and trainers,* LOUIS
VUITTON. *Gold and
lacquered wood earrings,*
TIFFANY & CO

This bold kit bag from
Roksanda and Fila's
collaboration is a knockout.

*Organic-cotton dress and
orange taffeta hood,*
ROKSANDA. *Duffel bag,*
ROKSANDA & FILA, *at
Fila.co.uk. Leather boots,*
BALMAIN. *Ear cuff,*
PAULA MENDOZA

Practice makes perfect:
drill down on dramatic
hues, courtesy of Versace
and Paco Rabanne.

Stretch-silk bra top,
VERSACE. *Latex and lace
shorts,* PACO RABANNE.
Trainers, GUCCI. *Socks,
stylist's own*

Go for gold: rely on Mac Cosmetics Pro Longwear Paint Pot
in Born to Beam, £18.50, for a winning payoff.

Asymmetric crêpe jumpsuit, JEAN PAUL GAULTIER HAUTE
COUTURE BY OLIVIER ROUSTEING

Moving the goalposts:
maximalists, seek out Ralph
Lauren and Versace's
game-changing gear.

Nylon jacket, VERSACE.
Strech-cady gown, RALPH
LAUREN COLLECTION.
Hat, KANGOL

Ballpark figures:
Burberry and Balenciaga
will ensure you won't get
lost in the bleachers.

*From left: Achenin wears
jersey jacket and jersey skirt,
BURBERRY. Patent-
leather shoes, VERSACE.
Headband, bra top, and
necklace, as before. Maty
wears windbreaker, ROKH,
at Shopbop.com. Dress with
asymmetric frill hem,
GIVENCHY. Spandex
boots, BALENCIAGA.
Hair: ISSAC POLEON.
Make-up: CHIAO-LI
HSU. Nails: SIMONE
CUMMINGS. Set
design: IBBY NJOYA.
Production: JANUARY
PRODUCTIONS.
Movement direction:
YAGAMOTO. Models:
AKON CHANGKOU,
MATY FALL,
ACHENRIN MADIT,
NYAGUA RUEA*

Squad goals: look to
your inner Lioness and
lead in Diesel's form-
flaunting cropped jacket
and micro-mini.

*Drawstring jacket and
miniskirt, DIESEL.
Trainers, GUCCI.
Socks, stylist's own.
For stockists, all pages,
see Vogue Information*

Soft focus: contrast double-layered, chunky chains with a snug, autumn-ready knit.

This page: rhodium-plated white gold and pavé-diamond necklace (top), VAN CLEEF & ARPELS. *Recycled silver necklace (bottom) and white-gold and pavé-diamond hoop earring (sold as a pair),* DAVID YURMAN. *White-gold and diamond ear cuffs,* ANA KHOURI, *at Matchesfashion.com. Wool sweater, leather top with gloves, miniskirt, and leather boots,* GIVENCHY

Mix your metals and your lengths for a neck mess we can all get on board with.

Opposite: gold earring (sold as a pair), GUCCI. *White-gold necklace and yellow-gold necklace,* DINH VAN. *Gold-plated AirPod chain,* TAPPER. *Varsity jacket,* ROKH, *at Harrods and Selfridges. Viscose rollneck,* ETRO

Opposite Effect

In JEWELLERY, *the latest* ADORNMENTS *are all
about* OFFSETTING *autumn's* SOFTEST
looks with a subtly TOUGH *edge. Study the*
CONTRASTS, *says* RACHEL GARRAHAN.
Photographs by AMIT ISRAELI. *Styling by* ENIOLA DARE

Go full monochrome with
Cartier's Juste un Clou in
white gold and Ruth
Leslie's silver rings for
every finger.

*White-gold and diamond
pendant necklace*, CARTIER.
Silver stacking rings, RUTH
LESLIE. *Vintage T-shirt*,
CONTEMPORARY
WARDROBE. *Wool sweater*,
EMPORIO ARMANI

Pomellato's full-volume
Iconica rings are a perfect
match for Louis Vuitton's
ultra-luxe layers.

Rose-gold hoop earring,
oversized coat, wool rollneck,
and miniskirt with scarf
detail, LOUIS VUITTON.
Rose-gold bands (on left
hand), POMELLATO.
Silver ring with woven
gold curb chain,
MEGAN BROWN

Boucheron and Chanel
make giving your jewellery
the personal edge a
sophisticated cinch.

*White-gold necklace,
yellow-gold necklace, and
white gold bracelet (middle),*
BOUCHERON.
*White-gold and diamond
bracelet and beige-gold
bracelet,* CHANEL FINE
JEWELLERY.
Cashmere/silk cardigan,
CHANEL. *Denim dress,*
Y PROJECT

Send your sense of touch
into overdrive with chains
in multiple textures.

Silver necklace,
GIOVANNI RASPINI.
*Braided silver chain
necklace,* EMANUELE
BICOCCHI.
Corduroy jacket and sweater,
DSQUARED2. *Jersey
rollneck,* WOLFORD

Tiffany & Co softens black
titanium with a splash of
rose gold and diamonds.

*Titanium, rose-gold and
diamond necklace and
bracelet,* TIFFANY & CO.
*Black-rhodium plated,
silver, gold and diamond
linked ring and bicolour gold
and silver linked ring,*
SPINELLI KILCOLLIN.
*Draped wool rollneck
dress,* LOEWE. *Socks,*
GLASSWORKS
LONDON.
Vintage trainers,
CONTEMPORARY
WARDROBE

Hannah Martin takes
piercings to a super-luxe
level while Messika's
carabiner chain toughens
up The Row cashmere.

*Gold and pearl earring
and gold hoop earring,*
HANNAH MARTIN.
Gold and diamond necklace,
MESSIKA. *Cashmere
jacket, wool rollneck, and
wool skirt,* THE ROW.
*For stockists, all pages,
see Vogue Information.
Hair:* KOTA SUIZU.
Make-up: LAURA
DOMINIQUE. *Nails:*
SASHA GODDARD.
Set design: PHOEBE
SHAKESPEARE.
Model: MALAIKA
HOLMEN

Treasure
ISLAND

As DOLCE & GABBANA *mark 10 years of* ALTA MODA, *the Italian house take over* SICILY *for a* BAROQUE-*inspired celebration of heavenly* COUTURE. *By* DANA THOMAS. *Photographs by* ANGELO PENNETTA. *Styling by* JULIA SARR-JAMOIS

"When you come to Italy you taste a good arancino, ice cream or glass of wine. Alta Moda is also all about this unique experience," say Domenico Dolce and Stefano Gabbana.

Silk-taffeta cape, georgette and lace petticoat dress, gloves, stockings, and shoes. Clothes, accessories and jewellery (throughout), DOLCE & GABBANA ALTA MODA

Corsetry fit for sultry Sicilian widows is a house icon. "Black is not just a colour, but a symbol of family and sensuality," say Dolce and Gabbana.

Tulle and lace corset, lace skirt, lingerie, stockings, veil, gloves, and jewellery

And for the blushing
Alta Moda bride? The
embellishment on this
jacket nods to sinuous
patterns on ancient friezes
and took 45 days to
hand-embroider.

*Embroidered faille jacket,
lace miniskirt, stockings,
shoes, veil, and gloves*

Think of the brand's founders as the baroque stars of Italian fashion. This headline dress and headpiece features gilded acanthus leaves sculptured from light Lurex.

Embroidered tulle corset dress, tights, shoes, gloves, and headpiece

S

icily has always been at the heart of Dolce & Gabbana. Domenico Dolce hails from Polizzi Generosa, a medieval town near Palermo, and the duo's opulent, maximalist approach to design and style embraces and builds upon the Mediterranean isle's rich baroque history. And so, how perfect that they chose Syracuse, a 2,700-year-old city on Sicily's Ionian coast, for their 10th anniversary Alta Moda event in July. For four days and nights – mainly nights – Dolce & Gabbana threw lavish shows and crazy-fun fetes to celebrate the beauty and charm of the region, honour Italy's artisans and ring up millions in sales (clients are said to drop an average of £85,000 each). No small affair was this: 20 hotels, 900 workers and 150 caterers all contributed to make the magic happen. And what magic it was.

On the first night, Alta Moda's more than 700 guests, including Helen Mirren and her husband, the director Taylor Hackford, Kris Jenner and the brand's top clients, drifted through the cathedral-like Grotta dei Cordari, or Ropemakers Caves, in the Neapolis Archaeological Park, ogling at vitrines displaying Dolce & Gabbana's Alta Gioielleria collection of Hellenic-inspired statement jewels and watching toga-garbed actors and musicians perform in classical tableaux. "Mmmm, delicious," Sharon Stone gushed to the mozzarella maker as she bit into his freshly made cheese at the jaunty market-like after-party, which closed with opera and a piano recital in the Teatro Greco, a fifth-century BC amphitheatre that is now a Unesco World Heritage Site.

The following afternoon, guests napped by hotel pools, toured the city's historic sites, dropped into the Dolce & Gabbana pop-up at the Grand Hotel Ortigia – where some serious shopping was done – and attended jewellery appointments, where even more serious buys were made. "We've already ordered the ear cuffs and a cross, and we're negotiating for a 100-carat diamond," one American client told me, referring to the Sicilia necklace, with a 100.1-carat pear-shaped yellow diamond.

At dusk, it was off to the women's couture show, Alta Moda, on the Piazza Duomo, where guests, including Mariah Carey and Drew Barrymore, outfitted in tiaras and shiny gowns, watched from café tables as the hour-long show – a procession inspired by Pietro Mascagni's opera *Cavalleria Rusticana* – unfurled before the looming cathedral. "It's not just the clothes, the two metres of pearls, of pleats… It's about the *sacro* [sacraments], about the *fede* [faith], about the family, about Sicily and – so important – it's about black," Domenico Dolce said. "It's a style of life."

Later that evening, everyone was ferried to a pasta-heavy beach supper, where everything – the tables, the chairs, the waiters, the cabana boy dancers and a good many clients – was dressed in Dolce & Gabbana's dazzling blue-and-white majolica print. On Sunday night was Alta Sartoria, the high-fashion menswear line, in the ancient fishing village of Marzamemi. Locals lined the streets, waving and snapping pictures as guests – many wearing new fashion and jewellery purchases – glided down the cobblestones to their seats along the quay. More than a hundred Byzantine-inspired handcrafted looks, including bejewelled tunics and breastplates, long silk skirts and lean lamé suits, passed before their eyes as the sun set across the bay. Like everything at Alta Moda, all was "Made in Italy". "Two-thirds will be sold before this is over," the guest to my left whispered as we watched. Indeed, more than three-quarters of the couture had been purchased by the end of the event. "Clients text pictures of what they want during the show."

The festive marathon closed on Monday night with a party at the 13th-century Castello Maniace, with vats of spaghetti pomodoro, lots of Dolce & Gabbana animal prints and Ciara, in a black gown and an enormous black picture hat, singing "1, 2 Step", as Dolce danced the night away. For some, the night ended at dawn. That much was clear at breakfast on Tuesday morning, when guests readied to head to Catania Airport. "What an exhausting weekend," one client, garbed in Dolce & Gabbana silk pyjamas, a Dolce & Gabbana thick gold chain with a large, gem-encrusted cross and Dolce & Gabbana sunglasses, said. "I can't wait for next year."

"It's not just the CLOTHES, the two metres of PEARLS, of PLEATS… It's about the FAMILY, about SICILY and about BLACK," said Domenico Dolce. "It's a STYLE of LIFE"

"We are looking to be surprised," say Dolce and Gabbana. This astonishing jacket blooms with a profusion of the brand's signature rose petals.

Draped Lurex chiffon jacket, stockings, and gloves

The brand are longtime devotees to heavenly bodies. Two mikado silk winged cherubs sit on each shoulder of this dress, their cascading curls shaped as if real locks of hair.

Duchesse-cotton and mikado dress, gloves, tights, and shoes

The history of Sicily
shines in Dolce &
Gabbana's designs. The
precious ornate details of
this suit are inspired by
the baroque treasures of
Syracuse Cathedral.

*Embroidered brocade
jacket and miniskirt,
lingerie, stockings,
shoes, and jewellery*

Eighty 3D flowers
festoon this breathtaking
skirt. They denote the
brand's mastery in
Italian chiaroscuro.

*Tulle and lace corset,
embroidered faille skirt,
lingerie, stockings,
gloves, and jewellery.
For stockist, all pages,
see Vogue Information.
Hair:* JORDAN
ROBERTSON. *Make-up:*
JENNA KUCHERA.
Production: SICILY
PRODUCTIONS. *Digital
artwork:* OUTPUT
LONDON. *Model:*
GRACE ELIZABETH

Mr BLUE SKY

Ahead of his latest album's RELEASE, STORMZY *recounts the heartbreaks and* EPIPHANIES *that led to its* CREATION. *Portrait by* OTIS KWAME KYE QUAICOE

T

he transition from boy to man is supposed to take years. Mine took two weeks. I went to Jamaica in the summer of 2020 a boy and came back a man. OK, don't get me wrong, I still have a hell of a lot of adulting to do and if you ever bore witness to the worst versions of me you'd find it difficult to see this man I've supposedly grown into but Jamaica changed a lot. I'm sure the setting helped. Caribbean waves lapping at your feet; lush trees hanging overhead; sun rising and setting like a classic oil painting. You wake up every day in the kind of stillness that can't be described, it can only be felt. Every day I would wake up with more clarity than the day before and more confidence in how I was going to face my future.

But it was the people I travelled with that made it happen. I was with people I could trust. People I could open up to. People I could be vulnerable around. Four clean-hearted souls. Friends very dear to my heart.

It was like therapy, every day – but no one intended for it to be like that. We were just supporting each other through our shit. Conversations in the pool would turn into moments of self-revelation. Chats at the dinner table became a time for unpacking trauma and healing. We took our fears to the ocean and gave it to the water. I never knew I'd left London with so much baggage. You don't realise how much stuff you're carrying until you decide to let it go. But I didn't just come back feeling lighter, I came back feeling different. I came back not just feeling like a man, but knowing what a man was and that was what I needed to be. I know that sounds like some hippy shit but one of the things I'd learnt in that transition is that you can't get hung up on what people think. You have to speak your truth. And the truth was that for all the success I had enjoyed and the wild ride I'd had and the love of my supporters, I realised that

if I didn't redefine what success meant to me, I would never be able to actually enjoy it.

Jamaica was my first holiday in years. I'd always hated the idea of chilling when the world's moving. Being still made me uncomfortable. From my early twenties I'd been on a relentless mission to make music, make noise and make my name. That same drive had propelled me from my ends in South London to headline the Pyramid Stage at Glastonbury in the blink of an eye so I can't claim there was no benefit.

But the pandemic forced me to stop and because everything stopped I didn't have to worry about the whole world moving while I stood still. My world tour was cancelled. So I had to rest. And I'd already made some life adjustments. I quit smoking weed because I knew that being alone in the house smoking weed would do no favours for my mental health. I quit social media because I had come to the conclusion that God didn't design us to consume that much information… but that's a story for another day. So when I landed in Jamaica, I was ready. God made sure I was ready. It was his purpose that I was serving. I know it was me who did these things but he was guiding me. In the evenings, as the sun started to dip and the others would be getting ready for dinner, I would go off by myself, walk to the water and pray – my own private ritual. I had time to think and plenty to think about. A year before I had broken up with an ex-girlfriend and my responsibility for that was still weighing heavy on me. It felt like I had blood on my hands from devastating the world that we had created for ourselves and the feeling became unbearable. Then, one evening, by the ocean, I sat and wrote out a long message. A message of accountability, not redemption. Seeking redemption at that point would have been both audacious >

"Ultimately, my FEELINGS all came down to how to BE a MAN. And more specifically how do I BECOME a man. ME. Michael. STORMZY"

and selfish but it felt like the beginning of the real healing process – a process that, even if I didn't know it then, would come to reshape me both as a man and an artist.

And then there was my father. He left when I was a child. We don't have a relationship. We don't speak. I know he used to drive cabs because random strangers would DM me, saying, "Your dad's so proud of you. I was in his car today, and he was saying so." But I used to think that I'd be very much fine to leave this earth in a position where he and I weren't talking. I was so ready to die with all the ill-feeling I had towards him. But after Jamaica I guess something shifted in me. In time I went from anger to a kind of acceptance; to wanting to say: "I

would rather forgive you." Because he, like myself, is a flawed man. He is a flawed man who made a mistake – granted, a huge one – and has had to live with that for 20-odd years. I can't imagine how that festers in the soul. How it haunts. The God I serve is one who gives us grace. And I know more than anyone what it feels like to want forgiveness and grace.

But, ultimately, my feelings about my ex, my dad, my career, my mental health and self-care really all came down to how to be a man. And more specifically how do I become a man. Me. Michael. Stormzy. The kind of man I want to be. That's what's changed.

Back when I was younger, my idea of masculinity was always rooted in violence: whoever could fight; whoever was more willing to go the extra mile to protect their name. But what we learnt about being men, about having all the girls and all the money and the violence, didn't turn out to be real manhood for me – it was somewhat the opposite. I found confidence and strength in my vulnerability. Saying "I'm sorry" and "I love you". Taking accountability. Strengthening my relationship with God. Spending time with my nephews. We had to unlearn and redefine what we were taught being a man was. I still understand that I'm deeply flawed. It's just that now I want to be better and I have a greater understanding of what "better" looks like.

This is the spirit that has guided my new album. In 2020, my record label's co-president Alec Boateng – also my mentor – suggested I get in the studio with producer-songwriter Kassa "PRGRSHN" Alexander and in our very first session he played a piano chord that kicked off what would become the first track on my new record. That chord resonated with my soul and made me go on a journey I had no idea I was even ready to go on. There was no pre-meditation. But the moment I heard that chord, it was just me and the music. In the studio, we wrote down our intentions for the album on a big whiteboard. Words like "freedom", "bravery", "feeling". I love music with all my heart and we made an album that I hope demonstrates this.

This album wasn't made for the "fans" or the "haters" or the "hip-hop heads" or the "R&B lovers". We considered no one. The audience who'll receive it were not catered to in any way, shape or form. The listener wasn't thought of once. Quite frankly, it's the most selfish thing I've ever made. Picasso never used a particular shade of blue because he thought people would like it, he used it because that blue was bubbling in his spirit and it had to hit the canvas.

Everything was in service to music, to art, to my truth and most importantly that indescribable feeling when sound would touch my soul and it just felt good. "Don't change that!" or "Let that guitar riff keep running" or "Keep that vocal exactly how it is." Sometimes unexplainable. Sometimes perfectly imperfect. But it always felt right.

This album is the musical incarnation of that journey that I've been on in every way you can imagine. It was actually part of the journey itself. Defining it as "highs and lows" or "from boy to man" would be a huge understatement and an injustice to all the intricate details that make this journey as beautifully complicated as it is. But as the title of one of my favourite tracks on the album says, somewhere down the line, "I Got My Smile Back".

Finally,
My eyes can see
There's sun behind my rain
There's colour in my pain
I may fall down
Feet don't fail me now
Cos through the storm
I found my smile

Good times: a selection of Stormzy's personal pictures. 1. On holiday in Jamaica. 2. The first time meeting his god-daughter Aniyah. 3. With his big sister DJ Rachael Anson. 4. At Aniyah's naming ceremony. 5. In New York for a fitting with Burberry ahead of the 2022 Met Gala. 6. On a date at Dinner In The Sky at The O2.

7. In Jamaica, dressed as Usain Bolt for a fancy dress night. 8. Doing the "Coke vs Pepsi" challenge in the studio. 9. At home in London with his boys, Boss and Enzo. 10. With his mum at Exeter University receiving a doctorate. 11. An album recording session. 12. Christmastime, with his nephews Allyas and Josiah. 13. In Dubai with friends

OUTWARD BOUND

The fastest ROUTE to autumnal chic?
Via versatile, go-your-own-way OUTERWEAR,
as MAX MARA's teddy bear COAT proves.
Photographs by SEAN THOMAS.
Styling by JORDEN BICKHAM

Blaze a trail in the
most snuggly of Max
Mara's classic coats.

*Camel-wool/silk coat
(throughout),* MAX
MARA. *Recycled-
cashmere dress and
leather boots,* CHLOE.
Hair: MUSTAFA YANAZ.
Make-up: ROMY
SOLEIMANI. *Production:*
DIRTY PRETTY
PRODUCTIONS. *Model:*
ABBY CHAMPION.
*With thanks to Greenport
Conservation Area, The
Secret Gardener Nursery,
West Taghkanic Diner and
Rivertown Lodge, New York*

Teddy bear's picnic: a crisp garden walk calls for a cosy cover-up, paired with Tory Burch's postbox-red skirt.

Wool minidress and wool skirt, TORY BURCH. Leather shoes, BROTHER VELLIES. Silver pendant necklace and red lacquered wood pendant necklace (joined together), TIFFANY & CO. Gold and emerald pin, PROUNIS. Oversized gold-plated pin with charms, LIZZIE FORTUNATO

Sweet treat: we've
got a taste for tactile
tailoring and The Row's
candy-stripe shirting.

*Cotton shirt, sleeveless
cashmere rollneck, and
wool/cotton trousers,*
THE ROW

Eat, chic, repeat. Pair a
comfy classic with Carolina
Herrera's fluid glittering
gown for glamour to go.

Metallic knit dress,
CAROLINA HERRERA.
Gold, steel, lacquer,
onyx and leather watch,
CHANEL WATCHES

RIVERTOWN
LODGE

TAVERN 7 DAY
SAT/SUN BR

HOTEL

Fuzzy feelings: a cuddly
coat and a heritage Gucci
check feel as good as a
Sunday sleep-in.

Cashmere sweater,
KHAITE. *Cotton shirt
and wool kilt,* GUCCI.
*Cashmere socks and leather
shoes,* LAFAYETTE 148
NEW YORK. *Leather bag,*
THE ROW. *Lapis pendant
necklace,* MATEO, *at
Net-a-porter.com.
For stockists, all pages,
see Vogue Information*

SHOOTING STAR

*For STEVEN MEISEL, 1993 was a stellar YEAR,
awash with supermodels, fashion LEGENDS and countless
VOGUE appearances. On the eve of a new EXHIBITION
celebrating his ANNUS MIRABILIS, the
photographer speaks to MICHAEL BENSON*

I

t's a balmy August evening when I meet Steven Meisel on the dockside in A Coruña, a port city in the Galicia region of northwest Spain. In November, a rare exhibition of his work, *Steven Meisel 1993 A Year in Photographs*, will open at the beautiful space that Elsa Urquijo designed for the MOP Foundation, chair of Inditex Marta Ortega Pérez's initiative to bring cutting-edge exhibitions to A Coruña. Steven has agreed to walk me through the show.

Except, of course, this is all in my imagination and we do no such thing. Steven, one of the world's most prominent photographers and, as such, impossible to pin down, is some 4,000 miles away in his studio in New York City, and I'm in France. Yet, thanks to a clever synthesis of technology, we spend an hour together, back in 1993. Bill Clinton is in the White House, Nirvana are blazing across the US, Prince has become a symbol, and Steven Meisel – fresh from his completion of *Sex*, his brilliant collaboration with Madonna – is set to embark on a blitz of creativity. Over the next 12 months, he will shoot 28 *Vogue* covers together with more than a hundred editorial stories, including the iconic "Anglo-Saxon Attitude" in the December issue of British *Vogue*.

He seems genuinely surprised by the scale of all this. "I don't sit and look back at my work unless I'm forced to. I was shocked when my agent showed me just how much I had done that year. I remember him saying, 'OK, do this job and do that job,' and I just went to work. The work just comes, instinctively, organically, you know. I've been seeing all these visions since I was a little kid."

The exhibition comprises a sequence of portraits, adds Steven: "This cast of amazing characters who I found really inspiring, really beautiful, really cool," he says. "I think I'm good with picking people, discovering people, whatever the word might be, whether or not they are a model. I see things in them that they might not see." His image of Marlon, Keith Richards's son, is a good example. In front of Steven's lens, Marlon seems to have been transported to a perfect rock star parallel universe. He isn't alone. The show features more than a hundred portraits of women and men from the worlds of fashion and film. And as we pass them by, we circle back to this idea of transformation several times; to the notion that these extraordinary images are the summation of everything that Steven has learnt. As he says, "What you really see in these portraits is me."

This moment in the early 1990s seems to have been a perfect time for him, and perhaps that goes some way to explaining his prodigious work rate. "I need to be inspired by great clothes and back then there were so many great designers. It was fashion, fashion, fashion…" We move on to a group of images made at Yves Saint Laurent's atelier on Avenue Marceau in Paris. We find Loulou de la Falaise reclining in the lounge where the great couturier's clients would await their moment. "I believe we were there for two days," he recalls. "One day we shot in the studio, where we took portraits of Catherine Deneuve. Then we went to the salon, where we shot Yves, Loulou and Paloma. It was very exciting for me to go to the original salon for the first time."

Steven's obsession with beautiful people, his encyclopaedic knowledge of all aspects of fashion, particularly his mental inventory of models and designers, reaches back to his schooldays. As we move from Saint Laurent to Twiggy – artfully arranged on a staircase – a little history creeps in. The 1993 shoot was one of the very few times they worked together professionally, though it was not, apparently, the first time he had taken her photograph. "I was a Twiggy fan. I was 12 or 13 years old and on a quest to meet her. So, I cut school and went to Melvin Sokolsky's studio because I knew that's where she'd be. I knocked on the door and the stylist – Ali MacGraw! – said no, but the cinematographer let us in. So, I got the photograph and an autograph! She was 17 or maybe 18, and it was her first trip to New York, I believe. I think she was caught up in the whole whirlwind of being Twiggy. She was so shocked when I told her this story all those years later."

This habit of cutting school to track down models seems to have been an important part of his education. "I used to do that a lot. I went to school on 57th Street. I don't know why, but I would always have an Instamatic with me. New York seemed small and back then you just saw models all over the place. They were hard to miss. So yes, it started when I was really young. I think maybe it began even before I started to take the pictures. I just liked fashion."

The exhibition opens with a small group of street photographs of passing women taken when Steven was in the sixth grade. Seen here for the first time, they are like mini-Garry Winogrands, and seem to hint at things to come. Steven is not so sure. "I think >

KRISTEN McMENAMY

"He makes a girl feel like a million dollars," Kristen McMenamy –
here, the star of a March 1993 *Vanity Fair* profile that labelled her
the "model of the moment" – told British *Vogue* in January this year.
"You know, I fell in love with him back in the day."

HAMISH BOWLES

Future *The World of Interiors* editor-in-chief Hamish Bowles
photographed in his New York apartment. As Steven recalls, "I
just said, 'Stand here by the window, just pose like this.'"

"*These* EXTRAORDINARY IMAGES *are the summation of* EVERYTHING *that Steven has* LEARNT. *As he says,* "*What you* REALLY SEE *in these portraits* IS ME"

that obviously looking at those pictures from a 12-year-old's perspective, I might have been dreaming of possible futures but no, I never thought that I would have a job as a photographer. Well, when you are that young you aren't thinking about jobs at all."

Maybe not, but these early obsessions with modelling, style and beauty enabled his ascent to the pinnacle of the profession. His understanding of all aspects of fashion is unparalleled and his influence has nurtured numerous careers, particularly those of the models featured in this exhibition. Perhaps no one more so than Linda Evangelista, who appears in it more often than anyone.

"Linda was over here yesterday, and I was trying to understand what it was about her. I don't know. What is it about Linda, or what was it from the minute I met her? The first thing we did together was US *Vogue*. Linda gives blood, literally. She'll stand on her head; she'll do this or do that. Besides the fact that she's a beauty. I mean, there are a lot of beautiful women that don't photograph and aren't photogenic and aren't willing to create with you and do the process. Linda was always willing to do everything, and happily so."

There's an intriguing image of Linda as Katharine Hepburn, which, it turns out, is almost accidental. "Starting with *Blow Up*, I have all these images from the movies in my head. It's who I am, it's part of me. But I wasn't going for Katharine Hepburn. Maybe by the time we took the first Polaroids I said, 'It kind of looks like Hepburn,' but it wasn't that we went in that day thinking, 'Oh, we're doing a Katharine Hepburn story.'" It reminded me of a particular style, and we went with that… but it wasn't premeditated."

Location has always been important for Steven and at that time nowhere more so than the corridors of the Ritz Paris. "I was obsessed with those wide hallways. Christy would be in one room. Linda would be in another. And then Madonna would be upstairs in the attic room. It was like a fun house." Fun is an important part of his creative process – a feeling of play that allows him to create an environment with models. "It's part of everything. We have to laugh. I mean I can focus on a dime when I need to, but I also need laughter and fun with everyone, and that includes the client and the models and the whole team."

This great, quintessentially Parisian hotel provided the perfect backdrop for Steven's work with numerous models including Kristen McMenamy, who we find slumped on a sofa wearing just a hat or striking a sequence of exaggerated doll-like poses. "Kristen

is another special one – there aren't that many. She interpreted me straightaway. Half the time I didn't even have to say anything to either her or Linda. By this time, I don't know if she needed my guidance anymore because I had been working with her for a while. It was like she instinctively knew what to do. She loved to create. Now that I'm looking at the poses. It's my body language but exaggerated because of her. Of course, I want to give Kristen the credit she deserves… but it's also me."

Steven, who is widely admired for his meticulous attention to detail, draws my attention to a small dog in his portrait of Isabella Blow. "That was in Paris. At a small café in an alleyway by the studios where I was working. That was Azzedine [Alaïa]'s dog so of course we used him in the pictures."

Nineteen-ninety-three also saw Meisel's first professional assignment in London, where he collaborated with Blow on "Anglo-Saxon Attitude". It was Blow, too, who first introduced him to Stella Tennant. "She had no interest. She had never modelled before. It just wasn't something that she wanted to do. Issie just gave me all these different pictures of society girls that she knew. And of course, I fell in love with Stella, everything about Stella. What an incredible model. She gave everything and I adored her. She would sit there reading books in Chinese. We took her to Paris to work on Versace with Linda and Kristen. And Stella was like, 'What the hell am I doing?' It was Linda who said to her, 'No, you're great.' And she really was."

Steven's remarkable year of 1993 included a 60-page feature on men's fashion for *Per Lui*, and the A Coruña exhibition is punctuated with images that are unlike any other images of men made at the time. He coaches his male subjects in the same way he works with women. The result is a group of images that are by turn innovative, warm, provocative and very often just great fun. Such as Hamish Bowles riffing on Cecil Beaton's 1920s images of the Bright Young Things. "I knew Hamish really well and this was organic. It was in his apartment and I just said, 'Stand here by the window, just pose like this.'"

And with that, Steven disappears into the night, leaving a trail of stories and a collection of images that, as Marta Ortega Pérez says, "remind us that he is an exquisite artist – a true master of style". *Steven Meisel 1993 A Year in Photographs is at A Coruña, Galicia, Spain, from 19 November to 1 May 2023*

ISABELLA BLOW

In July, fashion editor Isabella Blow posed in *Vogue* Italia beneath the
title Eccentric Today, wearing a velvet and muslin dress by Dolce &
Gabbana with a hat by Philip Treacy, the milliner she discovered. Her
co-star was borrowed from the dog's owner, designer Azzedine Alaïa.

TWIGGY

Wearing a leopard-print coat found at Manhattan vintage store
O Mistress Mine, 1960s icon Twiggy was pictured on a New
York stairwell, some 26 years after Steven first shot the model
on her debut trip to the city.

CAMILLA NICKERSON

The American *Vogue* fashion editor Camilla Nickerson took a turn
in front of the lens for an appearance in the magazine's Italian
edition. Styled by Joe McKenna for a shoot dedicated entirely to
white clothes, here she wears a knitted bikini by Prada.

LUCY FERRY

With Paris as his backdrop, Steven captured model Lucy Ferry – at the
time married to Roxy Music's lead singer, Bryan – in head-to-toe
Christian Lacroix, with the pictures later appearing in *Vogue* Italia.

STELLA TENNANT & PLUM SYKES

From left, model Stella Tennant and fashion assistant (later author)
Plum Sykes, appear in British *Vogue*'s story Anglo-Saxon Attitude. The
former wears an Alexander McQueen dress with Vivienne Westwood
heels and the latter a baby-blue mohair minidress by Jennifer Jones.

VOGUE INFORMATION

2 Moncler 1952 Woman
Moncler.com
16arlington.co.uk
A
Adidas Customised by Matty
Bovan Mattybovan.com
Aeyde.com
Akris.com
Alaïa 020 3057 7905
Alexandermcqueen.com
Alexeagle.com
Alighieri.com
Ambushdesign.com
B
Balenciaga.com
Balmain.com
Bottegaveneta.com
Boucheron.com
Breitling.com
Brothervellies.com
Brunellocucinelli.com
Bulgari.com
Burberry.com
C
Carolinaherrera.com
Cartier.com
Chanel 020 7493 5040
Chanel Fine Jewellery
020 7499 0005
Chanel Watches
020 7499 0005
Chloe.com
Chopard.com
Christianlouboutin.com
Coach.com
Completedworks.com
D
Davidyurman.com
Diesel.com
Dinhvan.com
Dior.com
Dolce & Gabbana Alta Moda
020 7495 9250
Dover Street Market
020 7518 0680
Driesvannoten.com
Dsquared2.com
E
Emanuelebicocchi.it
Emporio Armani
020 7491 8080
Etudes-studio.com
Etro.com

F
Fabianafilippi.com
Fendi.com
Framacph.com
G
Gianvitorossi.com
Giovanniraspini.com
Givenchy.com
Glassworkslondon.com
Gucci.com
H
Hannahmartinlondon.com
Harrods.com
Hermes.com
Herno.com
Hunterboots.com
I
Isabelmarant.com
Isseymiyake.com
J
Jean Paul Gaultier Haute Couture by Olivier Rousteing
Jeanpaulgaultier.com
Joseph-fashion.com
K
Kangol.com
Khaite.com
L
Thelacquercompany.com
Lafayette148ny.com
Libertylondon.com
Lizziefortunato.com
Loewe.com
Louisvuitton.com
M
Marc-cain.com
Marinarinaldi.com
Matildejewellery.com
Maxineshoes.com
Maxmara.com
Meganbrownjewellery.com
Messika.com
Michael Michael Kors
Michaelkors.co.uk
Miista.com
Millygrace.co.uk
Mintydiamonds.com
Miumiu.com
MM6 Maison Margiela
020 7493 2533
Mollygoddard.com
N
Neous.co.uk

Nike.com
Npeal.com
O
Omegawatches.com
P
Pacorabanne.com
Paulamendoza.com
Paulsmith.com
Pomellato.com
Prada.com
Proenzaschouler.com
Prounisjewelry.com
Puma & Dua Lipa Puma.com
R
Ralphlauren.co.uk
Roksanda.com
Rolandmouret.com
Therow.com
Ruthleslie.co.uk
S
Saint Laurent by Anthony Vaccarello Ysl.com
Salvatore Ferragamo
Ferragamo.com
Selfridges.com
Spinellikilcollin.com
Stellamccartney.com
T
Tapper Gettapper.com
Tibi.com
Tiffany.co.uk
Tillysveaas.co.uk
Tissotwatches.com
Tomford.co.uk
Toryburch.com
Toteme-studio.com
Tudorwatch.com
V
Vacheron-constantin.com
Valentino Garavani
Valentino.com
Vancleefarpels.com
Versace.com
Victoriabeckham.com
W
Wolfordshop.co.uk
Y
Yproject.fr
Z
Zankovstudio.com
Zenith & Watches of Switzerland
Watches-of-switzerland.co.uk

Vogue is distributed by Frontline, Midgate House, Peterborough, Cambridgeshire PE1 1TN (01733 555161). Subscription rates include delivery and digital editions. Full rates are £47.88 for one year in the UK, £119 for the rest of the world. To place your order, call +44 (0)1858 438 819. Special offers and exclusive promotions are published in this issue or online at Vogue.co.uk. To manage your subscription, log on to Magazineboutique.co.uk/solo. For enquiries, email vogue@subscription.co.uk. US distribution: Vogue, ISSN 0262-2130 (USPS 463390) is published monthly by Condé Nast, Vogue House, Hanover Square, London W1S 1JU, UK. US distribution: the US annual subscription price is $137. Airfreight and mailing in the USA by agent named World Container Inc, 156-15, 146th Avenue, 2nd Floor, Jamaica, NY 11434, USA. Periodicals postage paid at Brooklyn, NY 11256. US Postmaster: send address changes to Vogue, World Container Inc, 156-15, 146th Avenue, 2nd Floor, Jamaica, NY 11434, USA. Subscription records are maintained at Condé Nast Britain, Subscriptions Department, Tower House, Sovereign Park, Market Harborough, LE16 9EF, UK. Printed by Walstead Roche. Repro by Rhapsody. All rights reserved. Reproduction in whole or in part without written permission is strictly prohibited. All prices are correct at time of going to press but are subject to change. Manuscripts, drawings and other materials submitted must beaccompanied by a stamped addressed envelope. However, Vogue cannot be responsible for unsolicited material. The paper used for this publication is based on renewable wood fibre. The wood these fibres are derived from is sourced from sustainably managed forests and controlled sources. The producing mills are EMAS registered and operate according to the highest environmental and health and safety standards. This magazine is fully recyclable – please log on to Recyclenow.com for your local recycling options for paper and board. Copyright © 2022 THE CONDE NAST PUBLICATIONS LTD, Vogue House, Hanover Square, London W1S 1JU. VOGUE.CO.UK

CONDÉ NAST

recycle

GENDER EQUALITY IS NOT JUST A GOAL
IT IS CRITICAL TO THE SURVIVAL OF THE PLANET

GENERATION EQUALITY

CHIME FOR CHANGE

FIGHTING TO ENSURE GENDER EQUALITY IS AT THE FOREFRONT OF OUR GLOBAL RECOVERY
BECAUSE NONE OF US CAN MOVE FORWARD IF HALF OF US ARE HELD BACK

EQUILIBRIUM.GUCCI.COM/GENERATIONEQUALITY
#ACTFOREQUAL

Designer Profile

LOOMINATE

Loominate's holistic approach to sustainability focuses not only on using eco-friendly materials, but also in functional designs to create long-lasting pieces. This quilted jacket has a 100% rayon from bamboo lining and is reversible, offering more ways of integrating into the transitional season's closet. Check out the full quilted jacket collection on loominate-designs.com
Instagram @loominate.designs

COME ON

Come On present their new collection Fraternite' in Paris Fashion Week, featuring 27 genderless pieces. Their full colour pieces are formulations of classic tailoring, print shirts and knit vests, using sustainable fabrics and responsible production. Come On presented two previous collections at NY Fashion Week. Photography by Pat Battellini. View their new collection at www.comeonworld.com and Instagram @comeonworld.ig

LUNA AMADA

Luna Amada is a handmade brand by a young designer based in Turkey, combining the contemporary and the traditional to tell the story of timelessness. The brand symbolises the strength and patience of women while unifying heritage and contemporary fashion. Each product tells a woman's dream. Discover the collection www.lunaamadashop.com
Instagram @lunaamadashop

KAJAL NEW YORK

Consciously sourced. Woman owned. Climate neutral. Kajal New York is a NYC based label that has caught our eye. Founded on the idea of being stylish while doing good for the planet. Bold, glamourous, and eco-conscious designs for the modern woman. The purpose is to offer luxury ready-to-wear garments that are ethically made with high quality fabrication. The line supports female empowerment in India. Discover the collection at www.kajalnewyork.com Instagram: @kajalnewyork

VANTAGE ATELIER

Vantage Atelier is inspired by British country style, specialising in luxury tweed pieces that are designed and handmade in Great Britain. Priding themselves on creating items that are timeless yet contemporary, Vantage Atelier put a feminine edge on a tailored fit. All items are designed with quality, luxury and also comfort in mind, to treasure for a lifetime. Visit www.vantageatelier.com and Instagram @vantageatelier

NUAJE NUAJE

Nuaje Nuaje is the creator of versatile and sophisticated resort wear that puts you in a golden state of mind. Each piece is made with 100% luxurious natural fabrics and exquisite craftsmanship achieved by skilled artisans and BSCI-credited manufacturers, to be a wardrobe staple for years to come. Visit nuajenuaje.com Instagram: @nuajenuaje

KEEYA ISTANBUL

Keeya Istanbul is a brand created by designer Özem Kesk in her beloved city. Keeya underlines the theme of sustainabil. All fabrics used are natural alloys. All the needle lace details in their pieces are handcrafted by the artisan women of Anatolia, meaning each one is unique and none ever the same. Visit www.keeyaistanbul.c and Instagram @keeyaistanbul

OLARSGRACE

Olarsgrace is an all-inclusive women's wear bran known for its impeccable attention to detail in i designs (most notably their trousers). Olarsgrace definitely one to look out for in present-day fashi for modern and workwear looks. Their stylish ar high-quality yet affordable pieces aim to inspir confidence in every wearer, building a communi of strong women. The brand redefines contemporary fashion with its creative designs th stand the test of time. Visit olarsgrace.com and @olarsgrace on Instagram.

FOXGLOVE

Foxglove wish to contribute to the freedom and singular of unique people wit their dresses, bringi the lightness of bein able to take a single dress from day to nig The designer create dresses where movir fabrics meet exciting cut-out details. Believing day dresse should have the excitement of an evening dress, their dresses are designed as transitional pieces which can move from day to night with just an accessory change. Visit www.foxglovefashion.com and Instagram @studio.foxglove

NÈGLIGÈ

ew York based brand, Nègligè, creates unique and original designs at a more accessible price. Their goal is to create haute couture designs that you're not afraid to wear again and again. Nègligè embraces the idea that even red carpet ready clothes are made for the body and not the closet. Visit negligenyc.com Follow them on Instagram @negligenyc

BORN VILLAIN

Born Villain was founded in 2020 in Istanbul by Begum Ballar. Born Villain women are bold, powerful, unique, free spirits who are not afraid to take risks in their personal styles. Each season presents a collection of edgy and unique pieces and are available on www.bornvillain.shop Instagram @bornvillain.shop

DELLA TERRA

An ethically made Colombian brand, Della Terra creates timeless, high quality and sustainable pieces. With a hyper focus on material science and the minimisation of their environmental impact, they use a wide range of low impact natural, organic, and bio-based materials. They value transparency, so they trace their entire supply chain from farm to garment and make this information available to its customers via their hangtags with a QR code to display the full environmental and social impact of each style. Visit dellaterra.co and Instagram @dellaterra.co

MOHOLESS

MOHOLESS is a Parisian brand that offers a range of ultra-design accessories made from upcycled waste. These unique pieces are inspired by women's wardrobes, like the Top Bag: their best-seller with a minimal casual aesthetic. Join a bold project that also offers exclusive handcrafted travel-inspired capsules. Check out the full story on moholess.com and support the brand on Instagram @moholess

HEKSA

Founded upon the devotion of creating a better future, Heksa aspires to grow a platform allowing for diversity and freedom. Through the sustainable and creative nature of the designs, the brand offers you the freedom to create your own wardrobe thus allowing you to express your own individual style but most importantly giving you the freedom of choice. For more visit www.heksashop.com and follow @heksaofficial_ on Instagram.

TYPE B COLLECTION

Montreal-designed and Italian-made, Type B Collection was founded on the principle of quality while offering exceptionally creative designs. Designed to tell a story, each scarf is fabricated using hand-made materials and meticulous attention to detail. Art serves as the primary inspiration for Type B. The and embodies a strong sense of accessory pression - they believe that the way a scarf is apped around you, and the way the wind causes it sway from your body, reveals a different story th every outfit. Visit www.typebcollection.com d @typebcollection on Instagram.

THE C EDITION

The C Edition. A handmade bodysuits brand based in Athens, Greece is here to empower women from within and inspire confidence through their immaculate design and fit. Believing strongly that all women are a Circle and we should support and uplift each other, The C Edition uses its influence to transfer a strong message through its 300 different bodysuits styles all around the world. Visit www.thecedition.com and Instagram @thecedition_official

SIR BLUME

With a focus on sustainable and timeless garments for everyday wear, Sydney based brand, Sir Blume, has caught our eye. Effortless, modern, understated, and unisex designs for all things leisure. Inspired by the simple pleasures of life, Sir Blume stems from three sister's love for art and fashion, and is devoted to the production of limited quantities. A thoughtful curation of relaxed basics. Follow @sirblume_ on Instagram and visit www.sirblume.com for more information.

TERESA ESENCIA ENTRE HILOS

TERESA ESENCIA ENTRE HILOS is a story of a mother and daughter separated by cancer. Teresa, Johana's mother, was a woman who represented the purest form of maternal love: always present, understanding, and unconditional. Teresa is a Colombian luxury ready-to-wear natural fibre brand, presenting innovative and lusive designs printed in linen and cotton. But st importantly, through Teresa, Johana pays ute to the memory of her mother. t www.Teresa.com.co and follow eresaesenciaentrehilos and @johanarojasr Instagram.

FASHION HAUS

Fashion Haus is a clothing brand designed for those unique wardrobe staples that you will wear time and time again. The brand specialises in unique resort and ready to wear pieces that are bound to make a statement and get you noticed. Showcased here is the Felicity Corset. They offer shipping worldwide.

Visit www.fashionhausclothingltd.com and Instagram @fashion.haus_

LOU SWIM

LOU Swim is an Australian sustainable swimwear brand for smaller chests, with a focus on padded swimsuits designed specifically for the smaller chested woman in mind. Removing the awkward gaps that smaller chested women face, LOU Swim is helping women regain their confidence and emphasising that a small chest does not make a woman any less feminine. Visit louswim.com and @lou.swim on Instagram.

Designer Profile

ANNA ANTAL

Anna Antal was born in Hungary in 1922. After immigrating to Australia after WWII, she opened her first boutique in Melbourne in 1960. Her instincts about fashion were infallible. Her pieces were bold and uplifting and there was something reflexive about how they made women feel. Anna treated clothing like armour. She intimately understood the power of dressing up, using it as a non-verbal tool to communicate who she was and what she represented. Visit www.annaantal.com and Instagram @annaantalofficial

STANIEL

Staniel is a non-seasonal swimwear brand for the woman who enjoys both life and style – an approach that savours beautifully considered designs made to last. Known for their immaculate fit and soft-to-touch feel, Staniel couples timeless silhouettes with streamlined construction in celebration of the female form. Staniel's enduring quality and youthful sensibility redefines swimwear as an essential part of your wardrobe. Visit www.staniel.com and follow @stanielswim on Instagram.

MAEM DISKO

21-year-old founder, Margot Castor created Maem Disko with a commitment to ethical production and sustainability. Vibrant colours, playful accents and details of each piece are executed with eminent care. All her garments are handmade in Australia in small quantities using deadstock, recycled and natural fibres to help create less overall output and minimise textile waste! Visit www.maemdisko.com and Instagram @maem.disko to shop the full collection.

ANDRIDZ PARIS

ANDRIDZ PARIS offers fine leather goods meticulously made in their Parisian workshop while promoting eco-design. They select leathers of French origin from the dormant stocks of prestigious houses in order to offer you exceptional products. Sensitive, sensual and timeless, their creations express in colour the great refinement of artisanal leather goods and French excellence. Visit www.andridz.com and Instagram @andridz_paris

ALLOUR STUDIO

Allour is a prêt-à-porter luxury brand based in Italy, focused on women's evening wear. Each collection is designed by selecting fabrics and shapes that belong to history, introducing them into a contemporary setting. From start to end, every step of the supply chain is based in Italy to guarantee quality and a luxurious Italian finish. Experiencing the Allour means being surrounded by an enchanted aura, a mixture of elegance, opulence and playfulness. Visit allour-studio.com/en/ and follow @allourstudio on Instagram.

MOCHIL

MOCHIL combines the traditions, colours and patterns of Latin American culture into a modern fashion product, which values original craftsmanship, high-quality and responsible materials. Their first Shopper bag was made entirely from vegan cactus leather, and embroidered with the typical MOCHIL pattern of pearls. MOCHIL brings a touch of Latin spirit to your bohemian and effortless chic wardrobe. Visit mochil.com and Instagram @mochil_official

ANNA OTTON

Anna Otton is a brand that creates subtle fashion with soft, feminine lines, inspired by elements of the world of art, architecture and tasteful design. Their products are made in Warsaw, using sustainable materials. Original textile patterns, transferred to fabrics by digital printing, are hand-painted by the designer herself, who founded the brand in 2022 after graduating from London College of Fashion and perfecting her skills in the British fashion industry. Visit annaotton.com and Instagram @annaotton

OTKUTYR

Established in 2011 and based in Jeddah, OTKUTYR is a pioneering Saudi fashion house, renowned for its local and ethical production. OTKUTYR has its own in-house line, under the same name, with collections ranging from haute bridal couture to ready-to-wear. The fashion house is dedicated to showcasing local designers' internationally by offering services such as creative direction and local production, amongst others. Visit www.otkutyr.com and @otkutyrfashionhouse on Instagram.

KIMONOGIRL

Have you heard of Energy Fashion? Here it is... KimonoGirl is an Energy Fashion brand that creates magical clothing to empower women. All their handmade kimonos are charged with high frequencies. They aim to boost and elevate your mood whilst you wear their garments. Follow @realkimonogirl on Instagram and visit www.realkimonogirl.com

BELLE BUSINESS

Belle Business Wear was founded by Delali Agbele to reimagine the world of professional wear by showcasing that professional does not have to be boring. Designing luxury professional attire for the everyday working woman, their brand allows business, professional, corporate, and all around boss women to "handle business, while serving looks". Visit bellebusinesswear.co and Instagram @bellebusinesswear

FERAYE

For free spirited women who love the art of living, dance in bare feet, embrace the moment and laugh out loud, Feraye continues to celebrate life with their new Nomad Collection. All handmade and unique. Visit www.ferayes.com and Instagram @ferayebutik

KNITWRTH

Chicago-based brand, Knitwrth, turns iconic pop culture moments into luxurious wearable art. Founder and designer Kris Cantu's designs have proven to be one of the most 'Instagrammable' garments around the globe. Skilfully spun from its signature woven textile creating a one-of-a-kind jacquard piece that showcases individuality and style.

Follow @knitwrth on Instagram and visit www.Knitwrth.com Ships worldwide.

FANAA

'Fanaa' is the concept in which the individual discovers himself, his creation and his unity by breaking his ego. Founded by two friends, Fanaa originated from the same philosophy, guiding customers to find their true selves and style. Creating timeless fashion through minimalism, Fanaa keeps up with daily trends through bold and simple details. Conscious of nature, they also maintain sustainable production. Visit www.fanaa.uk and Instagram @fanaa.uk

ZAID

Zaid is an Australian label offering unisex leisurewear essentials. Founded on the philosophy of limited quantity with high quality, founder and designer Meg Marandola spent years scouting the globe for the highest quality fabrics. 'Edition One' is a unisex collection of versatile, functional and comfortable essentials, designed to transcend seasons and trends. Follow @zaidcollective on Instagram and visit www.zaidcollective.com to shop. Photography by @paristilleyphotography Brand Design & Creative Direction by @elizahillcreative

ZASTA

Zasta emerged in San Francisco through the intertwining influence of cultures, eras, and styles. Zasta has recently announced the launch of their Collection 2, which incorporates vibrant textile designs, handcrafted by master artisans. In other exciting news, Zasta has launched their first Studio located at 1764 Haight St. San Francisco, California, and showcasing all of their collections. Visit zastastudio.com and follow @zastastudio on Instagram.

RHODOCHROSITE

Rhodochrosite is a luxury fashion brand based in Turkey and founded by Cemre Inan. The energy of the Rhodochrosite stone is matched with the identity of the strong woman silhouette that the brand has created in every aspect. They wanted to unite the metal accessories, knitted fabrics and denim fabrics, with different forms and accessories, going beyond the standard perception. Each season's collection features limited edition and authentic pieces that will take you from sunrise to sunset. Shop at rhodochrositestudio.com and @rhodochrositestudio on Instagram.

MOTHER THE STUDIO

Mother The Studio uses top-quality materials that are ethically and sustainably sourced. They create 100% plastic-free clothing to order, in the USA. Their styles are flattering and contemporary. MTS believe in taking responsibility for their effect on the planet to honour future generations. Mother The Studio are slowly changing the fashion game in the name of love and care. Visit motherthestudio.com and follow @motherthestudio on Instagram.

TO APPEAR ON THESE PAGES, CONTACT 020 7152 3705 OR EMAIL CLASSVOGUE@CONDENAST.CO.UK

Designer Profile

YVETTE LIBBY N'GUYEN PARIS

ZAVIA WALKER

Zavia Walker's fashion and lifestyle brand fuses classic style with exclusive hand painted prints for those who want to look and feel good. By embodying their "self-accepting and fearless" message, with their effortless chic aesthetic, they invite you to embrace your individuality, while exuding confidence in your personal style.

Visit zaviawalker.com and @shopzaviawalker on Instagram.

Yvette LIBBY N'guyen Paris chooses time as their own fashion language. While offering a wide spectrum of collections and looks, the brand always stays true to their DNA: the beauty of timeless sophistication or retro-cool design. Fall in love with them for their gender-fluid fashion identity and ecological characteristic. Seizing the rhythm of the falling rain and young hearts falling in love, the brand presents a one-of-a-kind line of couture raincoats: waterproof, easy-care, and trendy see-through. Visit yvettelibby.com and @yvette.libby.nguyen.paris on Instagram.

KENZIE KAY

Kenzie Kay collections are designed for those who wish to be elegantly dressed whilst still showing a hint of coquettish femininity. The wearer values the luscious feeling of fine silk and Italian wools, quality nearly obsolete in today's market. Made to effortlessly turn heads. Visit kenziekay.com and @kenziekayfashion on Instagram.

BETTYVONCHIC

BettyVonChic is a vintage-inspired clothing brand. Owner and Designer, Mary Martin, founded the brand in 2018 and launched her original designs in 2021. BettyVonChic Originals are made in the USA with a focus on sustainability, moving away from fast fashion toward quality, limited edition, sustainable goods.

They are committed to providing their customers a unique and seamless shopping experience. Visit www.bettyvonchic.com and Instagram @bettyvonchic

Jewellery Designer Profile

FEJN

Clear and pure design – made for city nomads and urban heroines, fejn stands for puristic fine jewellery with a timeless and modern style. With their sustainable approach, they love reduced designs and clean looks. Founder Dagmar Kraemer brought her own label to life, realising her dream: a label for urbanists. Since then she has followed two clear policies: pieces of jewellery, inspired by purist fashion and sustainable action. Visit www.fejn.com and follow @fejnjewelry on Instagram.

STINA SIQIONG WEN JEWELLERY

Stina Siqiong Wen is a contemporary jewellery designer passionate about exploring alternative materials and observing everything in her daily life that infuses her creative process. She is known for the invention of unique soft concrete jewellery that challenges concrete property and ultimately provokes dynamic interactions between wearer and viewer, visually and actually. Visit www.stinajewelry.com and follow @stina_jewelry on Instagram.

DEAR KATIOPAE

Through modern and delicate jewellery, Dear Katiopae wants to tell the story of various African cultures Ashanti, Akan, Bamileke, Mas and others by reinterpreting ancestral forms and symbols enlightening the traditional skills and crafts. By wearing a Dear Katiopae jewel, you are helping to preserve century-old heritages and traditions. Shop the collection at www.dearkatiopae.com and follow @dear_katiopa on Instagram. Model: Angela Kwamba. Photographer: Andre Modeste.

HANNO

Hanno, exquisite, handmade jewellery designed by renowned Sako Hanno from Stockholm. By using an extraordinary combination of old-fashioned utensils with modern devices they create jewellery that is completely unique and made to order. Visit hannostockholm.com and follow on Instagram @hannostockholm

FLUX STUDIO

Flux Studio designs timeless jewellery fit for any occasion. Each pair of Pink Spinel Gradient Earrings is handcrafted, and each stone is intuitively hand-selected to fit within the gradient. No two gemstones are the same, so you'll be sure to have your own unique piece. Explore more at shopfluxstudio.com and Instagram @shopfluxstudio

PIA HALLSTROM

Swedish-born jeweller Pia Hallstrom creates precious jewellery with an element of the unexpected, designed to lift spirits and love forev. She focuses on design and wearability – at all time of the day and for women of all ages. These are beautiful jewels, handcrafted in London and designed to be worn season after season, generatio after generation. Visit www.piahallstrom.com and follow @piahallstromjeweller on Instagram.

COEUR DE LION

GENUINE FRESHWATER PEARLS make this yellow-gold jewellery special – consisting of a sophisticated necklace and delicate hoop earrings – a graceful, elegant choice. The combination of different-sized chains and pearls is not the only feature that stands out. The necklace also offers an innovative multiwear option, allowing it to be layered or worn in different lengths to suit the outfit.

Discover more on www.coeur-de-lion.org or follow @coeur_de_lion_jewellery on Instagram.

CRISTINA LUCIA

Based in Sweden, Cristina Lucia is a Polymer Clay Jeweller. Her style is contemporary and refined, without losing a sense of fun. Every handmade piece gets the same focus and attention to detail. The collections come in a variety of colours, textures and designs. Made using Hypoallergenic inless Steel, safe for sensitive ears. Visit stinalucia.se and follow them on stagram @cristinaluciasweden

EKENBERG

The latest design by Ekenberg Scandinavia ‹In your hand› has received a lot of attention with its symbolism. This beautiful pendant representing a hand holding a diamond, is available in various sizes and crafted from 18k gold with a high-quality diamond. Discover Ekenberg Scandinavia at Ekenberg.no and follow them on Instagram @ekenbergscandinavia

ANNA INSPIRING JEWELLERY

Dedicated to positivity and a lust for life. ANNA Inspiring Jewellery creates timeless fine jewellery and unique haute jewellery pieces. Each piece is conceived and created with immense care and passion. Add a personal engraving and make their pieces your pieces. Visit their ANNA London store on 16 Marylebone High Street. Shop online at www.annaij.com and follow them on Instagram @anna_i_j

HARPER KENDALL

Harper Kendall produce and craft beautiful fine jewellery from classic to contemporary designs using the finest gold and precious metals with diamonds and gemstones to t your specific style along with their unique line generator with a one-of-a-kind bespoke wellery Subscription Service assigning you a rsonal jewellery stylist Visit: harperkendall.com d follow-on Instagram and Facebook harperandkendall

FULLORD

FULLORD offers a beautiful range of jewellery by creative director Sandrine Thibaud. Seen here is the Ghost Ring in 18 carat rose and white gold with full pavé diamonds. The ghost ring features a minimal yet complex design that combines a rounded square outside with a circular inside giving life to unique volumes and proportions. Its iconic shape makes the ghost ring unusual and classic at the same time. Made in Italy.

Visit fullord.com and follow on Instagram @fullordgeneva

KBH JEWELS

KBH Jewels is a female founded, planet-first sustainable fine jewellery brand based in New York handcrafted with 100% recycled solid gold, cultivated luxury diamonds and sustainably cultured AA graded South Sea pearls. With a core commitment to clean material sourcing, circular practices and meticulous quality and craftsmanship, KBH's statement-making designs can be found at KBHJewels.com and follow @kbhjewels on Instagram.

VALERIE CHIC

Valerie Chic jewellery created by Victoria Kopp is more than jewellery; embracing effortlessly chic style, innovative design and sustainability. For the modern woman who wants to not only look chic, but also unique and confident. Designs are a blend of subtle, fun and statement, inspired by locations from tropical beaches, to ngapore, to London and are designed and ndmade in Munich, Germany. Versatile, these rings can be worn as hoops or dangles and from y to night. Visit valerie-chic.com and follow valeriechicjewelry on Instagram to find out more.

Jewellery Designer Profile

ALLISON AVERY

ALLISON AVERY is your new demi-fine jewellery brand designed to make every woman feel unique. Allison's fun and edgy pieces will make you feel like a goddess whether on holiday or in a board meeting. There's no such thing as too much bling.

Visit allisonaveryco.com
Instagram: @allisonaverycollection

NOE & MANE

Noe & Mane is an inclusive jewellery brand, created with the belief that everyone deserves to sparkle! The effortlessly elegant pieces can be layered or worn by themselves as an expression and celebration of indivduality. Pictured is the 'Extra Sparkle Pleat Necklace £52'.

Visit noeandmane.com and follow @noe_and_mane on Instagram for more inspiration.

ISABEL ALEXANDER

Isabel Alexander, creates distinctive, dramatic jewellery designed to be worn and loved everyday and everywhere. Handcrafted using high quality diamonds and the most luxurious gold and silver, their unique range is one to fall in love with and enjoy. UK and EU customers can now shop the collection on 1stdibs.com View their collection at isabelalexander.us and follow on Instagram @isabel.alexander

CHEE LEE DESIGNS

Chee Lee Designs, established by self taught artisan Cheena Mitchell, offers striking yet timeless, wearable works of art. Seen here is their Crescent Solitaire with precious stones in 22kt Gold vermeil or 14 kt Gold. A perfect statement piece with vibrant colours. Visit cheeleedesigns.com and follow on Instagram @cheeleedesigns

ANNIE AUSTEN

At the intersection of affordability and quality is Annie Austen, a brand focused on tarnish resistant, hypoallergenic, and size-inclusive pieces. From jewellery box staples to intricate pendants and adjustable rings, they believe every day is a special enough occasion to wear something you love. Find your perfect piece at annieausten.com and follow @shop_annie_austen

SETH MICHAEL

Seth Michael Carlson is a Philadelphia, USA based jeweller who creates each piece of his jewellery by hand to inspire wonder, curiosity, and a deep love of wildlife. Seth has partnered with Fairmined.org to source and promote ethically sourced gold. With an art therapy background Seth seeks to create pieces that excite the imagination. Visit sethmichaelstudio.com Instagram: @sethmichaelstudio

SIMPLY O JEWELLERY

Simply O is a young jewellery brand based in Germany who creates fine jewellery pieces with delicate pearls and fine gemstones for modern women of all ages. Their minimalistic and feminine designs are handcrafted with 14k Gold Filled to achieve luxury pieces for an accessible price. Find your everyday piece of luxury at www.simplyo.de follow on Instagram @simplyo.de or contact info@simplyo.de

SILVERWILLOW STUDIO

Erin Choi, designer and founder of Silverwillow Studio, produces artfully handcrafted jewellery and adornments that speak to your soul, exude personality and last for generations. With her extensive knowledge of metal arts, gemology and ornamental engraving, Erin uses mixed materials including ethically sourced gemstones and recycled metal to create fine jewellery pieces as unique as the person wearing them. Visit silverwillowstudio.us and follow @silverwillowstudio on Instagram to find out more

NOVITA DIAMONDS

Novita Diamonds gives you the opportunity to design your dream diamond ring with ethically sourced and conflict free lab-grown diamonds. As one of the largest lab-grown diamond retailers in the world you can buy with confidence the highest quality diamonds at affordable prices. Shop at novitadiamonds.co.uk or visit their London and Manchester showrooms. Follow @Novita.Diamonds on Instagram.

VIANNE JEWELLERY

New from Vianne Jewellery, the affordable demi-fine jewellery brand based in Manchester, UK, their new collection features exquisitely handcrafted gemstone jewellery including emerald, tourmaline and peridot (as pictured). All gemstones are natural and ethically sourced, these stunning pieces are must-haves for this season and are available in 18k gold vermeil and sterling silver. See more at www.viannejewellery.com and Instagram @viannejewellery

HIKARU PEARL

HIKARU PEARL create handmade accessories with mainly freshwater pearls which are known for their beautiful natural pastel colours, asymmetric shapes and variety of sizes These elements combined with minimalistic design give you a unique, elegant and precious charm. Shop via www.hikarupearl.com and follow @hikarupearl on Instagram.

SPINELLI KILCOLLIN

Spinelli Kilcollin is a luxury jewellery brand founded by husband and wife duo Yves Spinelli and Dwyer Kilcollin. Handcrafted in Los Angeles, Spinelli Kilcollin's jewellery is made by [loc]al artisans using ethically sourced materials. [Th]eir iconic linked rings are designed with mixed [me]tals and lustrous pavé-set diamonds offering [diff]erent variations in their signature silhouettes. [Vis]it spinellikilcollin.com [Ins]tagram: @spinellikilcollin

PRAIRIE SKY JEWELRY CO

Prairie Sky Jewelry Co explores the vast prairie landscapes as experienced by founder and one of North America's premier jewellery designers – Kenyon Lomax of Oklahoma. With each piece handcrafted in sterling silver and American turquoise, Kenyon's work both honours and emulates the expanse of the Prairie Sky. Visit prairieskyjewelryco.com and follow @prairieskyjewelryco on Instagram.

SOFIAH JEWELRY

Launched in 2020 by two sisters, named after their grandmother, Sofiah Jewelry is a luxurious jewellery concept. This Swiss brand of modular, customisable jewellery opens the door to a world of unlimited possibilities. Their unique and varied collections are designed to enhance the beauty of the modern woman. They believe in the beauty of simplicity and the importance of a detail with all unique designs crafted from the finest materials and gemstones. Visit sofiah.ch and follow @sofiahofficial on Instagram to find out more.

VICTORI

Victori creates ethical and sustainable jewellery out of recycled and Fairmined precious metals and lab-grown gemstones in Los Angeles. Inspired by the symbolism of Victorian jewellery, Victori's pieces are designed to be an emotional, symbolic keepsake and a luxury outfit accent. Discover more at www.victorijewelry.com Instagram: @victorijewelry

COMMON GROUND

Common Ground create beautiful jewellery from recycled materials and ethically sourced stones. Unique and durable adornments that will become a part of your every day ritual. Visit commongroundjewelry.com and follow on Instagram @commongroundgreenport

GGG JEWELLERY CO

GGG Jewellery Co established in Derbyshire in 2017 specialises in alternative fine jewellery created from ethically sourced precious metals and gemstones. Commissions undertaken. Shop their newest collections at gggjewelleryco.com follow on Instagram @gggjewelleryco

JONATHAN STEIN

Jonathan Stein is a second-generation South African diamond merchant and jewellery designer and manufacturer of 18kt and platinum custom-made fine jewellery. As per your design or theirs, every piece of their jewellery is a one-off bespoke piece. Specialising in fine quality diamonds and coloured stones. Visit jstein.com [an]d follow @jonathansteindiamonds on Instagram.

SHAWNA BUKER JEWELRY

Talented Canadian designer Shawna Buker creates beautiful jewellery just for you. Let them create your dream engagement or wedding ring using a lab grown diamond or moissonite stone. Visit shawnabukerjewelry.com and follow on Instagram @shawnabukerjewelry

KOOKY BLOOM

Kooky bloom is a small family-run business that specialises in handmade real preserved flower jewellery. No two items being the same allows you to own a special one-of-a-kind piece of nature. Fashion and precious items. Visit www.kookybloom.com and follow @kooky_bloom on Instagram.

URBAN STONES

The Stained Glass Dog-Tag by Urban Stones is a perfect Christmas gift for anyone. It features a depiction of a sunset, created with enamel to resemble the stained glass of old Church windows. The Dog-Tags are available in a range of colours and configurations starting at £1,499. Urban Stones was created by Nigerian designer, Manuchimso Opara, with a focus on sustainable jewellery practices. Manuchimso's influences range from ancient African architecture to modern [en]gineering and contemporary art. For more visit [ur]banstonesldn.co.uk and follow @urbanstones [on] Instagram.

HEIDI KJELDSEN

Heidi Kjeldsen, a talented fine jeweller based in Oakham, Rutland. Special commisions available to create perfectly bespoke pieces using the highest quality diamonds, gemstones and pearls. Visit heidikjeldsen.co.uk and follow on Instagram @heidikjeldsenltd

JOANNA ACHKAR JEWELS

Joanna Achkar fine jewels designs pieces inspired by the world and to be worn by sophisticated yet bold women. She creates eye-catching pieces for the lover of fun, the twisted and the outstanding. Featured is her Cosmic candy collection. Candy charms featuring white diamonds, cabochon centre stones and coloured enamel all set in 18k gold which can be customised. Visit www.joannaachkar.com to shop the collection and follow @joannaachkarjewels on Instagram.

Jewellery Designer Profile

CADMAN ROCK

Cadman Rock is a New Zealand based creator of artisan jewellery with designs inspired by the bold and courageous. The collections specialise in high quality sustainable materials and semi-precious gemstones. Each piece evokes a sense of history and adventure, making Cadman Rock truly collectable. For the wearer, there is no ordinary. Visit www.cadmanrock.com collections and follow @cadmanrock on Instagram.

XIAOTONG GUO

Xiaotong Guo was born in China, however it wasn't until she went to college that she embarked on her jewellery journey. Xiaotong finds beauty in imperfections and discovered a means of expression through her obsession with jewellery, utilising such imperfections in her work and elevating their charm into beautiful jewellery. Visit xiaotongguojewelry.com and follow @xiaotongguo_jewelry on Instagram to see more of her exquisite work.

MERAKI AND STAR

Ysabella Howard, the founder and creative mind behind Meraki and Star's unique style favours a delicate but bold approach to jewellery fashion. With an emphasis on dainty and classic but edgy design, these pieces are guaranteed to stun. Become a goddess today by visiting merakiandstar.com and following on Instagram @merakiandstar

DEON SMITH

A unique designer that hand makes jewellery in recycled silver and woods that are ethically sourced and indigenous to South Africa. Seen here is a brooch from their Botanical Collection, inspired by the special and beautiful Cape Floral Kingdom. Visit deonsmithjewellery.com and follow on Instagram @deonsmithjewellery

ADLIN HUE

The Japanese designer Mariko Abe makes the best use of the precious resources that already exist on the earth, with Adlin Hue designs. Materials include silver 925 recycled in the factory, deadstock stones cut by Japanese craftsmen, akoya pearls destined to be discarded, recycled glass and vintage deadstock chains. Shop the collection at adlinhue.com and follow @adlinhue on Instagram.

BALDUCCI

14k tanzanite and white gold ring. Contact Annette for your own bespoke design at Balducci Jewellers on 0151 336 5235.

EVERETT BROOKES

EverettBrookes is a multi-award-winning jeweller who offer fully customisable engagement rings, hand-finished by a team of world class jewellers, which can be ordered online and delivered with care, anywhere in the world. With a range of custom choices, such as lab-grown and natural-mined diamonds, their 'Designer Series' engagement rings can be hand-picked to suit each customer, as a budget friendly alternative to their bespoke jewellery. Visit www.everettbrookes.com.au and follow @everettbrookes on Instagram.

GIANO JEWELLERS

Giano Jewellers is a private jewellery designer and manufacturer based in South Africa. They specialise in creating fully customisable, one-of-a-kind pieces, allowing you to celebrate your individuality by creating a piece that is entirely unique to you. Bianca, the owner, works closely with her clients during the design process to ensure that they get exactly what they are looking for. Visit www.gianocustommadejewellery.com and follow on Instagram @gianojewellers

GABRIELLA ALICIA

Gabriella Alicia is an independent goldsmith who hand-makes each piece of her beautifully unique jewellery using ethically sourced precious materials such as gold, diamonds and gemstones. Gabriella Alicia is taking an innovative approach to elegant jewellery and creates skillfully crafted pieces to be treasured forever. Visit gabriellaalicia.co.uk

ENCELADUS

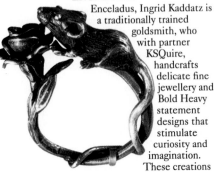

Enceladus, Ingrid Kaddatz is a traditionally trained goldsmith, who with partner KSQuire, handcrafts delicate fine jewellery and Bold Heavy statement designs that stimulate curiosity and imagination. These creations are future heirlooms emanating depth and mystery. Visit enceladus.ca and follow on Instagram @enceladus_studio

D BY DILYS'

DBD is here to elevate your everyday stack. With an Instagram feed chock-full of stacking inspiration, this Hong Kong brand is standing out with fun, one-of-a-kind fine jewels. Amongst its most covetable are the sweet, smooth and bold Montecristo Rings: featuring collectible cabochons and impeccable in-house craftsmanship. Visit dbydilys.com and follow on Instagram @dbd_finejewels

ANIMAH JEWELRY

Animah Jewelry was established by Anita Mahdavi, in 2014. Animah's eye-catching high pieces of jewellery with fascinating complications are the result of professional craftsmanship and meticulous designs. Designing and creating beautiful and classic jewellery is Anita's passion and she believes that hypnotic patterns with luminous diamonds and bright coloured gemstones create magnificent masterpieces. Visit animahjewelry.com and follow @animah.jewelry on Instagram.

DÁRÁ BY CREMA BELLA SPECIAL. Their evening clutch bag brand called Dárà, is a collection of evening minaudière bags for ...ned shoppers desiring that stunning accoutrement. Dárà offers peerless materials and elegant design to make their customers stand ... Visit cremabellaspecial.com to shop the collection and follow @cremabellaspecial on Instagram.

...OSE PARIS is the perfect blend of feminine, elegant, and effortless silhouettes. At the head of this label lies an unconditional lover ...ailoring who decided to sublimate this timeless garment. ... brand cultivates women's empowerment and is ...icated to preserving our precious planet: French ...ufacturing, noble and natural fabrics, flattering lines... ...will be charmed by a wardrobe of Parisian influences, to ...dopted day and night. Visit www.ose-paris.com and ...w @ose_paris on Instagram.

...MADELEINE TREHEARNE AND HARPAL BRAR ...sent Deep Sea Blue with a Tropical Garden: it tells a ...m story of luxurious shawls for this season in pink, both ... and strong, oranges, mango and beautiful blues; ...nningly hand embroidered with intricate detail with ...astical leaves, miniaturised flowers and trailing buds. ...by exciting design – the inspirational hand weaving and ...broidery of Kashmir – individual pure pashmina cashmere ...wls sourced exclusively by Madeleine and her small team, ...heers of the Kashmir shawl renaissance. Keen to support ...l communities, they obtain their shawls from renewable, ...ically produced sources in Kashmir. They send shawls all ...r the world. See the full collection at 20 New End Square ...don NW3 1LN or call for a brochure ...4(0) 2074356310, visit www.trehearneandbrar.com or ...w them on Instagram @madeleinetrehearne or ...ail mads@madeleinetrehearne.co.uk

...Greek brand, **IMISI COLLECTION**, are the creators of ...que fashion accessories. Motivated by Greek myth, all ...ir accessories carry inspirational quotes or words. The ...tured 'Gold play doh mood necklace' has been ...ted from gold plated Zamak and small crystal ...her beads. Two clasp loops allow for easy length ...ustment to suit any outfit. Visit ...w.imisicollection.com and follow @imisicollection ...Instagram.

...KURINJI is an Italian-Indian womenswear brand ...a mission to rediscover the traditional hand ...broidery and rich textile arts from India and bring ...m to a wider audience with Made in Italy ...houettes. Founder and designer Kavitha Vilvanathan ...s upcycled fabrics and natural dyes to create ...tainable collections with elegant, sophisticated and ...ly unique looks. Visit kurinji.it and @kurinjiofficial ...Instagram.

...HANRO has been producing the finest lingerie, ...htwear and loungewear since 1884. Premium ...ality, timeless design, and unique materials are at ...heart of every collection. As a result, HANRO ...ducts are particularly long-lived and often passed ...vn from generation to generation. Quality you can ...l on your skin – Made in Europe. Visit ...w.hanro.co.uk and @hanro.official on Instagram.

...Founded by Ebru Yalcuk and based in Izmir, Turkey, **LAMPEROS ATELIER** is a luxury ...achwear and resort wear label inspired by a chic Greek and Turkish summer lifestyle. Each ...ection is crafted from the highest quality fabrics, using unique colours and designs that ...'ll be wearing summer after summer. Shop the collection at lamperosatelier.com and follow ...amperos_atelier on Instagram.

...SK-NS are the creators of an inclusive lounge and shapewear brand, designed to enhance ...ery shape and size. At the heart of the British owned brand is the passion to promote ...fidence in women with all pieces designed to amplify and contour shape and curves, whilst ...t compromising on style or comfort. Shop the collection at www.sk-ns.co ...l follow @sknslabel on Instagram.

...Founded in 2004, **ELIZABETTA** are a small mother and daughter ...siness designing silk accessories for men and women. Their collections ... entirely produced in the Como region in Northern Italy, with the ...signer Elizabetta taking inspiration from the nature and culture around ...r to bring luxury Italian quality to the world. Visit elizabetta.eu and ...stagram @elizabettaboutique

...SOOD is a San Francisco founded brand designed in New York that ...ks to embody dualism, self-expression, representation, and collaboration. ...under and designer Sana Maqsood wants to help ignite confidence, ...mote inclusivity and re-define everyday jewellery basics. They are ...rrently selling their Edge series produced in sterling silver and 18k gold ...ted brass. Visit www.sood.co and follow @sood.clothing

...MIKAINE is a premium accessories brand redefining standards of ...mfort and refinement for unisex knitwear and caps. Their essentials ...lection features classic Swiss design combined with elevated Italian ...istry. By using only carefully sourced cashmere, merino wool and leather ...KAINE sought to ensure purity and quality whilst upholding the highest ethical standards to ...ate understated timeless accessories. The essentials collection is currently available online at ...w.mikaine.com and selected retailers in the UK. Instagram @mikaine

... Founded in Australia and sustainably made with smart and thoughtful compartmental ...signs, **UTOPPII** is an innovative travel backpack created for women going places while ...eking to make a positive impact on the world. Its minimalist black with gold hardware and ...ght colourful lining, inspired by the colours of sunsets, is bound to surprise. Visit ...w.utoppii.com and follow @utoppii on Instagram.

... The leather bags from LA-based label, **AALLYN**, stand out without having to shout. ...esigned for modern women by a modern woman, their pieces are effortlessly stylish, practical, ...d priced accessibly. You'll love the classic silhouettes and sturdy hardware for years to come. ...e pictured style comes with two strap styles. Shop online at AALLYN.com or @aallyn ...Instagram.

... NESSA by **BYLABRAND** features a square toe with lace up ankle design. The chocolate ...our heels are perfect for your weekend plans! Visit bylabrand.com and follow them on ...stagram @bylabrandofficial

... **JELANI** is a small brand founded by Natalia Gadd-Funes from her home in Sydney, ...stralia. The name 'Jelani' takes inspiration from the names of her angels. The Berry Burst ...cksuit, as seen, is just one of the latest thick and cosy tracksuit sets that this brand has to ...fer. Visit jelani.com.au and follow @jelani.thelabel on Instagram.

TO APPEAR ON THESE PAGES, CONTACT 020 7152 3705 OR EMAIL CLASSVOGUE@CONDENAST.CO.UK

Vogue's Beauty Shortlist

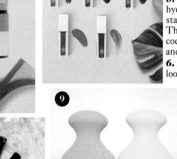

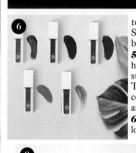

1. This creamy, caramel-scented leave-in moisturiser by **FAVEN ESSENTIALS** is a treat for the driest of hair. It can be used daily or as needed on damp or dry hair to help leave your hair feeling softer, stronger and moisturised. It can also be used as a beard and body moisturiser. Visit favenessentials.com Instagram: @favenessentials

2. BPERFECT COSMETICS have reached global success with a cult-like status amongst celebs, style influencers and beauty devotees across the globe. Their Chroma Cover Foundation is one of the first of its kind from any Irish born beauty brand, with 36 shades spanning a full spectrum of skin tones. Follow @bperfectcosmetics on Instagram and quote VOGUE20 for 20% off, valid until 31/12/22 (t&cs, excludes sale and bundle items) at www.bperfectcosmetics.com

3. TRUE NAIL POLISH is the perfect polish with a highly pigmented colour. Use the code VOGUE10 for a 10% discount (expires 31.12.22). Shop online at true-nails.co.uk and follow @true.nail.polish on Instagram.

4. It's time to Bare Your Bold and let the good times roll with the "must-have" set of the season from **BBOLD**. Introducing Bare Your Bold – a full-sized, 7-piece gift set available exclusively in selected Boots stores across the UK & Ireland and online. Now better than half price at £39.99 (was £85). Achieve the perfect looking golden glow with the TikTok viral Super Mousse Tan, sell-out Mist & Glow Face Mist, Smart Mousse with Colour Control technology, Hello Glow Gradual Tan, Nourishing Maintain It Moisturiser, Smooth Applicator Tanning Mitt and Exfoliating Glove. Also shop online at b-bold.co.uk and follow TikTok: @bbold Instagram: @bboldtan

5. FACETHEORY's Regena-C Moisturiser helps to leave the skin feeling hydrated and appearing brighter. It contains a combination of Retinol Ester, stabilised vitamin C, vitamin E, retinyl palmitate (0.6%) and hyaluronic acid. They are committed to sustainability and are certified cruelty-free. Use promo code VOGUE15 for 15% off (expires 24.12.22). Shop online at facetheory.com and follow @facetheory on Instagram.

6. NWADI is a cosmetics brand made for every BABE, regardless of how you look, they bring out the confidence and sassiness that lights up a room. Shop the stunning collection online at nwadibeauty.com and follow @nwadiofficial on Instagram.

7. LASHFACTOR LONDON's nanotechnology based bicellular under eye gel serum aims to reduce the appearance of under eye dark circles, puffiness, bags, and wrinkles. It contains carefully tested plant-based ingredients as Retinol, Vitamin C and Ginseng. The serum feels soothing and aims to reduce the appearance of fine lines and wrinkles around the eyes. Shop online at lashfactor.com and follow @officiallashfactor on Instagram. Get 15% discount now by using the code "VOGUE15" (expires 31.12.22).

8. At **AMPLIO**, their mission has always been to create a makeup range that will empower people everywhere to feel beautiful and confident wherever they go. Inspired by this mission, they bring you fabulous makeup products that work hard for you and that are suitable for sensitive skin and cruelty free! Visit www.ampliobeauty.com and follow @ampliobeauty on Instagram.

9. LILLYWHITE COSMETICS Hourglass Sponge is a must have for your beauty routine, it is the secret to a flawless looking makeup finish. Expanding in size once wet, applying liquid and powder formulas have never been so effortless. Visit www.lillywhitecosmetics.co.uk and follow them on Instagram @lillywhitecosmetic

10. WHIPPED CREAM BODY butter is a whipped blend of natural oils and butters fragranced with essential oils. This butter originated from the owner trying to assist a loved one with a dry skin issue. With consistent use their skin appeared to transform. Whipped Cream Body will supply you with the tools to experience soft and luxurious feeling skin even when you haven't been to the spa. Shop online at whippedcreambody.com and follow @whipp3d_cr3am_ on Instagram.

11. Soothe the look of dry, damaged skin with an artisan whipped blend of mango, tucuma, kokum, and tucuma butters. **VONAÉ**'s Mango Butter leaves skin feeling soft and supple. Enjoy chemical free, plant-based beauty products at www.vonaehair.com and follow @vonaehair on Instagram.

12. A true masterpiece lies in the essence of **MONA LISA**, a luxury fragrance oil created to awaken the visionary within. Each bottle radiates with the brilliance of Herkimer Diamonds, unparalleled in their ability to illuminate one's entire universe. Finally a luxury scent for the ultimate muse, for darling it is a work of art. Visit MonaLisaPure.com and follow @MonaLisaPureOil for inspiration on Instagram.

13. NIMONÉ BEAUTY offers a stunning collection of Lip S.O.SS (serum + oil gloss) from the boldest of colours, to the simplest of hues. Aiming to deliver the feeling of lasting hydration, all while activating your senses with aromatherapy. Cruelty free, Vegan and handmade by artisans – Nimone Beauty is lip care with flair. Shop online at nimonebeauty.com and follow @nimonebeauty on Instagram.

14. BUR BUR is a botanical hair growth oil. Originated from a family recipe this unique treatment includes high quality botanicals. Made with Burdock oil, Vitamin C and Bakuchiol. This product aims to support healthy looking hair growth and reduce the appearance of breakage. Learn more and at www.Burburcare.com and follow @burburcare on Instagram.

15. Be kind to your nails with **PRETTY PRO NAILS**, 100% vegan & cruelty-free nail polish. Shade Hot sauce comes in an 8ml bottle for you to have on the go with a visibly long-lasting pigmented colour available in 26 shades. Use code: Vogue20 for 20% off (expires: 31/01/2023). Shop at www.prettypro.com and follow @prettypro_ on Instagram.

16. SOAPSTAR creates skincare products that are suitable for everyone, including people with allergies to synthetic perfumes or synthetic preservatives. They only use what is really necessary and are transparent regarding the ingredients they choose. The Antares liquid hand soap for daily use is formulated to gently cleanse the hands. Enriched with inulin and 100% organic perfume. It leaves your skin scented and feeling moisturised. Shop online at soapstarofficial.com and follow @soapstar.official on Instagram.

17. EVME Colour Correcting Cosmetics are dedicated to supporting you to achieve an even looking skin tone with easy to use and highly pigmented colour correcting cosmetics. From brown and blue pigments found in hyperpigmentation and under-eye shadows, to redness and purple pigments found in blemishes and rosacea – they have got you covered. Made in the UK, Vegan and Fragrance Free. Visit www.evmecosmetics.com and follow on Instagram @evmecosmetics

18. VODUZ Velvet Crown is here to fight the appearance of frizz and keep your crown looking sleek and shiny. This thermal-activated blowdry aid aims to coat your hair in a lightweight layer, wrapping fibres around the hair to lock in humidity. The results can last for up to 3 shampoos, all whilst acting as a heat protector too! Shop online at voduzhair.com and follow @voduzhair on Instagram.

BYRDOUM is a Middle-Eastern inspired beauty brand powered by the desert date. [Fea]tured is their Night's Ode face oil containing vitamins A & E and cold-pressed from [so]ocert® certified organic desert dates. Vegan and cruelty free and suitable for all skin types. [Sho]p at byrdoum.com and follow @byrdoumofficial on Instagram.

NATALIA ME'GAN BEAUTY provide a beautiful range of high quality products to [enh]ance the look of your natural beauty. The brand's founder, domestic violence survivor, [tur]ned pain into purpose, creating highly pigmented, cruelty free, lip-glosses that feel [lig]htweight and long lasting. Shop online at nataliambeauty.com and follow [@n]ataliambeauty on Instagram.

GLASS GLOSS VEGAN LIP BEAUTY all-natural, organic, vegan lip oil is designed [to] help leave your lips feeling soft. Ideal as a daily lip moisturiser and nighttime lip [co]nditioner and it's so natural you can use it on your body. Visit glassgloss.com and follow [@]glassgloss_ on Instagram.

Achieve a salon quality experience at home with the KING HAIR & BEAUTY [Dr]ench and Repair Luxury Shampoo and Conditioning Hair Mask. Suitable for all hair [typ]es, the Vegan, SLS and Paraben free formula, produced using 100% renewable energy, [en]riched with Glycerine, Hydrolysed Wheat Extract and Hydrolysed Silk. It [hel]ps to leave your mane feeling silky soft. Drench and Repair leaves your luscious [loc]ks looking transformed and feeling strong and healthy. Shop online at [kin]ghairandbeauty.com and follow @kinghairandbeauty on Instagram.

SWEET SLEEP BY SWEET BEE ORGANICS. Get your beauty-sleep and [hel]p to boost your wellness with Sweet Sleep magnesium butter. Studies suggest [tha]t many of us are deficient in magnesium. Applying a grape-sized portion to your [ski]n, each evening, provides your daily dose, helping you to feel relaxed and sleep [we]ll. Shop online at sweetbeeorganics.co.uk and follow @sweetbeeorganics [on] Instagram.

PRETTY IN GLAM is a luxury, vegan and cruelty free cosmetic brand offering [a b]eautiful range of exceptionally high quality products. You need this lip gloss that [ai]ms to leave your lips feeling hydrated, whilst offering the feeling of an ultra smooth [an]d non-sticky application. Shop online at prettyinglam.com and follow [@]prettyinglamcosmetics on Instagram.

COMMAND COSMETICS is on a mission to make contour comfortable. The [bra]nd's universal 'Confidence' contour stick complements many skin tones, and its [wa]terproof, vegan, and cruelty-free formula can be used on the face and body! [Di]scover more at www.commandcosmetics.com and follow @commandcosmetics [on] Instagram.

Meet one of the internet's latest obsessions, MOONCAT. Their otherworldly [na]il lacquer is designed to last up to two weeks chip-free – for nails that look like [yo]u just left a high-end salon. You won't be able to look away from your nails. Shop [at] mooncat.com and follow @mooncat on Instagram.

The "Shampoo and Conditioner" Bundle from Canadian luxury beauty brand [T]RULY LIFESTYLE BRAND has gone from a TikTok sensation to an at home [fa]vourite. These vegan and cruelty-free products are formulated with a 3% keratin [ble]nd, silk amino acids, and 5 essential oils. They help to promote the look of long, [lu]scious locks. Shop online at www.trulylifestylebrand.com and follow [@t]rulylifestylebrand on Instagram.

Try these amazing EYECHA eco lashes which will make you look fabulous [wh]ilst helping the environment. Eyecha is one of the only brands that uses [re]cycled material to make its lashes and they support global tree replanting with [ev]ery purchase. Shop the range at Superdrug, at eyechalashes.com and follow on [In]stagram @eyecha_lashes

The RUMI COSMETIQUES' waterproof eyeliner aims to stay put all day [wh]ilst also nourishing with moisture. With its rich, easily blurrable and [qu]ick-fixing formula, their new LushLine+ eyeliner will let you create the look of [the] effortless line of your dreams whilst still being kind to your sensitive skin and [eye]s. They care for all ladies, having launched the eyeliner in 3 colours! Enjoy a [tru]ly elegant and sophisticated look with 10% discount code "VOGUE10" at [ru]micosmetiques.co.uk (expires 01/12/22) and @rumicosmetiques on Instagram.

BUSHNUT BEAUTY is an eco-luxury botanical skincare brand designed to [tra]nsform the look of dry, sensitive, blemish-prone skin into dewy, [re]silient, radiant-looking skin. The brand uses premium skin food [ing]redients of botanical plant butters, super seed oils, and herbal [ad]aptogens. Shop their collection at bushnutbeauty.com. Join their [In]stagram community @bushnutbeauty for more.

SOLANA BEAUTÈ is a new beauty brand whom have launched their [re]d eyeshadow palette named "Flourished Fantasies". This whimsical jewel [to]ned palette was also used in Milan Fashion Week for the founder's own [fa]shion Collection. This palette and other items from Solana Beautè can be [or]dered from solanabeaute.net

ZILLY is a Californian brand rooted in surf culture and obsessed [wi]th healthy, happenin' hair! Their spritz is a multitasking leave-in [co]nditioner that is formulated to leave hair feeling hydrated and [pr]otected against damage from salt and the sea. Zilly is vegan, [cr]uelty-free, and bottled in eco-friendly packaging. Shop at [zi]llyhair.com + @zillyhair on Instagram.

PRIME PROMETICS. Mascara created with and for [wo]men over 50. PrimeLash Mascara has a serum-base. It aims to leave your lashes [lo]oking longer and thicker. The mess-proof wand nourishes thin, sparse, brittle lashes [wi]th moisture. It contains bioactive nutrients and vitamins. Get 15% OFF with ["V]OGUE15" (expires 31.12.22) at primeprometics.com

New to the WAPHYTO hair collection, is this blend of plant-based botanical oils [in]cluding squalane, apricot kernel, canola, sunflower, safflower, and jojoba. What makes [it] especially unique is that it can be used multiple ways. You can add it to your hair [w]ashing routine as a pre-cleanse product, enjoy it as a massage oil for a scalp massage, [or] apply a few drops as the last step in your process and leave it in for a shiny look. [Sh]op online at en.waphyto.com and follow @waphyto on Instagram.

Make every day a good hair day with MONDAY HAIRCARE. Their award-[w]inning 0% SLS formulas instead contain ingredients such as shea butter and coconut [oil] to use on dry, winter hair. Visit uk.mondayhaircare.com and follow [@]mondayhaircare on TikTok and Instagram.

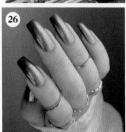

TO APPEAR ON THESE PAGES, CONTACT 020 7152 3705 OR EMAIL CLASSVOGUE@CONDENAST.CO.UK

8. **DECLARÉ**'s Derma Forte Cream is formulated for the darker time of the year when we are not as exposed to natural sunlight and our skin feels stressed, dry and tired. It aims to leave the skin feeling hydrated, firm and toned. Made with hyaluronic acid. Visit www.declareireland.ie and follow @declare_irl on Instagram.

9. **SELAURA** is a new perimenopause supplement. Created to target the feeling of brain fog, hot flushes, tiredness, hormonal fluctuations, thinning hair and aching joints, SELAURA will have you feeling like you again. Discover how you can live your best mid-life at www.selaura.com and follow @Selaura_Life

10. You will say "Oui!" To **BRUNETTE SKIN**. The new black-owned French brand founded by two sisters whose mission is to take your melanin to the next level. Shown here is their cruelty-free and vegan Cloud cream with rice ferments. It aims to diminish the appearance of imperfections and leave the skin feeling hydrated. Visit www.brunetteskin.com and follow @brunetteskin on Instagram.

21. **COCOON BOTANICALS** aims to leave your skin feeling balanced with natural, clean cosmetics. Featured is their Active Botanical Toner made with Rose Water, Aloe Vera, Panthenol, natural Cactus Extract and Green Tea. It leaves the skin feeling hydrated, soothed and nourished with moisture. Visit cocoonbotanicals.com and Instagram @cocoonbotanicals

22. UK based **BIOTRIUM** is a new premium pharmaceutical grade brand that manufactures cosmetics for women aged 35+. Their Intensive Brightening Serum is cleverly formulated with encapsulated Cysteamine. This product aims to brighten the appearance of your skin leaving it looking healthier and radiant. Use code AUTUMN for 30% off your first order. (Expires 31.12.22). Visit www.biotrium.co.uk and Instagram: @biotrium

23. Ran by its female founder and cosmetic chemist, **QT COSMETICS** creates well-rounded skincare that is inspired by self-care and stress-free moments. With ingredients like peptides, niacinamide, sodium hyaluronate and squalane oil, Cloud Eye Gels aim to deliver your best looking skin yet plus that cloud-nine feeling. Visit www.qtcosmetics.com and Instagram @qtcosmeticsusa

24. **RUBIFRESH** Skincare is a functional Australian skincare brand, using only natural and organic ingredients. The Coffee Seed Eye Gel helps to reduce the appearance of fine lines and wrinkles, aiming to leave your skin appearing brighter, smoother and refreshed. It contains active ingredients including green coffee seed extract, hyaluronic acid and natural silica. Shop online at rubifresh.com.au and follow @rubifresh on Instagram.

25. **SENSAB** is a gender neutral, vegan, organic and natural skincare brand based and created in London. Made by hand in small batches centred around the effectiveness of plant powered ingredients that are high quality and sustainably sourced. Discover their first product 'sensab cream deodorant' using the natural fragrances of tea tree and rosewood, this woody and floral mix offers a delicate touch for your skin and something that offers visible benefits, leaving it feeling fresh and cared for. Visit sensab-skincare.com and Instagram @sensab_skincare

26. **WIIG**. Correcting the appearance of unwanted brassy and yellow tones with PLEX technology and helping to protect against future damage. 3 miracles in one bottle. Developed by a leading London blonde specialist this "saviour for blondes" product gives you up to 10 to 15 uses per bottle. Try it and you will be converted. Shop online at wiig.co and follow @wiig.co on Instagram.

27. Give extra love to your skincare with **STARLA SKIN**'s innovative and wireless 7-in-1 LED Light Therapy Face Mask. It aims to boost collagen production to leave you with the appearance of healthy and glowing skin. Their mission is to empower women in the new era of aesthetic, where technology meets beauty in the most accessible and long-lasting way. Visit starlaskin.com and follow @starlaskin on Instagram.

28. Modern cosmetic science meets ancient holistic healing at **ÉPANOUIE SKIN**. Featured is the Éternelle Perfecting Crème, an overnight treatment made with premium plant oils, azelaic acid and essential vitamins. Use daily for radiant looking skin that feels softer and appears brighter over time. Visit www.epanouieskin.com and follow on Instagram @epanouieskin

29. Let your skin feel like a dream come true. **INDULG3 SKIN & BODY**'s Skin Lovin' Whipped Body Butters help to leave your skin nourished with moisture and with a glowing look. Specially handcrafted with clean and green ingredients, they are perfect for use as a daily ritual or anytime your skin needs some TLC. Featured are their new scents, infused with papaya extracts. Visit www.indulg3.com and follow @indulg3skinandbody

30. **CROCUS COLLECTOR** is a premium, awarded skincare brand devoted to bringing you a luxury spa experience at home. Crocus Extract is combined with handpicked active ingredients of natural origin. It helps to leave your skin feeling rejuvenated, firm, moisturised and nourished with moisture. It also aims to reduce the appearance of fine lines and wrinkles. Explore more at www.crocus-collector.com and Instagram @crocus_collector

31. **MILLION DOLLAR FACIAL**'s I'TX (pronounced "Eye-Tox") is an eye treatment that contains peptides, emollients, humectants and multi-vitamins. It nourishes your skin with moisture and helps to reduce the appearance of wrinkles around the eyes for a brighter, fresher appearance. To purchase visit shop.milliondollarfacial.com or follow them on Instagram @milliondollarfacialsystem

32. **CASMARA** Infinity Oil Elixir is formulated for mature skin with an advanced blend of 7 botanical phyto oils. This elixir is formulated with the aim to increase collagen production. This 98% natural advanced elixir blends nature's most precious treasures with the latest technology. It leaves the skin with a youthful looking glow. Follow @casmarairl on Instagram and visit www.casmara.ie

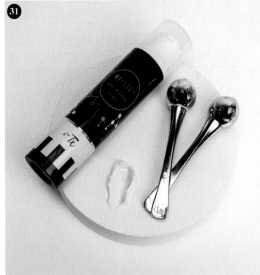

Pre-Party Pamper

33. The radically simple *FABILOUS CACAO BUTTER* is the rare beauty product that feels as good as it looks. It leaves the skin feeling restored, nourished with moisture, and air to reduce the appearance of stretch marks. Learn more at fabilouscacao.com and @fabilouscacao on Instagram.

34. Built from fine exotic, natural ingredients, and backed by science, *DAMANCI* haircare cruelty-free and vegan-friendly. Their lightweight Elixir Argan Oil is designed to leave all types of hair feeling healthy, strong and rejuvenated. Visit www.damanci.com and Instagram @damancihair

35. *NUDIFLORA* Botanica's entire skincare range consists of undiluted, 100% active plant extracts. They use the extraction method of Bakuchiol, Green Tea ar Kakadu Plum (the only ingredients) in their signature 'Collagen Rebuild' serum, access all phytonutrients of the plants. These products help to produce the look healthy and glowing skin. Shop online at nudiflora.com.au and follow @nudiflora_skincare on Instagram.

36. The Oasis Barrier Booster, by *ACADERMA*, is derived from ingredients fror Africa. Combined with Cactus, Olive leaf, Centella Asiatica extracts and Kinkelib tea. It aims to leave the skin feeling calmer and also helps to reduce the appearan of redness and inflammation. Visit www.acaderma.com and follow @acaderma on Instagram.

37. Nourish your skin with moisture with the *HIGHER EDUCATION*'s Greek Week Hydrating Probiotic Sleep Mask! Formulated with Lactobacillus Ferment 4 Glycolic Acid, and Sodium Hyaluronate. It aims to leave your skin feeling smoother and appearing brighter. It is formulated to leave the skin lookir radiant. Shop at @trndbty www.trndbty.com or on highereducationskincare.com

38. *SEVENTY HYAL* 2000 is a Next Generation Skin Booster, formulated with high molecular weight hyaluronic acid. Enhance the appearance of your skin's natural beauty, for a fresh and luminous lookin complexion. Visit www.seventyhyal.co.uk or connect with their socials @seventyhyal

39. The Recovery One from *HELLO SUNDAY* is a post-sun mask. Made with a blend of Cica, Oat Biotics and Provitamin-D. It nourishes the skin with moisture and leaves your skin appearing illuminated and brighter. Visit hellosundayspf.com and follow @hellosundayspf on Instagram.

40. Unlock the secret to youthful looking radiance with *BASZICARE*'s Collevo white lucent cream and Relevo white crystal serum. This duo aims to target the appearance of dullness t promote the look of luminosity. Find out more at www.baszicare.cc or follow @baszicare on Instagram.

41. Inspired by nature, *ARBŪ COSMETICS* Elements Extreme Nourishing Eye Cream is specially formulated to leave the delicat eye area feeling hydrated and appearing bright. Made with extract of rose oil, eyebright, Arctic oat, calendula and ginseng. It is creat by the highest standards of clean beauty. Visit www.arbucosmetics.com and follow @arbu.cosmetics on Instagran

A Very Vogue Wedding

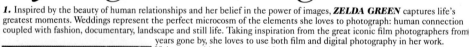

1. Inspired by the beauty of human relationships and her belief in the power of images, *ZELDA GREEN* captures life's greatest moments. Weddings represent the perfect microcosm of the elements she loves to photograph: human connection coupled with fashion, documentary, landscape and still life. Taking inspiration from the great iconic film photographers from years gone by, she loves to use both film and digital photography in her work. Visit www.zeldagreen.com and Instagram @zeldagreen

2. *TRAUFABRIK* is an award winning Design Studio for exclusive and luxurious wedding stationery based in Cologne/Germany, available worldwide. Specialised in bespoke stationery designs, Traufabrik only uses highest class materials, letterpress and hot foil printing for their unique looks. Visit www.traufabrik.com and Instagram @traufabrik

3. *AMELIA JANE* is a documentary photographer with a nostalgic, analogue style working candidly to tell the story of your wedding day by creating natural, timeless photographs. Amelia is the perfect choice for stylish, quirky and whimsical wedding North East based, she works worldwide. See more at www.ameliajanephotography.cc and check out her Instagram @ameliajanephoto

4. *LOLA*'s wedding photography philosophy: 'It's not about perfection. It's about real emotions and the in-between-moments.' With her photo documentaries she tells stories about loving, laughing, crying, hugging, partying and dancing people. Visit www.lolas-hochzeitsfotografie.com and Instagram @lolas_hochzeitsfotografie

5. *PAULINA WALSH*. Based in the Midlands but also shooting destination weddings, Paulina is a luxury editorial photographer with a fine art and romantic approach. Inspired by film, Paulina captures joyful love stories and creates timeless photos for couples intensely in love. Visit www.paulinawalsh.com or follow @paulinawalshphotography

6. Created for style conscious couples, *FOX & FLORA* curate florals that integrate seamlessly with your day. They take time to understand you and every detail of your wedding, so that your wedding flowers are truly bespoke to you. They are bold, creative, expressive, to deliver seasonally inspired floral design for weddings and events with impa Photo: Gail Secker. Visit www.foxflora.co.uk and Instagram @_foxandflora

7. Canadian designer *JOANNA DELANEY* creates one of a kind couture gowns for the modern bride. Her aesthetic boasts understated elegance with a focus on impeccable fit and quality tailoring. Available for online consultation worldwide. View more styles at www.joannadelaney.com Instagram: @joannadelaneystudio Photography: @lizrosa Makeup: @hannahschell Model: @akechyak

8. *PORTUGAL WEDDING PHOTOGRAPHER*. Distinctive through the beautiful use of natural light, Anastasia is a destination wedding photographer in Portugal. She takes aesthetically clean and elegant photographs, using a combination of photography techniques to capture gesture and emotions and create beautiful, meaningful wedding portraits. Visit portugalweddingphotographer.com and Instagram @portugalweddingphotograph

9. Australian based wedding photographer, *KATIE HARMSWORTH*, creates romantic imagery with a touch of drama. With a deep understanding of composition and light, she achieves beautiful photographs which capture her couples day perfectly. Available for travel worldwide, get in touch via www.katieharmsworth.com and Instagram @katie_harmsworth

10. With ten years experience photographing over 400 weddings, **EMMA LAWSON** creates timeless images with an editorial flair. Her informal, photojournalistic style lets her capture the candid and emotive moments. Specialising in UK and destination weddings as well as elopements, Emma is available all over the UK and Europe. Visit emmalawsonphotography.com and @emmalawsonphoto

11. TAWNY BALLARD PHOTOGRAPHY's perfect mix of genuine, candid moments and artful, directed portraits create an exceptional documentation of each couple's unique wedding day story. She is based in Chicago, IL and available worldwide. Visit tawnyballardphotography.com and Instagram @tawnyballardphotography

12. Inspired by fashion, art and architecture, California-based **DIANE SOTERO PHOTOGRAPHY** offers luxury clients incomparable and bespoke film and digital photography expertise. Serving couples across Europe, the United States and luxury destinations worldwide, Diane captures delicate, fresh and editorial-style imagery. Visit dianesotero.com and Instagram @dianesoterophoto

13. IMOGEN EVE matches an unobtrusive, documentary style of photography with a warm editorial feel, for modern couples in love. With a focus on storytelling through beautiful imagery, you'll look back on your gallery and relive the emotions of your day. Visit www.imogenevephotography.co.uk and Instagram @imogenevephotography

14. Inspired by the human experience, **BOBBI PHELPS** fuses both a photojournalistic and editorial approach within her imagery. She creates a personalised experience for each couple to ensure their photographs truly encompass their relationship. Bobbi is appreciated by her clients for her guidance, easygoing nature, and her emotion-driven storytelling. Visit bobbiphelps.com and Instagram @bobbi.phelps

15. BIANCA VIRTUE. Bianca's timeless compositions tell each love story exquisitely. Her frames are elegant, honest and imbued with an editorial-esque beauty. For the modern couple looking for romantic photographs that are stylishly framed and drenched in natural light. Visit www.biancavirtue.com and Instagram @biancavirtueweddings

16. With a decade in the industry, **ALICIA LUCIA PHOTOGRAPHY** has evolved into the blueprint for editorial and emotive wedding photography. Capturing the magic of each and every nuptial with aesthetic, culture and love in mind. Their team is set apart through their progressive values, elevated client experience and bespoke imagery. Visit www.alicialucia.com and Instagram @alicialuciaphotos

17. JACK ALDRIDGE is a documentary Wedding Photographer with a style for authentic storytelling. He knows the importance of capturing fleeting moments and his candid, relaxed approach achieves timeless frames with a sense of fashion for modern couples. Visit www.jackaldridgephotography.co.uk and @jackaldridgeweddings on Instagram.

18. Capturing all your dearest moments in a sophisticated way, **PHOTOGRAPHY BY MERLIN** artistically tells your love story in a timeless yet elegant series of photos. With her desire to capture the raw, vivid emotions, she connects with her couples to create magic to cherish forever. Visit www.merlinalink.nl and Instagram @photographybymerlin

19. Effortless and elegant, **NASTASSIA CHANTAL** is a fine art wedding photographer available throughout Europe. She is best known for her ethereal, natural style combined with an editorial approach. Visit nastassiachantal.com and Instagram @nastassia_chantal

20. Rui and Savannah of **THE LOPES PHOTOGRAPHY** are Lisbon based wedding photographers who curate emotive and intimate imagery for modern lovers. The husband and wife duo document your day in both film and digital format, using an editorial approach to capture your love with authenticity. As globetrotters themselves, they photograph destination weddings and elopements worldwide. Visit www.thelopesphotography.com and Instagram @thelopesphotography

21. TALI PHOTOGRAPHY, a sister duo with over 14 years experience in high-end destination weddings is a well established brand in the bridal world. Their distinctive, fashion forward style channels effortless elegance, to create dreamy and luxurious images which candidly capture your wedding day. Visit taliphotography.com and Instagram @tali__photography

22. LITTLE MISS BOYCO is a wedding photographer based in the Northeast of England and available to travel worldwide. Wiesia approaches her photography with a relaxed and natural style, with a focus on capturing the emotions of the couple and their guests. She creates a story of the day through her images so her clients can relive the feelings of their wedding day. Visit www.littlemissboyco.co.uk and Instagram @littlemissboyco

23. Photographer **AMY LOU** enchants couples and guests alike with her romantic style. Amy is passionate about genuine connections, shooting creative, contemporary couples across the UK. Those looking for relaxed, warm captures of intimate moments need search no more. Find her on amylouphotography.co.uk or Instagram @amylouphotography

24. JO GREENFIELD is an elopement photographer and filmmaker based in the Lake District with a passion for adventurous couples who love the outdoors. Visit www.jogreenfield.com and Instagram @jogreenfieldthephotographer

TO APPEAR ON THESE PAGES, CONTACT 020 7152 3705 OR EMAIL CLASSVOGUE@CONDENAST.CO.UK

A Very Vogue Wedding

25. LAUREN YOUNG is a destination wedding photographer based in Australia. With a background in fashion and beauty photography, Lauren captures the golden moments of your wedding day in a timeless and elegant way. These images captured on digital and film mediums are memories that can be cherished for many years to come. Visit www.laurenyoungphotography.com.au and @laurenyoung.weddings on Instagram.

26. VANESSA & IVO are a duo of filmmakers and photographers, passionate about creating artistic, intimate and cinematic images, with an editorial twist. Specialised in destination weddings, their art takes them to incredible weddings all over Europe and the rest of the world. Visit vanessaivo.com and Instagram @vanessaivofilms

27. PAUL AND NANDA are a British-Brazilian husband and wife team who seek to capture warm and romantic narratives for each wedding they shoot. Their respectful, storytelling style focuses on the uniqueness of each couple, creating timeless images across the UK and beyond. Visit www.paulandnanda.com and Instagram @paulandnanda

28. Portraying timeless elegance with an editorial aesthetic and emotive approach, **MASHA UNWERTH** draws her inspiration from black and white photography, fashion and modern art. She is passionate about storytelling and visual celebration preserving a wedding day story with pure artistry, raw emotion and love. Visit unwerth.co.uk and Instagram @masha.unwe

29. BRAUTLY has affordable designs and mix and match styles helping you feel unique, 100% you and proud to be a bride. With over 20 years experience in the bridal business and lots of passion for bridal fashion this brand is women-led and launched just last year. Find easy and ready to wear civil wedding pieces and bridal accessories. Visit www.brautly.de and Instagram @brautly.de

30. A husband and wife team who began filming weddings as a passion project, **FINESHAD FILMS** bring you luxury destination wedding photography and videography. Established in 2017, the duo capture weddings with a playful and elegant style. Danielle expresses the nuances of emotions and connections shown on a wedding day in a whirlwind between sunris and sunset, meanwhile Martin brings a meticulous, detail driven quality to their work and an impressive background in music technology. Visit www.fineshadefilms.co.uk and Instagram @fineshadefilms

31. UK and Destination wedding photographer **AMY WOODHAM PHOTOGRAPHY** specialises in vibrant, passionate and joyous photography for people in love. Her work echoes with all of the raw and honest moments from a wedding day, which make for the most treasure and romantic photographs. Visit www.amywoodhamphotography.com ar Instagram @amywoodham_photography

32. Based in Sussex, **LAUREN BETH PHOTOGRAPHY** creates timeless images that tell the story of your wedding day. Capturing your day naturally as it unfolds, Lauren photographs the special moments yo will hold in your memories for a lifetime. Find out more: www.laurenbethphotography.co.uk Instagram: @lauren.beth.photograp

33. CHARLOTTE GRIFFITHS PHOTOGRAPHY captures exceptional images for the modern couple. Based in Hampshire, availab throughout the UK and worldwide, her style blends candid emotion, elegance and romance, resulting in a timeless and chic collection that perfectly encapsulates your day. With an editorial feel and attention to detail, Charlotte perfectly captures the essence of your wedding, providing beautifully preserved memories. Visit charlottegriffithsphotography.com and follow on Instagram @charlottegriffithsphotographer

34. LIVIFAITH PHOTOGRAPHY is a Destination Wedding photographe based in the US. With a storytelling approach, she captures your day exactly it unfolds leaving you with authentic and meaningful images. Her portraits have personality, are creative, and contain candid and emotional interactions Available in the US and worldwide. Visit www.livifaithphotography.com and Instagram @livifaithphoto

35. IN LIEBE GEHÜLLT is a bridal concept store for modern and roman bridal looks. They stand for romance and elegance with a touch of casualnes For timeless, playful and delicate looks visit www.in-liebe-gehuellt.de and Instagram @inliebegehuellt

36. LOUISE GOLDING PHOTOGRAPHY's effortlessly elegant style captures natural, soulful, authentic moments whilst blending them with an edge of editorial glamour. Based in Portugal and travelling worldwide, Louise captures the love stories of the modern romantics. Visit www.louisegolding.com and Instagram @louisegoldingphotography

37. IMOGEN & JAMES capture cinematic wedding films in the dreamy and emotive signature style of videographer Frances McMahon. With an emphasis o unobtrusive filming and small details, Frances brings a unique style of visual storytelling. View her latest work at www.imogenandjames.com and Instagram @imogenandjamesfilms

38. Founded by Dominik Scherer, **EMOTIONAL PERSPECTIVE** developed a unique approach to photography which is more than anything about pictures that combine feelings with art. You will fall in love with how Dominik lets his heart speak through his camera! He is also dedicated to offer the most emotional Super 8 vintage films. Visit www.emotionalperspective.com and Instagram @emotionalperspective

39. CÉCILE DE FLEUR was created for the non-traditional bride. Inspired by sexy negligees, their sustainable wedding party dresses transcend long after your big day is over. The collection showcased, Vol. I Rebirth of the Goddess, expresses the death and rebirth that the brand represents, reminding women going through challenges they will transform like a butterfly with patience. 1% of every purchase will be donated to the Tree Sisters Organisation. Visit ceciledefleur.com and Instagram @ceciledefleur

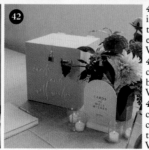

40. SALLY PINERA is a luxurious destination wedding photographer who is internationally acclaimed, award winning and specialises in high end weddings aroun the world for distinguished clients with high taste. Her style is contemporary, elevated classic photography that is editorial, elegantly candid and fashion forward. Visit sallypinera.com and Instagram @SallyPinera

41. AULINE-JEAN is the classical singer of the moment. The gift of together choosing the live soundtrack to enhance your day is her unique magic. Auline-Jean's breathtaking voice will be the soundtrack to the best day of your life. Visit auline-jean.com or email eventsajm@gmail.com

42. SIGNED BY G elevate your events to the next level with their bespoke collection. From table stationery to table numbers, welcome signs, seating charts, place cards and more, each piece is created with love and care to add the perfect finishing touch to any occasion and leave your guests speechless. Visit www.signedbyg.com and Instagram @signed_byg

Next Generation

Premium Danish brand **BIBS** is creating stylish essentials for children aged 0-3 years. Scandinavian in aesthetic, their dummies and baby accessories are available in a wide range of colours and are made from quality materials with the highest regard for sustainability, functionality and safety. Visit bibsworld.com and follow @theofficialbibs on Instagram.

EISSA & JUDE is a Kuwaiti wooden toy brand made to nurture children's imagination, creativity, and expression. Their philosophy focuses on translating the Middle East into play through imaginative creations. The toys are designed and produced by local talents using natural and sustainable materials. Visit eissa-jude.com and @eissa_jude on Instagram for more.

MATANA ORGANICS' vita rich sugar scrub is infused with organic sugar cane crystals, pure vitamin C and turmeric. This natural body scrub is designed to gently exfoliate leaving skin feeling softer, silkier, smoother and more supple. Explore more at matanaorganics.com and @matanaorganics on Instagram.

HONEY CAKE TIGER believes that together we have the power to make a difference to leave a rad planet for our future generations. Crafted ethically in California, their cosy, all-seasons organic collections are made with gender-neutrality in mind. Explore honeycaketiger.com and join them on Instagram @honeycaketiger

DIDRIKSONS' 'Ben' vest and trousers are both cool and cosy with Sherpa fleece and quilting. The insulation is made of recycled fibres and the lining has been dyed using Solution Dye, with PFC-free water repellent finish. This technique saves up to 80% water compared to conventionally dyed polyester/polyamide fabric. Explore more at didriksons.com and @didriksons on Instagram.

LIDA STUDIO creates hand-woven and embroidered clothing using traditional natural dyes and fabrics. With a focus on 'ahimsa' philosophy, they use peace silk to enhance sustainability, and create each piece to represent the birth of a butterfly. To explore their story, visit lidastudio.com and @lidastudio_ on Instagram.

AND SO IT BEGAN is a small Scottish brand creating luxury baby and children's wear. Specialising in hand cut and sewn baby sleepsuits with matching muslins, the range consists of classic hand painted prints created from the softest organic cotton fabrics. Visit andsoitbegan.co.uk and follow @andsoitbegan_ on Instagram.

CLOTH CLUB is bringing beauty and simplicity to the modern cloth nappy. Designed with love and first-hand experience, Cloth Club's innovative and ethically made reusable nappies are easy-to-use and essential for the sustainably stylish parent. Visit clothclub.com.au and @clothclub._ on Instagram. Shot by @rubinalucas.

JUNIPER STUDIO have a passion for treasuring the small things in life, crafting bespoke keepsakes, décor and gifts for families to look back on and treasure for generations to come. Based on the Hampshire Surrey border, they pride themselves on the sustainability and longevity of the memories they help create. Visit juniperstudio.co.uk and follow on Instagram @juniperstudiouk

9. The 'Matchy-Matchy' Beanies made by **JOLI NOUS** are an elegant and eco-friendly must-have for the whole family. Knitted in Switzerland from Italian Cashwool®, they are available in several sizes and unisex colours, and are OEKO-TEX, RWS and GRS certified. Visit jolinous.ch and follow @joli_nous on Instagram.

11. MILIN are a European company that crafts exquisite wooden toys to both entertain and teach through a world of imagination. They dedicate their toys to conscientious parents who are looking for ecological, educational toys made of only high quality materials. Explore their world at milin.pl and @milin_toys on Instagram.

12. LITTLE LADY EMPIRE creates timeless clothing that is unique and sophisticated. Produced in Australia by some of the leading, most experienced seamstresses, owner Jiji Darwiche aims to maintain quality and longevity, treating every garment as an art piece that can last for generations. Visit littleladyempire.com and follow @littlelady_empire on Instagram for more.

13. HEIRESS COUTURE NIGERIA creates stylish fairytale outfits that will make all of your dreams come true. They offer a wide range of luxury ballgowns for your princesses, charming outfits for little princes, and a 'Mum and Me' collection. Visit heiresscouturenigeria.com and follow @heiresscouturenigeria on Instagram to view the full, exclusive collection.

14. Say hello to the **BUGABOO** Giraffe, the adjustable chair designed for all ages. Whether your child is relaxing, playing, or enjoying mealtime, the Bugaboo Giraffe is made for discovery, and the beautiful, timeless design makes it a perfect centrepiece for the heart of any home. Visit bugaboo.com and @bugaboouk on Instagram.

15. LITTLE LOVE BLANKETS offer a luxury range of car seat blankets to keep your little one soothed and warm while on the move. Designed so that the straps of the car seat pull through the blanket, all you have to do is wrap your little bundle up! Find out more on littleloveblankets.co.uk and @little_love_blankets on Instagram.

16. BOHO RAINBOW creates sustainable rattan and cane furniture for children, designed with love by mum and owner, Nesrine, and handcrafted by artisans in Indonesia. The timeless design has a fable-like style, from cots to wardrobes, as well as exquisite organic cotton canopies from India and brass wall decor handmade in Morocco. Explore this world of beautiful children's pieces on bohorainbow.com and @boho_rainbow on Instagram.

17. The new **ICANDY** Core has been expertly designed for every journey; a truly ground-breaking new pushchair crafted by the iconic British company. Adaptable for every age and stage of a child's development, the exquisite new design showcases striking styling and cutting-edge features such as the pioneering Multi-Mode Wheelbase and LED Visibility Hub Light. Explore icandyworld.com and @icandyworlduk on Instagram.

Next Generation

18. With classic sartorial style, **COCO & IVES**' distinguished silhouettes are informed by the structure of iconic British and French fashion. Manufactured by some of the world's oldest and most renowned mills, they craft functional and elevated pieces designed for the everyday. Explore @cocoandives on Instagram and use code VOGUE for 20% off your first order at cocoandives.com (Expires 31/01/2023).

19. **HUGGABEAU** offers linen dolls with a capsule wardrobe that reflects modern children's fashion. Designed by Bo, a mama dreaming up stylish pieces that compliment minimalistic décor, their heirloom quality Loveys are ethically handmade in Canada using sustainable fabrics. Visit huggabeau.com and follow @huggabeau on Instagram.

20. **NATALIE ROWLEY** is a lifestyle photographer focusing on maternity, newborn and families. Natalie's gentle and friendly nature puts her clients at ease, ensuring she captures intimate, authentic photos and the true essence of her subjects. Covering London, Dorset and surrounding areas, Natalie specialises in photographing families in the comfort of their homes or sentimental locations. Visit natalierowleyphotography.com and follow @natalie.rowley on Instagram to view more examples of her wholesome, artistic work.

21. Mother, Creator, Image Taker, Light Follower, Memory Maker, Enthusiast of all Loves. **YAZMINE MAY** is a luxury family and wedding photographer, based in Bath/ Bristol UK and willing to travel pretty much anywhere to capture all stages of love. Her gift to you is an heirloom of art to pass down and treasure forever. Visit yazminemay.com and follow @yazminemayphotography on Instagram to view more of her raw emotive work.

22. **CARAMELLA** offer complete nursery design to transform your dreams in to reality. Elegant and timeless furniture and accessories of the highest quality, visit caramellainteriors.com to view the range and follow on Instagram @caramella_interiors

23. **OAK AND DAGGER** was established in 2020 by mum of two boys, Tyler Davis, to provide timeless clothing that captures the sweetness and simplicity of childhood. Oak and Dagger is made for every adventure, with every little wanderer in mind. Visit oakdagger.com and @oakdagger on Instagram.

24. **POLISHED PRINTS** is a mum-owned lifestyle brand bringing high-quality, ethically made clothes to everyone. Made of 100% organic cotton, the timeless designs spread messages of kindness, love, and acceptance, while also being kind to your skin. Use code 15VOGUE for 15% off (expires 15/12/22) at polished-prints.com and @polishedprints on Instagram. Shot by @wrightphotographs

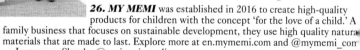
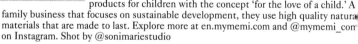

25. **NARZBABY** is a home-based, family-owned, and operated baby boutique in New York. Narzbaby carries baby apparel and accessories that are of exceptional quality, lovingly-made, and long-lasting whether it is for your first child or your last. Visit narzbaby.com and follow @narzbaby on Instagram.

26. **MY MEMI** was established in 2016 to create high-quality products for children with the concept 'for the love of a child.' A family business that focuses on sustainable development, they use high quality natural materials that are made to last. Explore more at en.mymemi.com and @mymemi_com on Instagram. Shot by @sonimariestudio

27. **FIN & VINCE** presents "Dreamer's World", an autumn/winter collection full of magic dust, adventure and imagination, sustainably made in Portugal and Peru. Jump into their whimsical world created for the dreamer and begin collecting moments. Shop at www.finandvince.com and follow @finandvince on Instagram.

28. **JACK DAVIS APPAREL** is an American brand featuring buttery soft organic cotton clothing with hand drawn prints by Brittany, a busy mum of two, focused on creating versatile and trendy basics for active boys (NB to 4T). Visit www.jackdavisapparel.com and follow @jackdavisapparel on Instagram, or email hello@jackdavisapparel.com for wholesale inquiries.

29. "Sparking imaginations through sleep and play!" **LITTLE SNOOZES** is an award winning children's furniture company boasting modern Scandinavian and adventurous styles. Their collection of stunning themed beds will revolutionise bedtimes whilst providing a safe and comfortable night's sleep. Visit littlesnoozes.co.uk and follow @littlesnoozes on Instagram.

30. **MY B** offer a curated selection of unique and stylish baby and children's clothing which capture cosy comfort and timeless simplicity that they can adventure in all day. To explore more, such as the Mummy and Me collection, visit mybkids.com and follow @mybkids.official on Instagram.

31. The perfect Christmas gift! **TINY ART** turns children's drawings into personalised modern art, exquisitely created by designers with an eye for detail. The work of your little artist will never be forgotten but have pride of place in your home. Create your own at tinyart.love/en and follow @tiny.art.prints on Instagram for more inspiration.

32. **INITIAL BAG CO.** is an Australian brand offering a premium range of personalised backpacks for you and your mini. Choose from a stylish collection of luxe colours in plush, teddy fabric with gold accent details which can be mix and matched with your choice of coloured initials. A unique gift customised with their first initial, these bags support letter recognition and are made for endless adventures. Visit www.initialbagco.com and @initialbagco on Instagram to view the collection.

MINI & MAE creates the softest Quilt Heirloom Playmats for ur little one, that can turn into a blanket and even a beautiful ll-hanging. Made from sustainable linen and filled with organic ton fleece, they are inspired by nature and ethically handcrafted in rmany. Visit miniandmae.com and @miniandmaeoffical Instagram.

TINY TEA – KIDS TEA is changing the way your mischief kers quench their thirst- and their imagination. Packed with perfoods and vitamins, this tea aims to help little bodies and minds ive and is made for even the fussiest little ones, in four fantastic vours. Explore the collection at tinyteakids.com.au and iny.tea.kids on Instagram.

. Ethical, sustainable, cosy and easy. **OAKS** was created by a ther who envisioned a better tomorrow for her children. Oaks' articles are made to mix and match ch each neutral piece having been carefully and lovingly designed with your children in mind. At ks, they believe that the quality and design of your children's clothing can impact the way they l. So let them be little and run free. Visit www.oaksdeeplyrooted.com and follow @Ohheyoaks Instagram.

MIMUBY is a clothing brand focused on gender-neutral and sustainable baby and children's clothing. Designed in rmany, each piece is produced in Portugal from soft organic cotton and is ko-Tex certified. This kind-to-skin collection is made for adventuring, and n be found at mimuby.de and @mimubykids on Instagram.

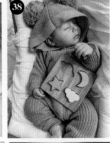

ULLABELLE baby products are inspired by California sunsets and are eated for modern parents who value practicality and timeless aesthetics. For autiful, high quality products you can cherish for generations to come, visit abellebaby.com and @ullabelle on Instagram.

THE NEUTRAL NURSERY is a children's boutique that provides fted wooden toys, exquisite nursery and children's room décor and ontessori learning products, as well as a beautiful Mama and Me clothing llection. Visit a world of imagination and nostalgia at theneutralnursery.net d @the.neutral.nursery on Instagram.

TENDER LEAF TOYS create quality wooden toys, made to last with a etime of love. Designed in the UK, made from renewable rubber tree wood, and nd-finished by skilled craftsmen in Indonesia, these timeless pieces will endlessly spire the imagination. Find out more on tenderleaftoys.co.uk and @tenderleaftoys Instagram.

GRIMM'S handcrafts open-ended wooden toys for all ages: from rattles and aspers for babies to huge building sets for older children and adults. Made from tural materials, their toys promote an early understanding of quality. Browse the alogue at www.grimms.eu/en and shop the products at ww.kidly.co.uk/brands/grimms Find them @grimmswoodentoys on Instagram.

. Inspired by the coastal lifestyle of Byron Bay, **BAREFOOT BABY USTRALIA** brings baby and toddler's wear back to basics, offering unique designs r those looking for premium quality and durable clothing for their precious venturers. Visit www.barefootbabyaustralia.com and follow @barefoot_baby_australia on Instagram.

Vogue's Gallery

DANUTA JAGEMANN is a German artist based in Frankfurt. She is influenced by the beauty of nature in er artworks and fascinated by structured surfaces and metallic accents in copper, gold or bronze. The varied rtfolio and further information can be found at www.jagemann-art.com or email jagemann.art@gmail.com llow @jagemann_art on Instagram.

ELIZABETH WOLD creates abstract objects inspired by rust, decay, and abandoned things. Exploring the otential of processes and mediums, the paintings are grown from accretion, time, and experiences. See more Elizabeth's work at www.elizabethwold.art and follow @elizabethwold.art on Instagram.

ANDREW BIRKS is a British multidisciplinary artist, working primarily in oil on canvas, and sculpture sing tagua nut. In these 'paintings of paint', figurative elements act as visual anchors, sampling presentations in otherwise entirely abstract works on the themes of love, death and allegory. Visit ww.andrewbirksart.com and Instagram @birksworks

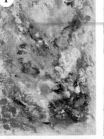

HOUSE OF HUSSEY aims to add intrigue and vibrancy to your home, spiring your interior journey with colourful, original artworks and limited edition ints. Co-founded by painter and set decorator Kimmy Hussey, alongside her usband Joshua Hussey, the studio focuses on colour psychology, palettes within e natural world and carefully selected, creative collaborations. Watch this space! isit houseofhussey.co.uk and follow their Instagram @houseofhusseyonline

JENNI MÄKI is a Nordic female artist, who has had her first art exhibition uring this autumn. This artist is inspired by nature, emotions, people and the resent moment. Her artwork is predominantly about freedom – freedom in the owing act of painting, using colour and brushstrokes. The direction and erspective of her work is never decided beforehand. Visit galleryartonline.com/jenni-maki and follow @jennilaurelina_paints on Instagram.

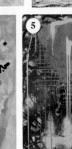
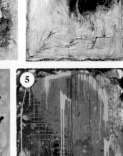

CHRIS KAMPRAD lives in Berlin as a freelance self-taught painter. She has en working in her studio, in Prenzlauer Berg. In her mostly bstract, colourful paintings, she searches for atmospheric lationships within certain colours, structures and light spectra. xpressive, accentuated shapes enter into dialogue with calmer, alanced reductions. Visit www.chriskamprad.art and follow artci.la on Instagram

JUDY CANTILLON COLLINS is an artist living on the South ast of Ireland. Her paintings are inspired by the seen and the agined. From the mystical side of the landscape to the fierce eauty of the ocean. This artist captures the barren yet beautiful ndscape, windswept and wild yet peaceful and perfect. isit judycantillonart.ie and follow @irishartbyjudy on Instagram.

Vogue's Gallery

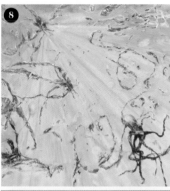

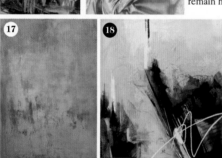

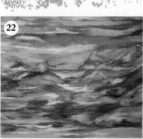

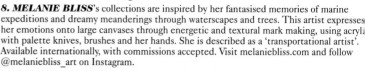

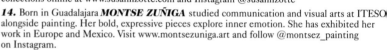

Czech abstract artist **JANETTE DE LA COLETTE** creates a variety of abstract art. She draws inspiration from her life, travelling, nature and history. Reality wasn't enough for this artist, so she created her own world. Art followed her throughout her life in whatever form it has taken, such as painting, drawing, photography and designing. Visit www.janettedelacolette.com and follow @janettedelacolette on Instagram.

IRENA BOOBYER is an award-winning Devon based artist, who creates bespoke papercuts from sketches, photographs, text, imagery and discussions with clients. 'Time and Tide', is an original hand-cut papercut inspired by coastal tranquillity. Using traditional single and double-fold techniques and skilful scissor work, Irena has created this original design. See irenaboobyer.co.uk for more. Irena is available for commissions. Follow @irenaboobyerpapercutting on Instagram.

DIANE HOLLAND is a San Fransisco-based, international artist. In her award-winning 'Mona Lisa Variations #01', she liberates the iconic 16th century Mona Lisa from her confinement, into a joyous, unique, modern portrait. Visit dianehollandart.com Instagram: @dianehollandart

AVRIL EGAN is an Irish artist and illustrator. Her art can be described as a triumph in perspective. These works are recognisable at a distance, due to the particular attention given to layering textures, detailing and personification. Visit her website eganart1997.wixsite.com/eganart and follow on Instagram @EganArt1997 or contact her via email eganart1997@gmail.com

EVA HENDRIKS is a Dutch artist who is Inspired by the flow of the elements, with wind and water as a metaphor for life. The fluidity, constant movement and change. She works with raw and natural materials, transforming them into elegant and graceful artworks which show their strength and softness, awakening our senses and exploring the art with our inner child. An earth tone palette and minimalistic approach are her nature. Visit www.evahendriks.com or on Instagram @eva_hendriks_art to view her work.

American Artist **LILY PERRY** creates bold and engaging paintings through a free experimental process. She paints with different mediums including acrylic, house paint, graphite, sharpies and pastels. She often adds unexpected elements such as glass or duct tape to her work and enjoys exploring contrast and scale. Her work can be found in galleries and private collectors' homes internationally. Find out more at lilyperryfineart.com and follow along @lilyperryfineart on Instagram.

LO HENNESSEY is a Massachusetts-based artist and Doctor of Physical Therapy. She specialises in oil, acrylic, and watercolour paintings inspired by her education, travels and imagination. Her work is characterised by vibrant colours, loud vision, and anatomical distortion. Learn more at www.LoHennyArt.com and Instagram @LoHennessey

The geometric abstractionism in **FABÍOLA SEGER KOLLING**'s work is subtle. Lines that meet by points of the composition create new geometric forms. The colours, always minimal, balance in contraposition. The point, always present, makes an allusion to Wassily Kandinsky's interpretation. Visit www.spectrogirl.com and follow @tetraktys5

Dutch Artist **ANGELIEN PETERS** is a free spirit. Her artworks are radiant, reflecting womanhood. Colourful and rich, these paintings evoke feelings of curiosity from the viewer. Her masks disguise contemporary life with a range of patterns and motifs. She is fascinated by the eyes and inspired by the beauty of nature and fashion. Visit www.angelienpeters.nl and follow @angelienpetersart on Instagram.

BUKOLA DAGILOKE is a British born, Nigerian award winning contemporary artist who uses her work to express and address concepts around race, identity and nature to create artwork that communicates powerful messages that might otherwise have gone unsaid. Her collection of original paintings is available at www.bukoladagiloke.com and Instagram @arts.by.kola

AURELIJA PESTENE is a Lithuanian artist based in Denmark with a bachelors degree in photography. She works with mixed media art. Her work is about time flow, change and memories, that are expressed through a unique combination of photography and pointillism. To find out more about this artist visit www.onthedotart.com or follow @aurelijapestene on Instagram.

Contemporary New York-based painter **MELISSA SCHAINKER** creates figurative/surrealist works from her studio in Tribeca. Her work has been exhibited in gallery and museum shows across the globe. Seen here is her recent oil painting, titled 'Emancipation'. Learn more about her work www.mschainkerfineart.com and follow @mschainkerfineart on Instagram.

NIGEL PROUD is a UK based portrait artist using charcoal and black/white pastel to enable him to capture a range of emotions. See how the musician becomes as one with the saxophone, truly lost in that magical moment as the melodies are transferred down his fingers. See his work www.nigelsportraits.co.uk and Instagram @nigels_portraits

KATRINA KOLTES grew up travelling worldwide, and is now a full-time artist based in Italy. Her paintings are a vivid expression of colour and light with striking contrasts, delving into mystical and magical worlds. She aims to inspire through soul expression, encouraging others to find their inner power and magic. Explore her online and exhibited works at www.katrinakoltes.com and on Instagram @katrinakoltes

STROKE OF A BRUSH British artist Josianne Cross is mainly an impressionistic artist whose heart lies with the skies. Her passion is painting land and seascapes inspired by memories, whilst also exploring realism. Her work aims to capture the viewer with the evocative emotion within. Visit www.strokeofabrush.co.uk Follow @stroke_ofabrush

LULU POPHAM is an oil and acrylic artist based in Hemyock, Devon. Lulu paints landscape and abstract landscape paintings along with seascapes, exquisite trees and local gardens. She recently exhibited for Devon Open Studios 2022. Commissions available. Visit www.artbylulu.co.uk email lulu.popham@btinternet.com and follow @art_by_lulu on Instagram.

REIF MYERS is a 30 year old artist who has been exhibiting for 11 years. Reif has developed his own style of modern art, combining bright colours and humour through his signature icons. His work is best described as art to be enjoyed rather than analysed. Ships worldwide. Visit www.reifmyersartist.com Instagram: @reifaxl

MAJA GRECIC is a UK based artist that forged her skills studying at Belgrade University of Arts in Serbia. Most of the paintings she painted over the years had an abstract etiquette, but were always based on elements from reality that appeared as fragments and symbols, more or less visible. It is always her personal experience and emotion that is a source of ideas for her next work. Visit majagrecicart.com Instagram: @mayasageisnow

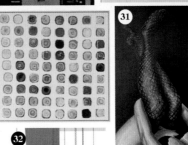

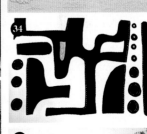

Vogue's Dream Home

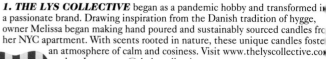

1. THE LYS COLLECTIVE began as a pandemic hobby and transformed into a passionate brand. Drawing inspiration from the Danish tradition of hygge, owner Melissa began making hand poured and sustainably sourced candles from her NYC apartment. With scents rooted in nature, these unique candles foster an atmosphere of calm and cosiness. Visit www.thelyscollective.com and on Instagram @thelyscollective

2. Inspired by Danish pastel design, bold colour clashes and abstract patterns, the **ZEBRA KNITS** 'Knitted Knot Cushion' is perfect for any room in the home. Available in two sizes, these bright and bold cushions are versatile and unknot for a unique cushion experience like no other. Explore the latest collection at www.zebraknits.com and on Instagram @zebraknits

3. STUDIO GABRIELLE is led by award-winning designer Louise Parker, who has a wealth of experience in the worlds of design and architecture. This year she's extended the business to launch a signature furniture range, including the La Gràce headboard, which we love in statement red-and-white stripes. To explore more of the collection visit www.studiogabrielle.co.uk or follow on Instagram @studiogabrielleuk

4. BARNBURY is a unique homeware and furnishings brand based in the Cotswolds. Jonathan Parkin and Jonathan Sellwood combine their creative talent to curate collections from around the world, including pure wool throws, luxury home fragrances, unique gifts, lighting and home accessories. Visit their showroom or shop online at www.barnbury.com and Instagram @barnbury

5. British brand **GRACE COLE** is the undiscovered gem of the Luxury Bathing world, offering pure, unapologetic luxury for your every day. Their indulgent bath, body and home fragrance products are available in six fragrances, designed and developed in England alongside world-class Perfumers. Use code 'VOGUE20' for 20% off sitewide (expires 15/11/22). Visit www.gracecole.co.uk

6. FLOREY CERAMICS is a U.S. based ceramic design studio creating a variety of sculptural and functional porcelain objects. Cubic abstractions of traditional ceramic forms, intersecting art, craft, and design. Each Slip-casted porcelain vessel is sculpted, sanded and refined by hand then fired to 2200 f. Explore more work online at www.floreyceramics.com and Instagram @floreyceramics

7. Discover the luxurious, eco-conscious candles, melts, and diffusers by **ARTESAO** an Australian brand founded in Sydney by designer Tanya Pillay. Hand-poured candles and home décor statement pieces made for every moment, with signature fragrances reminiscent of beautiful memories and olfactive experiences. Artesao products are non-toxic, vegan and cruelty free. Visit: www.artesao.com.au Instagram: @artesao__

8. ST. BROWN & CO. is a luxury California candle brand, consciously hand poured with vegan wax and non-toxic fragrance oils. The Frankincense + Myrrh is a Holiday favourite with its elevated musky holy aroma and crackling wooden wick. Follow @stbrownco on Instagram and shop at stbrownco.com

9. Ceramicist **LEO WONG** sculpts his characteristic flowers by hand, embracing the Japanese aesthetic tradition of Wabi-Sabi, accepting transience and imperfection. His background as an arborist informs the bespoke botanical objects that add a unique touch to any home. Find out more at www.la-ceramique.com and @leowongceramics

10. Inspired by the 1900's, comfortable in the 50's and reaching for the stars in the 21st century, these cosmic plant stands are crafted using Birch plywood. Based in London, **DOTTYPIX** are two designer makers who imagine and create objects that appeal to their aesthetics of minimal yet meaningful. Visit dottypix.co.uk and Instagram @dottypix.uk

11. IRIS LIFESTYLE brings together elegant + timeless, planet-conscious homewares to inspire slow living; responsibly-made artisanal pieces of excellent quality designed for longevity, using certified sustainable, ecological materials, fabrics + fibres… each with a story to tell. Instagram @iris.home.lifestyle and visit www.irislifestyle.store

12. FRANKIE CERAMICS is an independent studio in Suffolk specialising in hand thrown, bespoke ceramics strongly driven by shape and texture. Her distinctive colours are easily recognisable due to her own handcrafted glazes, formed from raw materials. From tablescaping to stunning sculptural centrepieces, Frankie's unique designs are made to order. Shop online at www.frankieceramics.com and follow on Instagram @frankieceramics

13. REX DESIGN ROOM is an upholstery, furniture and interior design studio. Designing one of a kind furniture pieces, taking a fresh look at how to reimagine your home with a planet conscious approach. Explore more, commission a piece and shop the "Dopamine" collection at www.rexdesignroom.co.uk and Instagram @rexdesignroom

14. Impact label **MOTHER** is on a mission to create sustainable products for better living. They make plant care easy with this timeless and modular green wall design. The integrated grow lights take care of your plants throughout all seasons. Create your own indoor forest. Visit www.mother.life and follow them on Instagram @mother.life.official

15. Elle chair armrest by Nataša Perković. **GOES** is an award-winning, design-oriented manufacturer that transforms solid wood into contemporary products. Their products present a reflection of the designer's vision, and they are here for a reason – to make your personal space more magical. Visit www.goes.ba and @goesfurniture

16. STUDIO CLAY was born out of founder, Noura Al Dhaheri's vision to educate and engage the curiosity of others about all aspects of pottery. Her studio is an open space so every stage of the process is purposely visible. By Studio CLAY is composed of 4 different collections, aiming to immortalise Emirati culture through ceramics and storytelling. The Midas Collection symbolises both humble origins and luxury and like 'Midas' a golden touch to epitomise affluence and strength. Visit: www.studioclay.ae to view the full collections. Instagram: @studioclay.ae

HALAROSIS is a New York based home fragrance company that is dicated to creating safe, clean, and effective formulations. The company s phthalate-free, essential oil infused fragrances to create soy wax dles, wax melts, and air + fabric fresheners that feature room-filling nt. Explore the collection at www.halarosis.com or Instagram @halarosis

ROSIE DALIA is a London based interiors and lifestyle boutique ering distinctive and colourful pieces for your home and wardrobe. turing handmade linens and homeware that create moments of magic und the table. Discover more at www.rosiedalia.com and tagram @rosiedaliacollection

Multidisciplinary artist *JULIANA MAURER* pushes against reasing alienation from nature with Stena, a hand-blown glass carafe ch makes use of the thermal function of soapstone. Rough, unworked he juxtaposes fragile-looking glass to make the carafe a sculptural nt even when empty. Every piece is handmade and unique. Find out re at www.julianamaurer.de and @julijanamaurer

At *LA CUSHIONS*, all orders are handmade using only the best lity materials and luxurious feather inserts, to ensure your cushions nd out from the rest. Discount code: VOGUE15 (valid until 31/12/22). inspiration be sure to check out: www.lacushions.co.uk and ow @lacushions

H+E GOODS COMPANY is a Los Angeles based home decor and ign store. Their carefully curated collection celebrates the work of master sans around the world and features a variety of handwoven vintage rugs, uthblown glassware, baskets, towels and more. Learn more at w.handegoodscompany.com and follow their journey @he_goodscompany

MESSY BY MAHLIA is a handmade ceramic brand, born in Byron Bay stralia. Their key foundations are creativity, sustainability, playfulness and nection, with an aim to make statement pieces that last and bring joy to r home. Find out more at www.messybymahlia.com l @messy.by.mahlia

Handpicked rustic décor by *FOX AND BEAU* offers a unique and eless collection of home accessories and interior inspiration. Based in ckinghamshire they are inspired by their surroundings which reflect oughout their brand and products. Visit www.foxandbeaushop.com and ow on Instagram @foxandbeau

Did you know there are 100s of ways to transform your home using yl? From kitchen surfaces to tables, windows, walls and more. That's NNIE & BOLD understand environment affects everything. y they help thousands of customers re-energise living spaces to uplift i inspire. Shop wallpaper and vinyl at: www.bonnieandbold.co.uk tagram: @bonnieandbold

AMII CERAMICS are handmade, functional, sculptural vessels. signed in Canada for collectors with the focus of brightening up interior ces. As seen at the 1000 Vases exhibition, Paris in September 2022. Visit amiiceramics.com stagram: @amii.ceramics

PIPER & OAK is a Canadian lifestyle boutique where functionality and style merge, offering simple uries suitable for your everyday. Gifts, home décor, and furniture make timeless statements through ughtfully chosen textural elements and Scandinavian influences. Shop online at piperandoak.com and ow on Instagram @piperoak2016

SOPHIE MCILWAINE CERAMICS — Northern Irish Ceramicist Sophie Mcilwaine Ceramics creates ndmade mugs focusing on empowering people to celebrate their bodies. She has created commissions for men with breast cancer, mastectomies, stoma bags, insulin pumps and caesarean scars. She also creates ury homeware items with unique glazes to make a statement in your home. Visit at w.sophiemcilwaineceramics.com and follow on Instagram @sophiemcceramics

Colourful home living is the ethos of *RINI*, seeking to add unique lifestyle and homeware accessories to ur home. Based in London their candles are hand poured using eco-friendly, vegan and cruelty free terials, to shop their candles and other creative treasures visit www.rinistore.com or follow on stagram @rini.uk

LULLEVIBES, a bold young brand celebrating sustainability by creating travel towels made from 17 ycled plastic bottles and designed by artists from around the world. Ultra light, incredibly soft and mpact, LulleVibes towels are the go-to choice for the ultimate sustainable gift experience. Visit w.lullevibes.com or Instagram @lullevibes for more.

THE SUFFOLK NEST started as a passion project that has now bloomed into an inspirational mmerce business dedicated to all things floral. Owned by husband-and-wife team Chris and Ashlee, they ecialise in faux flowers, wreath kits and home décor, available for delivery nationwide. Visit at w.thesuffolknest.com and follow on Instagram @the_suffolk_nest

DIAPHANE CANDLES was founded in 2020 by architectural and set designer ca Petrescu. Sitting somewhere between a candle and a centrepiece, her pure eswax creations are guaranteed to light up any room in more ways than one. Offering a tainable alternative to paraffin, these candles release a delicate honeycomb scent and as natural air purifiers. Visit diaphanecandles.co.uk Instagram: @diaphane_candles

UK-based lighting experts Scarlett Hampton and Niki Wright founded GHTS&LAMPS to bring innovative, design-led lighting solutions to the UK lighting rket. Their lighting collections offer something for everyone and their extensive owledge of materials and construction means every product is well-designed, offering e best value and quality across a broad range of contemporary styles. Find out more at w.lightsandlamps.com and @lightsandlampsdotcom

PRETTY VIBE are a luxury artisan candle brand from South Wales. They use nt based, Coco Rapeseed wax and all products are vegan and cruelty free. They ieve in creating intentional living, by making your safe place calm, cosy, full of sitive memories and a vibe that you can feel and remember. Visit www.prettyvibe.co.uk and low on Instagram @prettyvibe.candles

NURACHE (Nura: Light, Che: God will increase) is a memoir of Kennedy Raye's nsnational sojourning. These coconut wax, cruelty-free, vegan luxe candles pour forth the ayers of her heart: abundant peace and blessings. Experience the light and warmth at w.nurache.com and @nuracheshop

Turn your living space into your happy place with *NUMBER 55 HOMEWARE*. A luxury me accessories brand that sells unique handmade resin coasters to pure crystal drinkware. own here are their new Christmas tree ornaments. If you want these elegant pieces in your me, shop online at number55homeware.co.uk or on Instagram @number55__

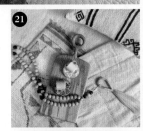

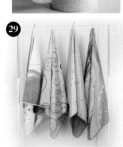

TO APPEAR ON THESE PAGES, CONTACT 020 7152 3705 OR EMAIL CLASSVOGUE@CONDENAST.CO.UK

Winter Wellness

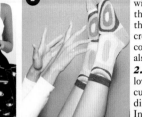

1. Complete your workout wardrobe and pump your personality into sweat sessions with Australian based, active accessories brand **REGENT RITUALS**. Mix or match their refreshing eco-conscious range of essentials and design your ideal set. Collect their bags, yoga mats, towels and bottles. This brand aims to empower women to create rituals that bring joy and improve wellbeing, while looking and feeling confident. Visit regentrituals.com and follow @regentrituals on Instagram. Products also available on theiconic.com.au and davidjones.com

2. Founded in 2020, **SOMATCHI** is a fun and cheerful accessory brand inspired by love and encounters. Their sustainably produced socks are designed to make their customers feel happy and positive when wearing them. They live by the motto 'a litt difference that makes big difference.' Visit www.somatchi.com and Instagram @somatchicom

3. CRADLE STUDIO blankets are beautifully crafted staple pieces for ever home. The long-lasting favourites have a sustainable value chain from cotton yarn to finished product. They are wonderfully soft, and available in a variety modern colours. The perfect gift for your loved ones (and of course, yourself) Visit cradle-studio.com Instagram @cradlestudio_home

4. Relax and unwind with **BOTANICAL BATH BLENDS** organic, carefully hand mixed botanical bath salts. This brand uses a divine blend of organic dri herbs, epsom salt and essential oils to enhance your bathing experience. Whether it is manifestation, celebration or relaxation in mind, shop now at linktr.ee/BotanicalBathBlends and follow @botanicalbathblends on Instagram

5. EVERYDAY CONNECTION, created by Alicia, encourages reflection an connection. The brand's hope is that their products help you on your journey, no matter what part of your life you are in right now. Whether it is journaling having open and honest conversations with your friends, taking care of yourse through your own version of self care. Visit www.everyday-connection.com Instagram: @everyday_connection

6. BASIC ECO designs stylish yet sustainable alternatives for the everyday. This brand offers a beautiful range of reusable pads and bamboo glass tumblers which are both highly durable and functional. Say goodbye to single use and switch to sustainable. Visit their website basicecostore.com and follow @basiceco.co on Instagram. Brand photography by Nikki Jones (@nikkijonesstudio on Instagram).

7. The **TAJII** water bottle is the ultimate reusable fashion hydration accessory. Its motivational messages and unique time markings provide gentle reminders throughout the day making it easy to stay hydrated, enabling you to practice self care as a priority. The sleek design combined with the BPA free plastic helps to make it lightweight, durable and drop resistant too. Visit tajii.com.au Instagram: @tajii_au

8. MOON SILK is a luxury beauty and lifestyle brand. Elevate your hair essentials with Moon Silk's hair ties. They help to protect your hair from kinks, breakage and snags and come in four different colou Create your own stack on moonsilkshop.com and follow @moonsilk_official on Instagram.

9. ST. EVAL – Whisk yourself away to a world of enchantment with playful characters and festive scents inspired by the magical Christmas season. Displayed with special gold and silver adornments, each candle tells a joyous festive story for the perfec gift. Certified B Corp. 10% discount code: VOGUE1 (expires 24/11/2022). Visit www.st-eval.com

10. Struggling to be more active? What better way t psych yourself than by getting a **SESES** yoga mat fo your home workouts. Seses have developed non-toxi eco-friendly, vegan suede yoga mats that are ultra-grippy and sweat absorbent. This brand have merged art, sustainability and performance into one. Shop at www.seses.store and get 15% off with the code VOGUE15 (expires 20/11/22). Follow on Instagram @seses_yogamats

11. Goodbye plastic bottles. Hello **BABY HAO'S PURIFYING WATER BOTTLE**. This stylish, eco-friendly bottle has a UV purification system that, at the touch of a button, eliminates up to 99.99% of bacteria, giving you clean, fresh tasting water anywhe anytime. An LED display screen for temperature display and reminder to drink function. Hello healthy hydration. Visit www.babyhao.com.au Instagram: @_babyhao

12. PURA COLLAGEN GLOW+ is a multi award-winning, powdered formula containing 10,000mg of the Bioactive Collagen Peptides® VERISOL®. It is designed to enhance the appearance of your hair, skin and nails. Take two scoops daily in your tea, coffee or smoothies fo optimum visible results. Shop online at puracollagen.co.uk

13. Wellness inspired by Mother Nature's Blueprint, **LANDKIND** is an entirely new class of sustainable supplements. They help you to feel healthier and more energetic without any of the byproducts that can be found in some other supplements. Visit www.landkind.health and follow @landkindhealth on Instagram

14. FELICIDADE yoga mats are visually stunning, eco-friendly yoga mats. They are all-in-one: yoga mat and towel, offering both the support of the yoga mat and absorption of the towel. These mats feel wonderfully soft and the prints are inspiring. Made to energise your practice. Durable and machine washable. Discover Felicidade, authentic yoga mat brand from Amsterdam at: www.studiofelicidade.co and follow @studiofelicidade

Vogue's Must-Haves

FIRETREE CHOCOLATE offer luxury sustainable dark chocolate, sourced from remote anic islands in the southern seas. The Firetree Luxury Collection contains seven single-estate etals in a stunning gift box. Ranging from 69% to 100% cocoa e collection is a true exploration in taste, much like fine wines. Gift Box contains 7 of their 65g multi-award-winning bars. p online at firetreechocolate.com and follow @firetreechocolate nstagram.

The latest addition to the **ILLIONAIRE SOCIETY** Reflective ection, the varsity jacket features the Illionaire World Logo in ective 3M on the back, with reflective and suede detailing on h sides of the front of the button down varsity jacket. The ective Strap Utility Pants are a perfect match, and feature the naire Society fonts in reflective 3M. The straps can be adjusted hange the look and fit of the pants according to how you feel. p online at illionairesociety.com and follow lionairesociety on Instagram.

NUDITEA is a small ethical brand based in the UK. sionately making delicious teas to give you little moments oy. Get 20% off with exclusive code 'VOGUE20' (expires 2.22) on www.nuditea.uk or follow their tea adventures Instagram @nuditea

Founder of **MOODLABBYLORRAINE** Lorraine Tam, ently won the Excellence and Best Visual Presentation ard at this year's Hong Kong Young Designer Competition h her collection 'I am not infected' which uses infrared erns and colours. Her standout item in the collection is "lung" shaped crossbody bag. Shop online at dlabbylorraine.com and follow @moodlabbylorraine Instagram.

SURREAL have taken the cereals you loved as a kid and reated them to be good for adults. Gone are the sugar and carb rloads – these tasty cereals are packed full of protein instead. ilable in four tasty flavours, SURREAL's the perfect breakfast midnight snack…) for your inner child. Visit eastsurreal.co.uk follow on Instagram @eat_surreal

44 FOODS is a pioneering online retailer redefining your food p. Nurturing a community of exceptional farmers and producers, nging you incredible quality with minimum waste. Discover rything you need for Christmas, from traditional roasts to treats gifts. Get £20 off when spending over £60 with code GUE20 (expires 31.12.22) at www.44foods.com and follow 4_foods on Instagram.

THE AUBURN COLLECTIONS is a small candle company ed in Texas with a wide range of scents, styles and gift boxes to ose from. Their focus is creating natural products that make r home smell amazing while being eco-friendly, vegan-friendly cruelty free. Shop online at theauburncollections.com and ow @theauburncollections on Instagram.

The **RUTLAND SQUARE GIN** unique Chai Spiced Gin ression is inspired by the refreshing and rich floral notes of long white tea sourced specially from the region of Dibrugarh, am. The aromatic and zesty lime adds citrus notes to the gin, dry Vetiver roots adds earthiness and dryness. The blend of erent tastes creates a softly spiced flavour profile with a kground hit of zesty citrus. Visit rutlandsquaregin.com and ow @rutlandsquaregin on Instagram.

VERITY MARSTON FLORAL DESIGN, renowned for utiful bespoke wreaths, are offering the opportunity for you to velop your own seasonal style at one of their workshops located in the nning Suffolk countryside with full tuition, equipment and gorgeous corations, November/December dates available. UK postal delivery for de to order wreaths. See all that is on offer online at veritymarston.co.uk follow @veritymarstonfloraldesign on Instagram.

. ANGUES, an exquisite liqueur that offers a unique drinking experience nks to the fresh fruit and its rustic crafting method. Contains no artificial youring and colouring, and only the finest quality ingredients are used en handcrafting this award winning (Great Gold medal – Spain IWSA and ver – USA Spirits Ratings) passion fruit liqueur. Shop online at gues.com and follow @angues.liquers on Instagram.

. EZRA OLIVE OIL produces cold-pressed olive oil, which is obtained m the early harvest green fruit of the olive trees grown without pesticides d fertilizers in the district of Mut, Turkey. This area has a microclimate ture and a high altitude, enriched with bitter almond and grass aromas. it ezraoliveoil.com.tr and follow @ezraoliveoil on Instagram.

. Esther Leslie founded ELLY HOME DECOR to help others de-stress and bring peace and llbeing into their homes. Her soy and coconut wax scented candles and pillows are handcrafted h love and beautifully packaged in her studio in Trinidad and Tobago. Her candles are available four sizes and nearly 40 scents. Use code Vogue15 for 15% off (expires 30/11/22). Photographer: cia Pierre. Visit ellyhomedecor.com and follow @ellyhomedecor on Instagram.

. GOOD IN BREAD delivers fresh artisan Sourdough loaves to your doorstep on a oscription or a la carte basis, always ensuring that you are receiving not only the best tasting ead but a wide variety of loaves, buns, rolls and bagels to suit every taste in your household. Use e VOGUE50 for 50% off your first subscription (expires 31.12.22). Order now at aregoodinbread.com and follow @goodinbreaduk on Instagram.

. This nut butter from KORO mixes festive flavours into a raw, nutty spread. Made without m oil, their cinnamon and vanilla almond butter is creamy and warming, best served drizzled er your breakfast on a cold winter morning. Get 5% off with the code ALMOND (expires 2/12/22). Shop online at koro-shop.co.uk and follow @koro_uk on Instagram.

. SWISH offers exquisite, expertly crafted ready-to-drink cocktails including both alcoholic d non-alcoholic ranges in a host of unique, experimental flavours. The deliciously bitter and tumnal "Breakfast Fizz" crafted with Premium Orange Spirit, Distillate of Toast, Clarified Pink apefruit and Orange Juices, evokes a happy memory of marmalade on toast. It's an absolute st-have this season. Use code VOGUE15 for a 15% discount, expires 30.11.2022. it swishcocktails.com and follow @swishcocktails on Instagram.

TO APPEAR ON THESE PAGES, CONTACT 020 7152 3705 OR EMAIL CLASSVOGUE@CONDENAST.CO.UK

Vogue's Must-Haves

16. Gift nature this Christmas. **SECRET GARDEN DISTILLERY** celebrates the wond of nature with its premium festive gin, where rich, spicy notes capture the essence of the season. Botanicals are hand-harvested and dried naturally, resulting in unique flavours and only the purest taste in every bottle. Secret Garden Gins – rooted in nature. Shop at the secretgardendistillery.co.uk and follow @secretgardendistillery on Instagram.

17. THE ARTISAN have created a gin which infus Croatian flavours, perfectly balanced to transform th way you experience and savour premium London dr gin. Carefully crafted with 14 organic botanicals and cold vacuum distillation, The Artisan creates distinctive flavours and a delicious aftertaste. Delivered from Croatian fields fresh to your glass. Enjoy it with some lime and your favourite tonic. Visit theartisangin.com and follow @theartisangin on Instagram.

18. MYDRINKBOMB. Summer's over but stay with FIT BOMB®. Just add sparkling water or spring water and you're all set to hydrate, or add a extra kick to your work out! Great for a skinny cocktail with a 1/3 of the calories – sugar free, low calorie and tastes great! Visit MYDRINKBOMB.c and follow @mydrinkbomb on Instagram.

19. A small batch organic Cornish gin crafted usin natural botanicals from the coast. Created by a female founder, **KINGSAND GIN** utilises only th high quality heart of the spirit in the distillation process to produce a truly clean and smooth gin. Reminiscent of those summer days by the sea wherever you may be and perfect for those who love a refreshing tipple at sundown or après-sea. Save 10% with exclusive code 'VOGUE' (31.12.22). Follow @kingsandgin on Instagram and order yours now at www.kingsandgin.com

20. LOVERAW - the indulgent plant-based chocolate brand, have recently launched Nutty Choc Balls, delivering the ultimate treat without palm oil or artificial ingredients. Available in Holland & Barrett at £1.89, these vegan goodies are made using whole hazelnuts dipped in a smooth hazelnut cream. Shop online at eatloveraw.com and follow @loveraw on Instagram.

21. THE CHEESE LADY offer a curated selection of the finest farmhouse and artisan cheeses for the most sophisticated palates. Procured from across Europe and the British Isles, their complex and wholesome cheeses are matured to perfection after being crafted with love, care and precision by masters of the cheesemaking profession. Source the finest cheeses and gifts online at www.thecheeselady.co.uk and enjoy free UK shipping for orders over £30 using the code VOGUESHIPPING. (Expires 31.12.22). Follow @TheCheeseLadyUK on Instagram.

22. OTC BEVERAGES is a multi award nominated and a multi award winning brand of non alcoholic drinks. Current flavours include gingerbeer and sorrel – each based on traditional Caribbean flavours. In 2020 they launched their new flavour Butterflypea flowe with Lime juice. All beverages are designed to have visible health benefits and are available in 250ml cans. Shop their offerings at otcbeverages.com and follow @otcbeverages on Instagram.

23. Forget all your preconceptions of rum. This is **HITCHHIKER** – an intriguingly uniqu British small batch botanical rum whose flavours are inspired by the diverse trade routes from the Caribbean to the shores of the UK. Explore Hitchhiker's story and range at www.hitchhikerrum.com and follow @hitchhikerrum on Instagram. Use code VOGUE10 fo 10% off (expires 31.12.22).

24. Slip into a little bit of luxury with **KIM+ONO** silk and charmeuse kimono robes. Handcrafted with heritage and designed with you in mind, every modern kimono robe is the wearable self care you deserve. Visit them at kimandono.com and on social @kimandono_

25. Sent every three months and aligning with each season, the **FLOURISHY** Cottage Garden Subscription Box makes the perfect gift for nature lovers. The subscription box is £39.95 every three months, and you will receive four boxes year. Shop online at flourishy.co.uk and follow @flourishyuk on Instagram.

26. "…a life lived in flow, with body and mind nourished, and you focused o what matters." True to their philosophy, a warm cup of Golden Milk by the enchanting, Scandi-born **INIKA SUPERFOODS** may be all you need to fee your flow this winter, and help to keep your wellness levels holistically in check. Always nutritious, delicious, and 100% natural. Shop online at inikasuperfoods.com and follow @inikasuperfoods on Instagram.

27. UBILAM MALIBU is a niche candle studio in Malibu, California. Upscale fragrances in slow burning coco soy wax. Collaborating with A-listers to create signature candles! Find this stylish brand in local Malibu shops suc as Jonathan Colombini's John Henry Salon, Malibu Market & Design and Bleusalt. Shop online at UbilamMalibu.com and follow @ubilam.malibu on Instagram.

28. CAORUNN SCOTTISH RASPBERRY GIN is expertly infused with Perthshire Raspberries to delight your palate with a vibrant fruity flavour that perfectly complements the hand-picked Scottish botanicals at Caorunn's heart. T result? An award-winning gin that delivers a bright and clean burst of fruit, with raspberry and the tartness of the rowan berries to the fore. Shop the Caorunn range at shop.caorunngin.com and follow @caorunngin on Instagram.

29. Steeped in British Heritage, **VINERS®** is a highly distinguished and much-loved brand, adding finishing touches to dining tables across the world. Dating back to the early 1900's, Viners® continues to maintain its tradition of high-quality materials whilst incorporating modern styles to create a varied selection of elegant cutlery, barware and serveware, answering all of your entertaining needs. Visit viners.co.uk and use code VINERSXVOGUE15 to get 15% off your order (expires 31.12.22) and follow @Vinerscutlery on Instagram.

30. NIELSEN-MASSEY VANILLAS is a family company that has been crafting premium vanilla and flavours since 1907. Its century-long promise is to provide one of the world's highest quality and most alluring flavours to elevate your recipes. Find at your local store, visit nielsenmassey.com and follow @nielsenmasseyUK on Instagram.

31. HAUTE FLORIST have introduced a new dimension to the ar of floristry. Meet The Oban, a truly spectacular bouquet featuring Twisted Willow and Scottish Thistle, complemented with beautiful deep Red Roses and gold coated Ruscus, a must have this season. Sh online at hauteflorist.co.uk and follow @hauteflorist on Instagram.

32. SPRUCE makes multi-award-winning refillable cleaning products. Made with natural, ethically sourced, vegan ingredients an fragranced with organic geranium and eucalyptus essential oils. Free from harsh chemicals. Buy the bottles once and get plastic-free refill delivered to your door. Get 15% off with the code VOGUE15 (expire 31.12.22) at wearespruce.co and follow @we.are.spruce on Instagram

SERENA DAYS has you covered for luxury pyjama gift shopping Christmas. Once you slip into their super-soft pieces made from utiful bamboo, you won't want to wear anything else. Plus, we've r seen a pj set look so chic! You can also shop with free monogram, he ultimate personalised treat. Visit serenadays.com to shop the Ivory trouser set and robe, and follow @serenadayslondon on agram. Image: @mxh.photos

MALDON SALT, a Royal Warrant Holding Brand this year brated it's 140th Birthday, available in all UK leading supermarkets. a a pinch of Maldon Salt you can elevate any dish from simple to aordinary. Shop online at maldonsalt.com and follow along on agram @maldonsalt for recipes and inspiration.

Devilishly delicious! **THE NAUGHTY VEGAN** is committed to ging the joy of chocolate to everyone aligned to a kinder planet. y have created a range of vegan 'mylk' chocolate treats and spreads, without compromising e. For their full range of mouth-watering delights, visit www.thenaughtyvegan.com.au w @the_naughtyvegan on Instagram.

HOT N SAUCY is your classic hot sauce reimagined. Vegetable-based, vegan sauces curated nall batches by Chef Sam Davis-Allonce. Their bright, bold and colourful sauces with flavours Beet N Fresno, Garlic N Pepperoncini and Sweet Potato N Habanero give you the heat you t and need at no added cost. It's all sauce and all natural. Visit hotnsaucy.co and follow otnsaucyco on Instagram.

JULES AND GEM HAWAII carefully selects and blends fragrances inspired by the vaiian islands fruits and florals. Seasonal fragrances are available for a limited time during the . Lychee is the Summer collection and has notes of lychee, strawberry, and rose. Coffee is the collection with notes of coffee bean, caramel and vanilla. Lastly, the Coconut Christmas Tree e Holiday collection with notes of fraser fir, coconut and vanilla. Shop the seasonal collection lles in this 3 oz candle size. Visit www.julesandgemhawaii.com Instagram @julesandgemhi

ARIE is a biotech-led company that makes health drinks for Gen Z's wellbeing. As an istry pioneer, they are one of the "World's First" integrated microalgae farm-to-bottle. rently launching into global mainstream distribution – at their Pre-Series A, contact them at arieliving.com for more information. Visit arieliving.com and follow @arie.living on Instagram.

MIJENTA's award-winning, additive-free, sustainable tequila uses a meticulous process and best ingredients to create an elegant and complex profile that is fruity and floral with hints of erality. One of the first tequila producers to earn B Corp certification, Mijenta's products are on neutral and its packaging is eco-friendly. Shop online at mijenta-tequila.com and follow ijentatequila on Instagram.

PEACE LILY GIFT BOX HAMPERS are about bringing calm, joy and wellness, and g good for the environment and society, using high quality great British products. Their pers are beautifully and sustainably packaged by hand with love, and delivered at pace with ndary service. They save you time and any gifting-related stress with an easy to navigate site a growing curated range of gifts. Shop at peacelilygifts.com and follow @peacelilygiftboxes nstagram.

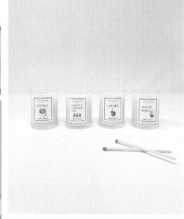

Pampurred Pets

LOVEHOUND is a boutique pet apparel brand that prides itself on creating fun and colourful an-friendly products. The Australian founder carefully hand-designs each piece with a focus safety and comfort. Her vision is to share her love for pets through unique designs that capture hearts. Visit www.lovehound.com and follow @lovehound on Instagram.

CAPRIPET is the original Capri style for furry friends and the people who love them. signed and handmade in Italy and inspired by the iconic fashions and natural beauty of the nd, this luxury pet-wear is a symbol of Capri style anywhere in the world. Find it on ripet.com and @pet.capri on Instagram.

BARX is an online-based brand creating unique, colourful and comfortable accessories dogs. They focus on statement pieces for the bold and brave that are also handy entials for owners. Join the club, visit www.barxdogs.nl and @barx.dogs on Instagram.

LITTLE HOUND DESIGNS combines a love of pets and art, to create bespoke pet traits and accessories. They turn your favourite photo of your fur-baby into an exquisite ce of art. Drawn by hand and entirely customisable, these portraits are the perfect gift. yours at littlehounddesigns.com and follow their Instagram @littlehounddesigns

FABIO THE CAT is a British online boutique providing curated collections of designer furniture. From exquisite shelf beds to discreet litter trays, products are designed in rope and carefully selected to fit any modern interior. Visit fabiothecat.com/vogue for a prise promotion and follow @fabiothecatshop on Instagram.

PAWSHMERE is a luxury dog clothing brand offering our furry friends the same h-end cashmere as their owners. Their knitwear is made from the finest cashmere fibres manufactured to the highest standard. They pride themselves on a range of inclusive and comprehensive sizes for every dog breed. Use code VEVOGUE (expires 31/12/22) at pawshmere.com and w @pawshmere on Instagram.

Born out of love for their four-legged family members and ir families, **TADAZHI** produce timeless designs that don't npromise on the aesthetics of your home, quality or practicality. Their ducts are sewn in organic cotton, adopting beautiful muted colours h reference to nature. Visit www.tadazhi.com and follow adazhiofficial on Instagram.

STUDIO ZORYA is owned by Marta Edmunds, who d-paints dog tags with intricate, bespoke designs made n rare, sustainably sourced deer antlers. Each piece is npletely unique and exquisitely crafted in Toronto, ngside a curated collection of dog collars and bandanas. Visit diozorya.com and @studio_zorya on Instagram to explore limited releases. Use code "Vogue15" for 15% off. xpires 30/11/2022).

TO APPEAR ON THESE PAGES, CONTACT 020 7152 3705 OR EMAIL CLASSVOGUE@CONDENAST.CO.UK

Pampurred Pets

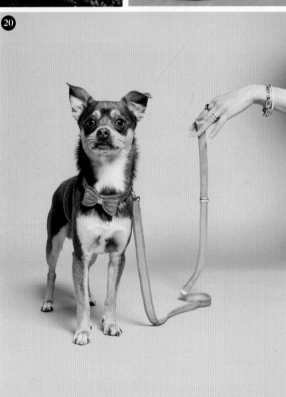

9. HAUS OF PAWS was founded by Jade Wilkinson, who creates adorable designs that purr-fectly suit the personality of your pooch. Her matching sets of harnesses, collars, leads and more provide style with a smile at hausofpaws.co.uk and @hausofpaws.uk on Instagram.

10. CATASTROPHIC CREATIONS is a luxury modern cat furniture brand specialising in modular systems that include hammocks, shelving, scratching poles, and bridge. Build a totally unique habitat for your cat using the modular design. Use code Voguepicks for 10% off your order (expires 1/1/23) at catastrophicreations.com and follow @catastrophicreations on Instagram.

11. SWOOF. is a UK based luxury doggy department store housing some of the world's most exclusive pet brands as well as some independent pet boutiques. Shop all of your dog's needs in one place, from stylish collars and great quality walking gear to pet caves and beautifully handmade food bowls that match your home aesthetic. Use code VOGUE22 for 10% off your first order (expires 31/12/23) at swoof.co.uk and follow @swoofuk on Instagram.

12. RUFF DIAMOND DOGWEAR is an Australian-based coat and accessori brand here for all of your four-legged friend's needs. Their focus is dog owners looking for high quality, boutique products for their pet All of their products are hand crafted and they offer a wide variety coats, sets, and accessories for all seasons. See more at ruffdiamonddogwear.com and follow @ruffdiamonddogwear on Instagram.

13. PUPREPUBLIC was founded by a pair of dog-loving sisters t source 'Seriously Good Stuff for Dogs'. They provide a curated rang of leads, harnesses and supplements, bringing beautiful quality, sty and ease to dogs and dog parents, and are known for beyond-the-ca customer service. Check out the monthly 'Pawparazzi' newsletter a visit puprepublic.co.uk and @puprepublic on Instagram.

14. VELVETIER® is a premium couture brand dedicated to elegant leads and luxury collars for your four-legged friends. Always fashion-forward, their products are designed with comfort and exceptional experience in mind. For affordable and sustainable products that last, enjoy 20% off your first purchase with code Vogue22 on velvetier.de (expires 30/11/22) and follow @velvetier_official on Instagram.

15. ROWAN is one of the world's first clean beauty brands for dogs. They use clean, vegan, human-grade ingredients. Their products leave coats appearing shiny, skin looking healthy, and everyone smelling like coconuts. This brand believes that the products we use for our dogs should be as good as the products we use for ourselves. Explore their mission at rowanfordogs.com and @rowanfordogs on Instagram.

16. PETNAH is a brand that provides luxury comfort for your beloved pet and always makes a statement. Their unique, beautiful products range from collars an leads to beds and teepees and are hand-made by coutu artisans. Explore this exquisite craftsmanship at petnah.com and @petnahpp on Instagram.

17. BONDI PUPS is an Australian pet boutique creating super-soft knit jumpers made from a luxurious wool blend that will keep your pup cute and cosy durin winter. They offer international shipping, so explore all seven colours on Instagram @bondipups and use code VOGUE for 15% off at bondipups.com (expires 20/12/22).

18. Toronto brand **SHOP JUJU** is a luxury pet boutique with a curated range of produ including beds, toys, treats, walking accessories, and more for dogs and cats. As an extension of their grooming salon, Juju Grooms, they strive to provide some of the best products to help enrich the lives of y pets. Explore more at shopjuju.ca and @jujugrooms on Instagram.

19. THE BETTERBONE has developed innovative pet products that are founded on 25 years of sustainable manufacturing. They create better options for pet parents to make decisions that are not only healthier for their dogs and family, but also the planet. Visit thebetterbone.com and follow @thebetterbone on Instagram.

20. Upscale brand **MEOMARI** operates around the core tene of luxury and artistry. Flawless patented designs, hand made b Italy's top artisans and from high-quality materials. While these jewels have a rare, delicate appearanc pet owners can rest assured these items are made be worn, not just admired. Visit www.meomari.cor and follow @meomari on Instagram.

21. ARDEN GRANGE is a British pet food bran built on the core philosophy of 'nutrition without compromise'. Their no-nonsense, naturally hypoallergenic recipes are packed with quality ingredients and powerful natural supplements. Their 'Sensitive' range provides pets with sensitive skin or tummies delicious grain free food and treats. Visit ardengrange.com and follo @ardengrangeuk on Instagram.
Shot by @hugoandursula

22. Ready your bowls, **NOOD PREMIUM PE FOOD**'s irresistible recipes are full of real mea that even the fussiest cats and dogs will love. Packed full of ethically-sourced protein, superfoods, probiotics, vitamins and minerals. NOOD promotes healthy looking skin and a shinier coat for the ultimate glow up. Available exclusively via Tesco, visit uk.noodpetfood.com and follow @noodpetfood on Instagram.